Greed and the Dark Powers in Luke-Acts

Greed and the Dark Powers in Luke-Acts

The Cosmic Battle from Jerusalem to Rome

Michael Blythe

WIPF & STOCK · Eugene, Oregon

GREED AND THE DARK POWERS IN LUKE-ACTS
The Cosmic Battle from Jerusalem to Rome

Copyright © 2025 Michael Blythe. All rights reserved. Except for brief quotations in critical publications or reviews, no part of this book may be reproduced in any manner without prior written permission from the publisher. Write: Permissions, Wipf and Stock Publishers, 199 W. 8th Ave., Suite 3, Eugene, OR 97401.

Wipf & Stock
An Imprint of Wipf and Stock Publishers
199 W. 8th Ave., Suite 3
Eugene, OR 97401

www.wipfandstock.com

PAPERBACK ISBN: 979-8-3852-4989-3
HARDCOVER ISBN: 979-8-3852-4990-9
EBOOK ISBN: 979-8-3852-4991-6

VERSION NUMBER 07/11/25

Scripture quotations marked (LEB) are from the Lexham English Bible, copyright © 2012 by Logos Bible Software. Used by permission. All rights reserved.

Scripture quotations marked (NASB) are from the (NASB®) New American Standard Bible®, copyright © 2020 by The Lockman Foundation. Used by permission. All rights reserved. Lockman.org.

Scripture quotations marked (NET) are from the NET Bible®, copyright © 2019 by Biblical Studies Press, LLC. Used by permission. All rights reserved. http://netbible.com.

Scripture quotations marked (NIV) are from the Holy Bible, New International Version®, NIV®, copyright © 2011 by Biblica, Inc.® Used by permission of Zondervan. All rights reserved worldwide. www.zondervan.com.

Scripture quotations marked (NRSV) are from the New Revised Standard Version Bible, copyright © 1989 by the National Council of the Churches of Christ in the United States of America. Used by permission. All rights reserved worldwide.

To my wife, Kristen:
Without your unwavering intellectual, emotional, and practical support, this work would not have been possible. Your partnership has been my anchor, enabling me to complete this project and to pursue biblical studies as an emerging scholar. You are my companion in all facets of life, and for that I am endlessly grateful.

Contents

Preface | ix
Definition of Terms | xi
Abbreviations | xiii
Introduction: Setting the Stage for the Cosmic Battle | xxiii

Chapter 1: Jesus and the Forces of Darkness—The Cosmic Battle from Nazareth to Jerusalem | 1

Chapter 2: Satan, Judas, and Betrayal: Prelude to Darkness (Luke 22:1–6 and Acts 1:15–20) | 12

Chapter 3: Ananias and Sapphira: Greed and the Spirit of Deception (Acts 5:1–11) | 28

Chapter 4: Simon Magus in Samaria: The Temptation to Bribe Divine Power (Acts 8:4–25) | 43

Chapter 5: The Death of Herod Agrippa I: Divine Justice and the Fall of Hubris (Acts 11:27—12:24) | 55

Chapter 6: Bar-Jesus/Elymas in Paphos: Confronting the Powers of Deception (Acts 13:4–12) | 72

Chapter 7: The Spirit of Python and the Philippian Encounter: Economic Exploitation and Spiritual Resistance (Acts 16:11–40) | 83

Chapter 8: The Cult of Artemis in Ephesus: The Struggle over Economic and Religious Allegiance (Acts 19:1–41) | 100

Chapter 9: The Cosmic Duel from Jerusalem to Rome: The Culmination of the Battle (Acts 20–28) | 113

Chapter 10: Subverting Empire—Limited Good, Symbolic Challenges, and Social Upheaval in Acts | 126

*Conclusion—From Darkness to Light: Greed and
    Liberation in Luke-Acts* | 147

*Appendix A—The Cosmic Duel of Luke-Acts and African Traditional
    Religion(s): Implications for the Contemporary Prosperity Gospel* | 159

Appendix B—Further Research Opportunities | 164

*Appendix C—Bridging the Gaps: Socioeconomic Ethics,
    Spiritual Opposition, and Rome in Scholarship* | 176

Bibliography | 185

Preface

Watch out and guard yourself from all types of greed.
—Luke 12:15 (NET)

This monograph began its life as my PhD dissertation, shaped by a long-standing passion for Luke-Acts that has underpinned my preaching, Bible study leadership, conference presentations, and earlier published work on the Lukan corpus. I have long been inspired by Luke's double concern for ethical transformation (especially regarding greed) and spiritual phenomena; my hope has been to bridge what I perceived as a scholarly gap in treating these dimensions in concert. As a disciple who takes Luke's vision seriously, I am convinced that an in-depth exploration of these themes contributes meaningfully to the church's formation and mission.

I owe deep thanks to my mentor, Dr. Richard Thompson, whose world-class Lukan expertise and patient encouragement allowed me to flourish as a researcher—my appreciation to Dr. Mark Mann for connecting us in the first place. I remain indebted to Rev. Dr. Filimao Chambo, whose affirming words were integral in my journey as a scholar laboring in the heart of the church's mission, and to Dr. Gift Mtukwa, whose guidance was a continuous reassurance across two major projects. Africa Nazarene University, with its vibrant African context, profoundly shaped my academic horizon; Dr. Russell Frazier further supported me along the way. I am also grateful for the friendship of Rev. Halissone Nefitala (PhD ABD) and the ongoing Luke-Acts conversations I shared with Rev. Dr. Chuck Crocker. Nor can I fail to thank the congregations I serve—Salem UMC, Shiloh UMC, and Centenary UMC in Mecklenburg County, Virginia—as

PREFACE

well as the faithful at the midweek study at First Baptist Church (Chase City, Virginia). Their support and fellowship have made me a better pastor and scholar. Ultimately, it is my prayer that this project, rooted in devotion and careful study, will bless disciples and strengthen the church for which it was written.

Definition of Terms

Cosmic duel: A theological motif of conflict between divine forces and evil powers, symbolic of spiritual or universal struggle

Cosmic war: An overarching spiritual or apocalyptic battle between good and evil forces in religious or theological narratives

Dark powers, or dark spiritual forces: The presence of the devil; Satan; unclean, evil, or impure spirits associated with possession, divination, sorcery, idolatry, and the imperial cult

Greed: Excessive desire for wealth or possessions, often depicted in Luke-Acts as a tool of the dark powers, accompanied by exploitative practices

Imaginative reading: This project employs the phrase "MacMullen's imaginative reading" to denote the application of his exercise "to imagine oneself a devout pagan while reading various Christian writings"; first discussed in chapter 5 (see MacMullen, *Christianizing the Roman Empire*, 111)

Socioeconomic ethics: Moral principles addressing justice, equity, and relationships in societal structures, especially regarding wealth, poverty, and community

Spiritual warfare: The struggle against dark spiritual forces, often linked with socioeconomic greed in Luke-Acts

Spirituality: The intersection of divine and dark forces with human life, institutions, and systems, particularly in how these forces influence socioeconomic realities and ethical behavior; encompasses both the empowering presence of the Holy Spirit and the opposing dark spiritual forces (e.g., Satan, demons, idolatry), which operate through greed, socioeconomic exploitation, and systemic injustice; this spirituality is not abstract or private but manifests in concrete actions, systems, and relationships

Abbreviations

Reference Works

ABD	*The Anchor Bible Dictionary*. Edited by David Noel Freedman. 6 vols. New York: Doubleday, 1992
CGL	Faculty of Classics. *The Cambridge Greek Lexicon*. Edited by James Diggle. 2 vols. Cambridge: Cambridge University Press, 2021
CHB	*A Cultural Handbook to the Bible*. John J. Pilch. Grand Rapids: Eerdmans, 2012.
DJG	*Dictionary of Jesus and the Gospels*. Edited by Joel B. Green, Jeannine K. Brown, and Nicholas Perrin. 2nd ed. Downers Grove, IL: IVP Academic, 2013
EDB	*Eerdmans Dictionary of the Bible*. Edited by David Noel Freedman. Grand Rapids: Eerdmans, 2000
EDNT	*Exegetical Dictionary of the New Testament*. Edited by Horst Robert Balz and Gerhard Schneider. 3 vols. Grand Rapids: Eerdmans, 1990–1993
HBD	*HarperCollins Bible Dictionary*. Edited by Mark Allan Powell et al. 3rd ed. San Francisco: HarperOne, 2011.

ABBREVIATIONS

HBSV	*Handbook of Biblical Social Values.* Edited by John J. Pilch and Bruce J. Malina. 3rd ed. MBMC 10. Eugene, OR: Cascade, 2016
L&N	Louw, Johannes P., and Eugene A. Nida, eds. *Greek-English Lexicon of the New Testament: Based on Semantic Domains.* 2nd ed. New York: United Bible Societies, 1996
LBD	*Lexham Bible Dictionary.* Edited by J. D. Barry. Bellingham, WA: Lexham, 2016
MGS	Montanari, Franco. *The Brill Dictionary of Ancient Greek.* Edited by Madeleine Goh, and Chad Schroeder. Leiden: Brill, 2015
REHJ	*Routledge Encyclopedia of the Historical Jesus.* Edited by Craig A. Evans. New York: Routledge, 2008
TDNT	*Theological Dictionary of the New Testament.* Edited by Gerhard Kittel and Gerhard Friedrich. Translated by Geoffrey W. Bromiley. 10 vols. Grand Rapids: Eerdmans, 1964–1976
TLNT	*Theological Lexicon of the New Testament.* Ceslas Spicq. Translated and edited by James D. Ernest. 3 vols. Peabody, MA: Hendrickson, 1994

English Bible Translations

LEB	Lexham English Bible
NASB	New American Standard Bible
NET	New English Translation
NIV	New International Version
NRSV	New Revised Standard Version

Commentaries, Series, Journals, and Important Terms

AcBib	Academia Biblica
ANTC	Abingdon New Testament Commentaries

ABBREVIATIONS

ASMS	American Society of Missiology Series
ATR	African Traditional Religion(s)
AYBC	Anchor Yale Bible Commentaries
BAFCS	Book of Acts in Its First Century Setting
BBR	*Bulletin for Biblical Research*
Belief: TCB	Belief: A Theological Commentary on the Bible
BibInt	Biblical Interpretation Series
BTB	*Biblical Theology Bulletin*
BtEE	Beware the Evil Eye: The Evil Eye in the Bible and the Ancient World
BTNTS	Biblical Theology of the New Testament Series
ConcC	Concordia Commentary
COQG	Christian Origins and the Question of God
CSC	Christian Standard Commentary
CTBS	Critical Theory and Biblical Studies
EBC	Expositor's Bible Commentary
EGGNT	Exegetical Guide to the Greek New Testament
ESS	Emerging Scholars Series
EvQ	*Evangelical Quarterly*
FBPC	Fortress Biblical Preaching Commentaries
Hermeneia: CHCB	Hermeneia: A Critical and Historical Commentary on the Bible
HNTC	Holman New Testament Commentary
HTR	*Harvard Theological Review*
IBC	Interpretation: A Bible Commentary for Teaching and Preaching
IBT	Interpreting Biblical Texts Series
ICC	International Critical Commentary
IDS	*In die Skriflig*
Int	*Interpretation*
IRUSC	Interpretation: Resources for the Use of Scripture in the Church
IVPBBC	IVP Bible Background Commentary

ABBREVIATIONS

JETS	*Journal of the Evangelical Theological Society*
JGRChJ	*Journal of Greco-Roman Christianity and Judaism*
JHebS	*Journal of Hebrew Scriptures*
JJS	*Journal of Jewish Studies*
JSNT	*Journal for the Study of New Testament*
JSOTSup	Journal for the Study of the Old Testament Supplement Series
LHJS	Library of the Historical Jesus Studies
LNTS	Library of New Testament Studies
MBMC	Matrix: The Bible in Mediterranean Context
NAC	New American Commentary
NBBC	New Beacon Bible Commentary
NBC	New Biblical Commentary
NCBC	New Cambridge Bible Commentary
NCCS	New Covenant Commentary Series
NCollBC	New Collegeville Bible Commentary
NICNT	New International Commentary on the New Testament
NT	New Testament
NTC	New Testament Commentary
NTFE	New Testament for Everyone
NTL	New Testament Library
NTS	*New Testament Studies*
ONTC	Osborne New Testament Commentaries
OT	Old Testament
Paideia: CNT	Paideia: Commentaries on the New Testament
PBM	Paternoster Biblical Monographs
PEHWW	Princeton Economic History of the Western World
PPSJ	Pentecostals, Peacemaking, and Social Justice
PTMS	Princeton Theological Monograph Series
SBL	Society of Biblical Literature

ABBREVIATIONS

SBLDS	Society of Biblical Literature Dissertation Series
SGBC	Story of God Bible Commentary
SNTSMS	Society for New Testament Studies Monograph Series
StBibLit	Studies in Biblical Literature (Lang)
THNTC	Two Horizons New Testament Commentary
TNTC	Tyndale New Testament Commentaries
TTCS	Teach the Text Commentary Series
VT	*Vetus Testamentum*
WBC	Word Biblical Commentary
WCS	Wisdom Commentary Series
WestBC	Westminster Bible Companion
WUNT I	Wissenschaftliche Untersuchungen zum Neuen Testament 1
WUNT II	Wissenschaftliche Untersuchungen zum Neuen Testament 2
ZECNT	Zondervan Exegetical Commentary on The New Testament
ZIBBC	Zondervan Illustrated Bible Backgrounds Commentary
ZNW	*Zeitschrift für die neutestamentliche Wissenschaft und die Kunde der älteren Kirche*

Ancient and Classical Sources

1 En.	1 Enoch
1 Macc	1 Maccabees
1QM	War Scroll (Cave 1, Qumran)
1QpHab	Pesher Habbakuk (Cave 1, Qumran)
1QS	Rule of the Community (Cave 1, Qumran Serekh)
2 Bar.	2 Baruch
2 Macc	2 Maccabees

ABBREVIATIONS

3 Macc	3 Maccabees
4QSd	Document d (Cave 4, Qumran Serekh)
Ach. Tat. *Leuc. Clit.*	Achilles Tatius, *Leucippe et Clitophon*
Aeschylus, *Prom.*	Aeschylus, *Prometheus Bound*
Apuleius, *Metam.*	Apuleius, *Metamorphoses*
Arist. *Eth. nic.*	Aristotle, *Ethica nicomachea* (*Nicomachean Ethics*)
Arist. *Pol.*	Aristotle, *Politica* (*Politics*)
Ar. *Plut.*	Aristophanes, *Plutus* (*Wealth*)
Athenagoras, *Leg.*	Athenagoras, *Legatio pro Christianis*
Aulus Gellius, *Noct. att.*	Aulus Gellius, *Noctes atticae* (*Attic Nights*)
Cassius Dio, *Hist.*	Cassius Dio, *Historia romana* (*Roman History*)
Chariton, *Chaer.*	Chariton, *Chaereas and Callirhoe*
Cic. *Agr.*	Cicero, *De Lege agraria* (*On the Agrarian Law*)
Cic. *Att.*	Cicero, *Epistulae ad Atticum* (*Letters to Atticus*)
Cic. *Cat.*	Cicero, *In Catilinam* (*Catilinarian Orations*)
Cic. *Leg.*	Cicero, *De legibus* (*On the Laws*)
Cic. *Nat. d.*	Cicero, *De natura deorum* (*On the Nature of the Gods*)
Cic. *Off.*	Cicero, *De officiis* (*On Duties*)
Cic. *Phil.*	Cicero, *Philippicae* (*Philippics*)
Cic. *Rosc. Amer.*	Cicero, *Pro Sexto Roscio Amerino* (*For Sextus Roscius of Ameria*)
Cic. *Verr.*	Cicero, *In Verrem* (*Against Verres*)
CIG	*Corpus Inscriptionum Graecarum*
CIL	*Corpus Inscriptionum Latinarum*
Dio Chrys. *Or.*	Dio Chrysostom, *Orations*
Dio Chrys. *Rhod.*	Dio Chrysostom, *Rhodiaca* (*The Rhodian Discourse*)
DK	Diels-Kranz, *The Fragments of the Presocratics*
Epictetus, *Disc.*	Epictetus, *Discourses* (alternate title for *Diatribes*)
Eur. *Andr.*	Euripides, *Andromache*

ABBREVIATIONS

Eur. *Phoen.*	Euripides, *Phoenissae* (*The Phoenician Women*)
Euseb. *Hist. eccl.*	Eusebius, *Historia ecclesiastica* (*Ecclesiastical History*)
Galen, *De alim.*	Galen, *De alimentorum facultatibus*
Hdt. *Hist.*	Herodotus, *Histories*
Herm. Mand.	Shepherd of Hermas, Mandate(s)
Herodian, *Hist.*	Herodian, *History of the Empire*
Homer, *Il.*	Homer, *Iliad*
Horace, *Od.*	Horace, *Odes*
IEph.	Wankel, Hermann, et al., eds. *Die Inschriften von Ephesos*. 8 vols. Bonn: Habelt, 1979–1984
Josephus, *Ag. Ap.*	Josephus, *Against Apion*
Josephus, *Ant.*	Josephus, *Antiquities of the Jews*
Josephus, *J.W.*	Josephus, *Jewish War*
Josephus, *Life*	Josephus, *The Life*
Jub.	Jubilees
Justin Matyr, *1 Apol.*	Justin Martyr, *Apologia i* (*First Apology*)
Juv. *Sat.*	Juvenal, *Satires*
Livy, *Hist.*	Livy, *Ab Urbe Condita* (*History of Rome*)
Lucian, *Alex.*	Lucian, *Alexander the False Prophet*
Lucian, *Peregr.*	Lucian, *De morte Peregrinus* (*The Death of Peregrinus*)
Lucian, *Vit. auct.*	Lucian, *Vitarum auctio* (*Philosophies for Sale*)
LXX	Septuagint
Mart. *Epigr.*	Martial, *Epigrams*
Mart. Pol.	Martyrdom of Polycarp
Minucius Felix, *Oct.*	Minucius Felix, *Octavius*
MSF	Major Semitic Family
MSS	Manuscripts (e.g., P74, א [Aleph], A, B, 1175)
MT	Masoretic Text
Origen, *Cels.*	Origen, *Contra Celsum* (*Against Celsus*)
Ovid, *Metam.*	Ovid, *Metamorphoses*
Ovid, *Trist.*	Ovid, *Tristia*

ABBREVIATIONS

Paus. *Descr.*	Pausanias, *Description of Greece*
Petron. *Sat.*	Petronius, *Satyricon*
Philo, *Flacc.*	Philo, *In Flaccum* (*Against Flaccus*)
Philo, *Spec. Laws*	Philo, *De specialibus legibus* (*Special Laws*)
Philostr. *Vit. Apoll.*	Philostratus, *Vita Apollonii* (*Life of Apollonius of Tyana*)
Philostr. *Vit. Soph.*	Philostratus, *Vitae sophistarum* (*Lives of the Sophists*)
Pind. *Nem.*	Pindar, *Nemean Odes*
Plato, *Leg.*	Plato, *Leges* (*Laws*)
Plato, *Resp.*	Plato, *Respublica* (*Republic*)
Plaut. *Com.*	Plautus, *Comedies*
Pliny, *Ep.*	Pliny the Younger, *Epistulae* (*Letters*)
Pliny, *Nat.*	Pliny the Elder, *Naturalis historia* (*Natural History*)
Pliny, *Pan.*	Pliny the Younger, *Panegyricus* (*Panegyric*)
Plut. *Alc.*	Plutarch, *Life of Alcibiades* (part of *Parallel Lives*)
Plut. *Brut.*	Plutarch, *Brutus*
Plut. *Def. Orac.*	Plutarch, *De defectu oraculorum*
Plut. *Demetr.*	Plutarch, *Demetrius*
Plut. *Garr.*	Plutarch, *De garrulitate* (*On Talkativeness*)
Plut. *Mor.*	Plutarch, *Moralia*
Plut. *Per.*	Plutarch, *Pericles*
Plut. *Pomp.*	Plutarch, *Pompey*
Plut. *Quaest. conv.*	Plutarch, *Quaestiones convivales* (*Table Talk*)
Porphyry, *Abst.*	Porphyry, *De abstinentia* (*On Abstinence*)
Porphyry, *Christ.*	Porphyry, *Contra Christianos* (*Against the Christians*)
Pss. Sol.	Psalms of Solomon
Seneca, *Ben.*	Seneca, *De beneficiis* (*On Benefits*)
Seneca, *Ep. Mor.*	Seneca, *Epistulae morales ad Lucilium* (*Moral Letters to Lucilius*)
Sib. Or.	Sibylline Oracles

ABBREVIATIONS

Soph. *Oed. tyr.*	Sophocles, *Oedipus tyrannus* (*Oedipus Rex*)
Strabo, *Geogr.*	Strabo, *Geographica*
Suet.	Suetonius, *De vita Caesarum* (*The Lives of the Caesars*)
Suet. *Aug.*	Suetonius, *Divus Augustus*
Suet. *Cal.*	Suetonius, *Gaius Caligula*
Suet. *Claud.*	Suetonius, *Divus Claudius*
Suet. *Dom.*	Suetonius, *Domitianus*
Suet. *Nero*	Suetonius, *Nero*
Suet. *Otho*	Suetonius, *Otho*
Suet. *Tib.*	Suetonius, *Tiberius*
Suet. *Vesp.*	Suetonius, *Vespasianus*
T. Mos.	Testament of Moses
Tac. *Agr.*	Tacitus, *Agricola*
Tac. *Ann.*	Tacitus, *Annales*
Tac. *Hist.*	Tacitus, *Historiae*
Tert. *Apol.*	Tertullian, *Apologeticus* (*Apology*)
Tert. *Scorp.*	Tertullian, *Scorpiace*
Vergil, *Aen.*	Vergil, *Aeneid*
Wis.	Wisdom of Solomon
Xen. *Eph.*	Xenophon, *Ephesiaca* (*The Ephesian Tale*)
Xen. *Hell.*	Xenophon, *Hellenica*
Xen. *Hier.*	Xenophon, *Hiero*
Xen. *Mem.*	Xenophon, *Memorabilia*

Introduction: Setting the Stage for the Cosmic Battle

Greed is usually the root of crime:
no fault of the human mind causes more poison to be mixed,
or a more frequent rampaging about with a blade
than the uncontrolled desire for extravagant wealth.[1]

—Juvenal

Luke's Framework for the Cosmic Duel

Themes and motifs in Acts should not be read abstractly or used to formulate systematic ideas in isolation from their broader context. Rather, readers should treat narrative components in unison with their relationship to the larger scope and shape of Acts, observing how various literary streams flow together to weave a tapestry of theological design.[2] With this in mind, this study demonstrates how two prominent themes that flow throughout Acts are intertwined. Scholarship has established an interest in socioeconomic ethics regarding the marginalized and issues of wealth, money, material possessions, and greed in Luke-Acts.[3] Likewise, Luke's writings emphasize matters of spirituality, which includes the Holy Spirit's activity, and phenomena associated with Satan, the devil, demons, and

---

1. Juv. *Sat.* 14.107–88.
2. Gaventa, "Toward a Theology," 146–57.
3. See appendix C, "Socioeconomic Ethics."

INTRODUCTION: SETTING THE STAGE FOR THE COSMIC BATTLE

other unclean, impure, or evil spirits.[4] However, seldom are these two vibrant Lukan features treated as intersecting themes and motifs.

This study identifies a recurring overlap between socioeconomic exploitation and spiritual activity, focusing on seven key Lukan pericopes. These passages were chosen because they graphically illustrate evil powers operating in tandem with greed, present the most vivid narratives depicting resistance to the Jesus group in Acts, and uniquely feature explicit naming or identification of characters.

The first key narrative involves Judas, setting the stage. In Luke 22:1–6, as Jesus approaches Passover, the evil powers' resistance culminates in Jerusalem, a strategic location. These dark powers' efforts are induced by Satan's entrance into Judas (Luke 22:3), who is present at Gethsemane as evidenced by Jesus's remark on the ascending hour of darkness (Luke 22:53). Satan's direct influence on Judas demonstrates the first aggressive attempt by the dark powers to circumvent the christological mission and forthcoming church. Subsequently, the introductory material of Acts is also dedicated to Judas (1:15–20), verifying the event's significance—that the occasion of his betrayal is more than a Gospel motif; it is also a bridge into Acts, establishing the tone for the remainder of Luke's writings.

Alongside Judas's betrayal (Luke 22:1–6; Acts 1:18–20), six other passages—Ananias and Sapphira (Acts 5:1–11), Simon the Magician (Acts 8:4–24), Herod Agrippa I (Acts 12:24–28), Elymas/Bar Jesus (Acts 13:4–12), the Python spirit possessing a Philippian slave girl (Acts 16:11–40), and the seven sons of Sceva along with Demetrius (Acts 19:8–41)—share core elements of the Judas account, including explicit character naming.[5]

Through a textual analysis of these seven accounts, this study explores how these passages reinforce Lukan theology, showing greed as a weapon of the dark powers whose defeat in Rome—as in Ephesus (Acts 19)—would yield systemic consequences. Then, although a socioeconomic emphasis is less conspicuous in Acts 20–28, this project contends that the cosmic battle and its accompanying socioeconomic overtone continues in these chapters.

---

4. See Appendix C under section titled "Spiritual Phenomena."

5. The one exception is the slave girl of Acts 16:16–21, who is not a named figure. As an exploited character, she is left anonymous; however, the πύθωνα spirit attached to her indicates a specific named entity. Also, much more could be stated concerning other potential criteria for delimiting these seven narratives, including the strategic geographic locations where they occur and the literary occasions for their presentation, which are often near narrative turning points.

INTRODUCTION: SETTING THE STAGE FOR THE COSMIC BATTLE

The confrontation continues into the empire's core, extending the motif of greed and spiritual conflict "to the end of the earth" (Acts 1:8).

To develop the connection between avaricious socioeconomic activity and dark spiritual phenomena in Luke-Acts, this study approaches the passages in question from a variety of angles. It explores sociocultural, political, historical, theological, and literary dimensions, including, but not limited to, the following eleven elements:

1. The activity of magic, sorcery, and comparable phenomena in conjunction with dark forces within the theological worldview of Luke-Acts (Acts 8:4–24; 13:4–12).
2. The practice of idol worship and its theological connection to evil in Luke-Acts (Acts 19:11–41).
3. Spirits of divination and their theological association to darkness in Luke-Acts (Acts 16:16–21).
4. The first-century socioeconomic perspectives of land accumulation in Jewish Palestine (Acts 1:15–20).
5. The narrative trajectory both in terms of real-estate devotion (Acts 1:15–20) and honor acquisition within the early church of Luke-Acts (Acts 5:1–11; 8:4–24).
6. The context of various intertextual connections between Luke-Acts and the LXX (Acts 5:1–11; 8:4–24, etc.).
7. The socioeconomic exploitative power and influence from which magicians benefited in antiquity (Acts 8:4–24; 13:4–12).
8. General sociocultural perspectives of ancient Mediterranean audiences toward those who perform magic or exorcism for hire (Acts 8:4–24; 13:4–12; 19:8–41).
9. The sociohistoric dynamics of slavery in the first-century Mediterranean context (Acts 16:11–40).
10. The sociohistoric background to the deification of royalty, including the connection to the imperial cult (Acts 12:20–24).
11. The exploitation of agricultural products by imperial rulers and their brokers within the first-century Palestinian setting (Acts 12:20–24).

Investigating these aspects of the text, this study addresses financial greed, social greed, and spirituality as overlapping features, especially in terms of Luke's narrative flow. This, in turn, forms a panoramic view of socioeconomic greed that consistently coincides with dark spiritual powers in Luke's writings. From such a narrative interlocking of these two elements, it is evident that a cosmic duel with evil begins in the Gospel and begs to be considered in terms of the culmination of Acts at the time of Paul's arrest and journey to Rome.

Historical-Critical, Social-Scientific, Narrative Analysis, and Intertextuality

This investigation uses several techniques or methods of study. It incorporates historical-critical methodology to "illuminate the text by exploring the world in which the text came into being."[6] It also uses the social-scientific method, a sub-branch of the historical-critical approach, which analyzes the "social and cultural dimensions of the text."[7] Since one of this project's significant goals is to consider the implications of the narrative flow toward Rome in Acts, these two related disciplines are useful in analyzing how the empire served as a primary agent of greed by means of systematically exerting policies of socioeconomic exploitation.

Both historical and social studies provide evidence that forms an overall framework for investigating the text itself. The sociohistorical approach works well in tandem with narrative analysis, which helps to construct an overall image of the story arc.[8] Narrative analysis determines answers to the questions, (a) What is the story about? (b) What happened, to whom, whereabouts, and why? (c) What consequences arose from this? (d) What is the significance of these events? (e) What was the outcome?[9]

Although intertextuality is secondary, this project adopts an abbreviated version of G. K. Beale's step-by-step methodology[10]—identifying Old Testament references, analyzing their context in both Testaments, surveying Jewish interpretive traditions, and exploring the theological and rhetorical implications—to ensure a careful rather than casual handling of Old Testament echoes and allusions in Acts.

---

6. Gooder, *Searching for Meaning*, xviii. See also Chilton, "Historical Criticism," 7.
7. Elliott, *What Is Social-Scientific Criticism?*, 7.
8. Malbon, "Narrative Criticism," 81.
9. Coffey and Atkinson, *Making Sense of Data*.
10. Beale, *NT Use of OT*.

INTRODUCTION: SETTING THE STAGE FOR THE COSMIC BATTLE

A Prophetic Historiography

Luke's writings are best encapsulated using James Morgan's proposed theory of prophetic historiography. Through this, Morgan does not suggest that Lukan writings are "predictive," but rather that they offer a "retrospective" and "interpretative" assessment of history from a divine perspective.[11] In this manner, Luke's style is akin to Jewish tradition, including the former prophets of the historical division of the Old Testament (Joshua, Judges, 1–2 Samuel, and 1–2 Kings) and the Chronicler, who retells history to meet specific aims. This was an accepted approach in Jewish tradition, recognized even by the unconventional historian Josephus, who claimed that only prophets were qualified to write histories.[12]

According to Morgan, the traits of prophetic historiography include: (1) weaving divine content into history; (2) authoritative and prophetic speech associated with the writer; (3) unique knowledge of the divine; (4) the formulation of a worldview and/or theological understanding for the reader; and (5) reinforcement of religious foundations, including intertextuality.[13] Each of these qualities applies to Luke-Acts, in which events are relayed as an instructional tool. The narrative develops theological progression, frequently adding material beyond the historical facts, which, though likely unverifiable, serves the prophetic perspective. Accepting prophetic historiography does not necessitate suspicion regarding Luke's integrity, but it implies a shaping of history to obtain theological recognition and appeal to specific societal segments.

The prophetic historiographic assessment is applicable to both the Gospel and Acts. However, Luke's approach in Acts deviates enough to raise questions about shared authorship and common genre. Luke relies heavily on Mark, possibly the "Q" document or other manuscripts ("L"), as well as the Septuagint and perhaps Paul's letters and Josephus's writings. By using these documents, Luke surrenders some degree of creativity, particularly due to his dependence on Mark. Conversely, these primary sources (Mark, "Q," and "L") do not contribute to Acts. As a result, Luke's artistry becomes more apparent in the second volume.

To complement his prophetic historiography, Luke likely drew inspiration from ancient writers such as Homer and Vergil and appears to have

---

11. Morgan, "Prophetic Historiography," 76.
12. Morgan, "Prophetic Historiography," 77, 79.
13. Morgan, "Prophetic Historiography," 82–83.

used literary parallelism with those ancient writers.[14] Additionally, Luke used the LXX and his own Gospel structure to communicate the early church's narrative and theological formation in an engaging way.[15] Luke's prophetic historiography, enriched by elements of an epic, serves as a literary vehicle that enables him to craft narratives with both creativity and theological precision. This approach not only showcases his literary artistry but also reinforces his theological agenda, allowing his work to engage readers with depth and rhetorical sophistication.

Having identified Luke's writings in the genre of prophetic historiography, it is relevant to note this study's perspective regarding the text's dating and audience. Concerning Acts of the Apostles, "no particular proposed date . . . is absolutely compelling"; therefore, a summarized range is most suitable.[16] The bulk of scholarly opinion affirms a range of 85 to 100 CE following Nero's reign.[17] This project accepts this span as the earliest plausible date for the completion of Luke-Acts while allowing for the possibility of a second-century composition. The significance of a later dating lies in its potential to expand Luke's theological agenda. Rather than merely presenting a historical account culminating in Paul's journey to Rome, a later date allows a more reflective and analytical prophetic analysis. This perspective includes the persecutions under Nero, Vespasian, and possibly Domitian. Additionally, it may have enabled Luke to draw upon the writings of Josephus and, potentially, those of Tacitus and Pliny the Younger.

In addition to his genre and dating, Luke's intended audience is relevant. An important clue is that the writer addresses his reader with the title κράτιστος, "most excellent" (Luke 1:3). This appellation is employed in three other New Testament locations, each by Luke in his second volume, and in each instance to designate a Roman official (Acts 23:26, 24:3, 26:25). In ancient literature, when κράτιστος is utilized as a superlative adjective, its relationship is to a "proper name" and often applied to the political elite of the Roman world.[18] In Josephus's multiple attestations of the term, the designation is applied exclusively to prominent leadership, including Epaphroditus,

---

14. MacDonald, *Synopses of Epic*; see also these sources by the same author: *Does NT Imitate Homer*; *Gospels and Homer*; *Politics of Homeric Imitation*; and *Luke and Vergil*.

15. Talbert, *Literary Patterns*; Edwards, "Parallels and Patterns," 485–501.

16. Keener, *Acts: Exegetical Commentary*, 1:383.

17. Perrin, *Luke*, 6.

18. Creamer et al., "Who is Theophilus," 2.

INTRODUCTION: SETTING THE STAGE FOR THE COSMIC BATTLE

who likely had a prominent role with either emperor Trajan or Nero.[19] The honorific is also ascribed to Vitellius, the governor of Syria, to King Agrippa I's royal family, and John Hyrcanus.[20] This leads James D. G. Dunn to acknowledge that Theophilus was "a man of some rank and influence."[21] Some propose Theophilus was a pseudonym for a Roman agent needing to remain incognito, possibly acting as a patron for Luke's publication.[22] A century ago, B. H. Streeter contended that "Theophilus" was an alias for Titus Flavius Clemens, the cousin of Domitian, whose interest in the faith came by way of his converted wife Domitilla.[23] More recently, Werner Marx interestingly argued that Theophilus was, in fact, King Agrippa II, in part because of the near persuasion to become a Christian (Acts 26:28).[24]

Another key point is that Luke's novelistic method may render Theophilus's historical identity irrelevant. The author might care more about how readers perceive Theophilus as a literary figure that serves as a representative persona. The title that Luke employs to his addressee, κράτιστος, its role referring to key Roman leaders in his other usages, and its similar role in Josephus's writings, all point to the idea that the function of the word is to identify political influencers. The use of this honorific, plus Luke's interest in political leadership, point to his audience being perceived as being a Roman official. Along with Acts' narrative ending in the city of Rome, this evidence suggests that Luke wanted readers to perceive Theophilus as a member of the Roman governing elite. The characterization of Theophilus as a Roman influencer enhances the literary intrigue, as Luke's narrative agenda is centered in the imperial capital.

How to Read This Book

This introductory section briefly explains how this project is organized. The study's primary focus revolves around Acts. However, chapter 1 covers relevant themes and motifs in Luke's Gospel, including Luke's socioeconomic ethics and spiritual phenomena, to establish a foundation for the subsequent interpretation of Acts.

19. Josephus, *Life* 1.430; *Ag. Ap.* 1.1.
20. Josephus, *Ant.* 20.12.
21. Dunn, *Acts of the Apostles*, 10.
22. Garland, *Luke*, 56.
23. Streeter, *Four Gospels*, 534–39.
24. Marx, "New Theophilus," 17–26.

INTRODUCTION: SETTING THE STAGE FOR THE COSMIC BATTLE

Chapters 2 through 8 provide textual analysis of the seven primary pericopes in Acts that form the foundation of this study. The first four, chapters 2 through 5, include four narratives that take place in the Palestinian context—Luke 22:1–6 with Acts 1:15–20, and Acts 5:1–11, 8:11–40, and 12:24–28—addressing the stories of Judas, Ananias and Sapphira, Simon Magus, and Agrippa I. The next three, chapters 6 through 8, address four passages that are set in the broader Mediterranean context—Acts 13:4–12, 16:11–40, 19:8–41—assessing the stories of Paul in Paphos, Philippi, and Ephesus.

The final two chapters, 9 and 10, offer a culmination of the prior arguments, discussing the significance of the findings from the seven focus pericopes for Lukan theology. Chapter 9 briefly reiterates the progression of the cosmic battle in Acts 1–19 and then extends these findings to the conclusion of Acts (chapters 20–28), which portrays the momentum of the gospel as it approaches Rome. Chapter 10 then discusses implications of the cosmic duel through the application of several theories, including the concept of limited good, the symbolic portrayal of Legion, and the subversive elements to empire.

The socioeconomic and political pedigree of these chosen texts generates an ideal opportunity to identify further research possibilities. With this in mind, this book's appendices, drawn from the original dissertation, offer robust examples of potential applications of this study's themes as well as related relevant literature.

Appendix A provides examples of applying this study's thesis to themes of liberation and postcolonial theologies, using the African contexts of African Traditional Religion(s) and the prosperity gospel. The study's implications are also relevant for the modern prosperity gospel and New Apostolic Reformation movements and sociopolitical criticism as applied to Western settings.

Appendix B offers avenues for further academic engagement of this study's themes within contemporary contexts. For example, the spiritual phenomena associated with this research offer potential for conversation with studies involving demonology and exorcisms. Other examples in this appendix signify the remarkable expansive capabilities of this research.

Finally, appendix C describes relevant existing scholarly works that intersect this study's themes. These writings are divided into to three categories with relation to Luke-Acts: socioeconomic ethics, spiritual phenomena, and Luke's view of empire, including judicial scenes, Acts' narrative conclusion, and Rome.

Chapter 1: Jesus and the Forces of Darkness—The Cosmic Battle from Nazareth to Jerusalem

Every creature of greed shall wither quickly away [like a flow]er at ha[rvest time. . . . Come,] strengthen yourselves for the battle of God, for this day is an appointed time of battle [for G]od against all the n[ations].[1]

—THE WAR SCROLL

Luke's Gospel

TO GAIN A CONTEXTUAL perspective, this chapter explores specific thematic features of Luke's Gospel, beginning with material immediately following the prologue (Luke 1:1–4). This study first navigates the background to Jesus's ministry (Luke 1:1—4:13), then Jesus's Galilean activity (Luke 4:14—9:51), followed by the travel narrative to Jerusalem as the third critical division (Luke 9:51—19:27). Finally, this chapter concludes by considering the events in Jerusalem in Luke 19:28—22:1 just prior to the initial pericope of this study (Judas's betrayal in Luke 22:1–6).

This material introduces the cosmic duel between Jesus and the dark powers along with the principles of socioeconomic ethics, including the reversal motif, denoting various political implications. The Gospel narrative heightens the anticipation during Jesus's journey to Jerusalem of the culminating event that occurs in his feud with evil forces. Other vital background

---

1. 1QM 15:11–13.

elements will be considered later within the textual analysis section when these factors arise.

Prologue to Jesus's Ministry (Luke 1:1—4:13)

The earliest section of Luke's Gospel identifies Jerusalem as a center of concern, foreshadowing Jesus's battle with the dark forces there. Additionally, the reversal theme is critical early in the Gospel, depicting stark socioeconomic and political realities. The opening narrative is the announcement of John the Baptist's forthcoming birth, a scene which takes place at the Jerusalem temple (Luke 1:5–25). The role reversal is evident in the contrast between Luke's portrayal of Zechariah and Elizabeth. The honorable male priest Zechariah was rendered mute and socially shamed, while his previously dishonored wife (due to barrenness), Elizabeth, was restored—both her womb and voice were opened, removing her shame. Elizabeth, in contrast to societal conventions, continued to act as the primary representative of Zechariah's household, maintaining important speech and social relations within the community (Luke 1:39–45, 56–63). When Zechariah's voice is restored, he relays the "political acts" (Luke 1:64–79) of salvation as a deliverance from enemies (1:69, 71, 74, 77), and God's gift of "light to those who sit in darkness" (1:79).[2] The "political and military language"[3] of the Benedictus reads as if the "Messianic Jesus advanced by Zechariah's son John was destined to lead a David-style thrashing of Roman legions on the battlefield."[4]

John the Baptist's ministry was set within the context of "scrutiny by powerful—and potentially punitive—political and religious authorities,"[5] which "underscores the danger of prophetic ministry" (Luke 3:1–2).[6] John was imprisoned and eventually executed due to his confrontation with the political leaders (Luke 3:19–20). His prophetic tone was also situated in the context of the Isaianic new exodus, when exiles returned from imperial captivity (Luke 3:4–6). Furthermore, the "political symbolism" of John's wilderness baptism bears comparison to others who sought to re-create the Jordan crossing, mimicking the Egyptian liberation of the past as a means

---

2. Marshall, "Political and Eschatological Language," 158.
3. Marshall, "Political and Eschatological Language," 157.
4. Spencer, *Luke*, 59.
5. Spencer, *Luke and Acts*, 139.
6. Reid and Matthews, *Luke 1–9*, 285.

of contemporary Roman protest.[7] The Jordan baptism also evoked memories of Naaman's leprous cure (2 Kgs 5:1–27),[8] a mechanism that earned the Syrian military leader's allegiance toward God. Furthermore, socioeconomic ethics were an essential companion to John's baptism with the prophet's insistence to eschew greed while demonstrating radical generosity, a principle even applying to political operatives (Luke 3:10–14).

Jesus's birth announcement was delivered with Messianic connotations (Luke 1:26–38), including the extension of an everlasting Davidic dynasty (Luke 1:32–33) juxtaposed with Israel's illegitimate leadership. Upon receiving the news, Mary departed Galilee for Judea, in proximity to Jerusalem (Luke 1:39–45). The prophetic speech in Mary's Magnificat (Luke 1:46–55) underscores Messianic implications, including "political and military deliverance."[9] It calls for socioeconomic reform: "He has brought down the mighty from their thrones, and has lifted up those of lowly position; he has filled the hungry with good things, and has sent the rich away empty" (Luke 1:52–53 NET).

Jerusalem remained the epicenter of Jesus's destiny. An imperial decree prompted his family to travel from Nazareth to Bethlehem, reinforcing the Davidic connection (Luke 2:1–7). Jesus's birth was humble; however, the angelic announcement was filled with parallels to "Roman imperial theology."[10] From the "good news" (Luke 2:10) of a birthed savior to the world (Luke 2:11) with an "army" of messengers (2:13) declaring "peace" upon the earth (Luke 2:14), the imagery is striking. Each element of this event aligns with an imperial context.[11]

The remaining information regarding Jesus's early life also occurred in Jerusalem. First, at his temple presentation, prophetic validation highlights the destiny of this young child (Luke 2:25–40). Israel's "salvation" (Luke 2:30) and Jerusalem's "redemption" (Luke 2:38) find confirmation in Jesus. He is to be "a light, for revelation to the Gentiles" (Luke 2:32 NET), causing the "falling and rising of many" (Luke 2:34 NET). At age twelve, Jesus remained at the Jerusalem temple during Passover, remarkably engaging the teachers (Luke 2:41–51). Later, around age thirty, the Holy Spirit attached

---

7. Reid and Matthews, *Luke 1–9*, 287.
8. Spencer, *Luke and Acts*, 140.
9. Marshall, "Political and Eschatological Language," 158.
10. Borg and Crossan, *First Christmas*, 187. See Luke 2:8–21.
11. Borg and Crossan, *First Christmas*, 187.

to him at baptism with an affirmation of divine sonship (Luke 3:21–22), supplemented through his Davidic genealogy (Luke 3:23–38).[12]

His initial duel with the dark forces was the critical event marking the transition from Jesus's formative years into his ministry. Following his Holy Spirit reception, Jesus resided in the wilderness for forty days of testing with the devil (Luke 4:1–13). Each test, to some degree, involved a selfish, and perhaps a covetous, need. The first was food (Luke 4:3), and the last involved the Jerusalem temple (Luke 4:9), again referring to Jesus's destiny on those premises. The central testing marker was the devil's offering to Jesus "all the kingdoms of this world" (Luke 4:5–6 NET). This pericope conveys that "a spiritual fight rages for control of God's world."[13] Its worldview suggests that earthly powers—from Egypt and Babylon to Rome's first-century empire—were under the influence and control of the dark spiritual powers.

This introductory bridge to Jesus's ministry highlights Jerusalem and its temple as a geographic core of his life. Additionally, the reversal implications are noted throughout this section with specific socioeconomic factors as indicated by Mary's Magnificat (Luke 1:46–55) and John the Baptist's ethics of greed and generosity (Luke 3:10–14). As Jesus transitioned into his Galilean ministry, the feud with the evil powers became clear, especially when the devil left him "until a more opportune time" (Luke 4:13 NET).

Jesus's Galilean Ministry (Luke 4:14—9:51)

The initial noteworthy event of Jesus's Galilean ministry occurs in his hometown, Nazareth, resulting in a key programmatic pronouncement that is essential in understanding his mission. He proclaimed the Isaianic Jubilee: "The Spirit of the Lord is upon me, because he has anointed me to proclaim good news to the poor. He has sent me to proclaim release to the captives and the regaining of sight to the blind, to set free those who are oppressed, to proclaim the year of the Lord's favor" (Luke 4:18–19 NET).

In Jesus's initial remarks, "the political language of the text is unmistakable. Greco-Roman auditors would associate with these prophetic words the kinds of expectations that were pronounced at the beginning of

---

12. Considerable work has been done concerning possible parallels to the "son of God," divine birth, and potentials in literary comparison between Jesus and Caesar Augustus, adding further weight to Luke's invitation to read his writings in an imperial context. See Kochenash, "Adam, Son of God," 307–25.

13. Spencer, *Luke and Acts*, 146.

an imperial reign."¹⁴ Moreover, the overlap between visible governmental structures and the captivity by the dark forces is implicit. As the initial Jubilee mandate (Lev 25) was a response to Egyptian exploitative economic practices, so also the Jubilee endorsed by Jesus was intended to confront greed in all forms.[15]

Jesus's own commentary affirms his fulfillment of the Isaianic passage paralleling him to Elijah and Elisha, both of whom served gentiles, including Naaman (Luke 4:22–30). From this foundation, both direct and indirect Roman agents play essential roles in Jesus's proclaimed kingdom of God. These include the distinguished centurion, a patron in Galilee (Luke 7:1–10), and the tax collectors in fellowship with Jesus (Luke 5:27–32). The intersect of these two Lukan categories is intriguing—that those serving imperial interests were simultaneously taught the ethics of God's kingdom (Luke 4:42–44).

The effects of the kingdom conveyed by Jesus were to be demonstrated not merely through ethics, but also by power—the expulsion of dark forces inhabiting people and society. Jesus's mastery over the dark forces was evident across multiple events. Examples include the unclean spirit and anonymous demons in Capernaum (Luke 4:33–37, 38–41), the demons plaguing his female disciples (Luke 8:2), and the distressed father with a demon-afflicted son (Luke 9:37–43). The command over the evil powers extends to his disciples (Luke 9:1). Luke 8:26–39 presents a particularly detailed and compelling scenario depicting Jesus's involvement of demonic spirits when confronting a "Legion" (Luke 8:30). There are representative qualities present in the demon-tormented man who functions as a surrogate of the "disruption and oppression caused by military occupation of the land by the Roman legions."[16] Richard Horsley has convincingly engaged this story, assessing multiple linguistic and conceptual parallels beyond the reference of Legion to argue the stark political implications of Jesus's activity.[17] Perrin provides another example of recent scholarship compelled by this imagery, as he also weighs the idolatrous nature and effects of Roman domination.[18]

The narrative sequence demonstrates that when dark forces were confronted, Jesus's healing ministry was also possible (Luke 5:12–26; 8:38–56),

14. See Reid and Matthews, *Luke 1–9*, 339n58.
15. Brueggemann, *Money and Possessions*, 52.
16. Carroll, *Luke: A Commentary*, 193.
17. Horsley, *Jesus and the Powers*, 127.
18. Perrin, *Jesus the Temple*, 166.

extending even to the resurrection of the dead (Luke 7:11–17, 8:40–56). Jesus's healing also propelled controversy, prompting various forces, including the Pharisees, to devise a solution to this perceived threat (Luke 6:11). Furthermore, Jesus treated social disorders. For example, the feeding of five thousand men (Luke 9:10–17) was a symbolic gesture in a world in which imperial policy governed the production of agrarian life. Jesus's actions sufficiently demonstrated his regard for the needs of the people in contrast to that of the tyrannical reigning powers.[19] Likewise, Jesus's miracle that generated a great catch of fish had subtle economic implications in a setting of an exploited fishing industry subject to Roman oversight (Luke 5:1–11).[20]

Furthermore, Jesus's self-identification as "Lord of the Sabbath" was commensurate with food provision, depicting that true Sabbath can only be experienced with sufficient nourishment. In addition, by invoking the Sabbath's roots, he portrays himself as a liberator akin to Moses's protest against Pharaoh's oppressive rule.[21] Therefore, Jesus exerted control over nature, multiplying food and calming the storm, providing further demonstrations of power over the dark forces (Luke 8:22–25).

When Jesus subdued the dark powers, he also resisted their human subordinates. This is evidenced in his crafty remarks concerning Herod Antipas in two specific instances (Luke 7:24, 9:7–9). The Herodian economic system under Roman patronage was well-attested as generating high taxation and significant debt. To address this, Jesus assigns such imagery in parabolic form. He not only shows reversal between the honorable Pharisee juxtaposed with the shamefully reputed woman in the parable of debtors but also indicates the economy of God's kingdom of Jubilee (Luke 7:36–50).[22] These ethics were further demonstrated in Jesus's Sermon on the Plain. After highlighting his control over dark spirits (Luke 6:17–18), he blessed the poor and hungry (Luke 6:20–21), contrasting them with the rich and well fed (Luke 6:24–25). Likewise, the ethics of generosity were remarkably conveyed to the extent of giving to everyone who asks without requiring a return (Luke 6:29–30, 34), a contrast to greedy economic practices within his context.

Jesus's ministry in Galilee began with important Lukan themes. He taught a Jubilee that relinquished the stronghold of the dark powers in

19. Food was about Roman power; see Carter, *Roman Empire and NT*, 110.
20. Hanson, "Galilean Fishing Economy," 99–111.
21. Brueggemann, *Sabbath as Resistance*, 2.
22. Oakman, *Jesus, Debt, Lord's Prayer*, 95.

many aspects of life, which was accompanied by the ethics of this release noted in the Sermon on the Plain. There, the hallmark of a life absent of greed was conjoined with Jesus's demonstrated command over evil operatives, including socioeconomic and political factors. Finally, in the latter part of the Galilean section, Jesus reiterated Jerusalem's narrative destiny when he communicated impending events that would transpire in that city (Luke 9:22, 31, 43).

The Travel Narrative to Jerusalem (Luke 9:51—19:27)

The lengthiest division of Luke's Gospel is the travel narrative to Jerusalem, a literary device which reminds the reader that Jesus's destiny lies in that location.[23] As the cosmic duel intensifies in that section, so the sense of urgency reiterates in several passages. Potential disciples had no time to bury their own dead (Luke 9:57–62). Moreover, Jesus expressed his intention to bring fire and division (Luke 12:49–53), which was symbolically indicated by perceptive audiences recognizing changes in the weather, like an approaching storm (Luke 12:54–56). Furthermore, Jesus issued a metaphoric call to respond with similar urgency to settle debts and avoid drastic legal action (Luke 12:57–59). All of these are hyperbolic components anticipating the anxiety associated with Jesus's aim toward Jerusalem. Furthermore, the holy city must bear fruit or risk enduring continuous actions of violence (Luke 13:1–9), leading to Jesus's lament over the location (Luke 13:34–35).

Along the way, Jesus dispatched seventy-two disciples. These operatives were announcing the kingdom of God (Luke 10:1–3, 11) in the war with evil, whose success is self-surprising, prompting Jesus's observation, "I saw Satan fall like lightning from heaven. Look, I have given you authority to tread on snakes and scorpions and on the full force of the enemy, and nothing will hurt you" (Luke 10:18–19 NET). With echoes of the demise of the king of Babylon (Isa 14:13–15), this "apocalyptic vision"[24] signifies the rise of Christ and the conquering of dark forces, resulting in ramifications for the earthly kingdoms.

Jesus continued to overcome the dark powers when casting out demons. Some attribute his success as being enabled by the "ruler of demons" (Luke 11:14–15), prompting Jesus's response, "So if Satan too is divided

---

23. Regarding Jesus's destiny in the direction of Jerusalem, see Luke 9:51, 53; 13:22, 31–33; 17:11, 25; 18:31; and 19:11, 31–34.

24. Bovon, *Luke 2*, 31.

against himself, how will his kingdom stand? I ask you this because you claim that I cast out demons by Beelzebul. But if I cast out demons by the finger of God, then the kingdom of God has already overtaken you" (Luke 11:18–20 NET). This echoes the exodus, as the power of God was revealed in superiority to the forces of Egypt (Exod 8:15; 31:18; Deut 9:10). Moreover, the "finger of God" evokes possible allusions to Babylon's fall and the mysterious divine message on the wall to King Belshazzar (Dan 5:5). The adjacent parable (Luke 11:21–22) of binding the strong man leads Perrin to consider the potential that Rome, by way of the spiritual forces that it represents, was Jesus's target.[25] As the narrative progressed with Jesus continuing toward Jerusalem, his command over evil grew stronger. He healed a woman, attributing her physical condition to being "bound by Satan" (Luke 13:10–17), which he clearly subdued.

A vivid aspect of Jesus's ministry involved controlling dark forces that occupied human bodies. He affirms this with the words, "Look, I am casting out demons and performing healings today and tomorrow" (Luke 13:32 NET). Furthermore, Jesus's Sabbath healings (Luke 14:1–6), the cleansing of ten lepers (Luke 17:11–19), and the restoration of sight to a blind man (Luke 19:35–43) further demonstrated his power over physically disrupting forces.

As Satan began to fall, the Gospel's central section further emphasizes socioeconomic ethical teachings. These range from the story of the generous Samaritan whose personal sacrifice demonstrated genuine commandment-keeping (Luke 10:25–37) to the parable of the wealthy fool who hoarded excess harvest and boasted of his extravagance (Luke 12:13–21). Additionally, both brothers within the traditionally identified parable of the prodigal son exhibited forms of greed (Luke 15:11–32). Jesus juxtaposed the hungry, ill, and poor character Lazarus with a well-fed, indulgent rich man, unconcerned about those hovering on the outside of his gates (Luke 16:19–31). That story is told adjacent to the narrator's remark that the Pharisees challenged Jesus because they loved money (Luke 16:14).

Jesus's teachings on banquet ethics conveyed critical socioeconomic principles. He taught that humility is a chief value by reversing societal honor positions (Luke 14:7–11). As he puts it, "For everyone who exalts himself will be humbled, but the one who humbles himself will be exalted" (Luke 14:11 NET). The social currency of reciprocity should not be the dominant motivation for extending invitations; rather, the picture of God's kingdom was realized when the dishonorable were received as guests, even

---

25. Perrin, *Luke*, 217–18.

to the exclusion of the elite (Luke 14:12–24). Later, the rich ruler initially appeared to be a law keeper yet was mournful of Jesus's command to detach from his wealth to benefit the needy and acquire inheritance in the kingdom of God (Luke 18:18–24). This led to Jesus's commentary, "How hard it is for the rich to enter the kingdom of God!" (18:24 NET). Immediately before Jesus's arrival in Jerusalem, Zacchaeus served as a prime example of positive reception of kingdom ethics. He relinquished half of his assets to the poor and paid restitution on his fraudulent activity at a 400 percent interest rate (Luke 19:1–10).

The reversal motif, notably indicated by socioeconomic concerns, continued, as a widow's dedication to justice enabled her to disrupt the activities of an unholy judge (Luke 18:1–8). Furthermore, the notorious tax collector departed the temple vindicated by God, while the holy Pharisee was the subject of rebuke (Luke 18:9–14). Likewise, Jesus's disciples experienced a reversal when he corrected their attempt to reserve his attention. Instead, he directed them to not only permit children to have access to him, but also to emulate those youths (Luke 18:15–17).

Unsurprisingly, the travel narrative to Jerusalem referenced the city multiple times, heightening the reader's expectations regarding Jesus's arrival there. At the same time, the battle against the dark powers continued, both through specific activity between Jesus and agents of evil, as through his expression of socioeconomics ethics. Among these, the "great reversal" served as a vital weapon in the ongoing feud with darkness. Early in this lengthiest division of Luke's Gospel, Jesus celebrates Satan's falling. Then, as the travel narrative approaches its close, Jesus notes that unlearned people perceive the hidden truths of God's kingdom instead of the supposedly wise and intelligent (Luke 10:21–22). The pertinent question for Jerusalem, which took its place as the epicenter of the war with evil, is whether that city would see and recognize the time of their visitation (Luke 19:44).

The Events in Jerusalem (Luke 19:28—22:1)

In the concluding section of Luke's Gospel, events in Jerusalem contrast Jesus's humble entry with a powerful Roman procession entering the city. This demonstration of strength was intended to underscore imperial might near the start of Passover week (Luke 19:28–40).[26] Jesus's entrance included expressions of kingship (19:38), a political exercise symbolizing a threat to

---

26. Borg and Crossan, *Last Week*, 1–3.

Roman dominance. Moreover, Jesus's next action was his temple protest, targeting the monetary transactions symbolizing an act of terror and social disruption (Luke 19:45-48). With Jerusalem and its temple, then, the ground zero of the battle against evil, Jesus lamented over that location (Luke 19:41-44).

Furthermore, Jesus remained in the temple, receiving honor challenges. He met opposition from the chief priests and experts in the law (Luke 20:1-8), agents discussing Roman taxation (Luke 20:20-26), and Sadducees regarding resurrection (Luke 20:27-44). To some extent, these temple challenges reflected the ongoing feud with the dark powers in conjunction with socioeconomic ethics. Jesus supplied his motivations when quoting from Isa 56:7 and Jer 7:11, highlighting concerns about socioeconomic injustice.[27] This is reinforced by his later temple statement observing how members of his opposition "devour widows' property" (Luke 20:47 NET). He then juxtaposes the wealthy givers of Jerusalem with the poor widow and her gift (Luke 21:1-4).

The temple stood as the main stage of the conflict with darkness. There, Jesus contrasted the temple's grandeur with prophecies of its downfall (Luke 20:5-9). He foreshadowed the coming opposition (Luke 21:10-19), Jerusalem's destruction (Luke 21:20-24), and the Son of Man's return (Luke 21:25-38). This section, the precursor of Judas's betrayal, illustrates the ongoing conflict, so much so that Jerusalem becomes a place of controversy, with various parties resisting Jesus, presumably under the influence of evil.

Synthesis

This chapter surveyed Luke's Gospel from its introductory material, through Jesus's ministry and travel narrative, to his temple interactions immediately preceding Judas's betrayal. Upon the launch of his ministry, the kingdom of God was pronounced, and a cosmic battle proceeded between Jesus and the dark powers, first noted through the devil's wilderness testing (Luke 4:1-13). This feud was further depicted through Jesus's commandeering of demons and unclean spirits. This conflict with darkness was apparent

---

27. The context of Isa 56:1-8 is the ethics of justice and inclusiveness with the return from exile with the reception of socially marginalized foreigners and eunuchs. Moreover, the referenced section to Jeremiah's temple speech (Jer 7:1-29) conveys the prophetic concerns over a variety of abuses, including the neglect of the "foreigner, the fatherless or the widow" (7:6) among other socioeconomic rebukes.

when, upon directing his steps toward Jerusalem, Jesus dispatched his disciples, whose success illustrated Satan falling (Luke 10:1–17). Multiple sub-elements comprise the weaponry of this war, including socioeconomic ethics that are often portrayed through Luke's reversal theme, by which the dark powers were confronted and fall, and societal structures were disrupted and reorganized. Luke's readers see a summons to reject greed and adopt the generous principles of God's kingdom. In this vision of societal rebalancing, the humble, poor, and dishonored rise, while the proud and wealthy assume greater responsibility.

Those with excess were exhorted to relinquish their claim on assets to the benefit of those who suffered from deficient resources. Such variables not only argue for the downfall of darkness but also pose a threat to any system which excels based on socioeconomic imbalances. Clearly and prominently, to Luke's audience, this would have been that of the Roman Empire itself. From the outset of this feud with evil, Jesus rejected the devil's invitation to become an ally or client in exchange for political power (Luke 4:1–13). Instead, Jesus directly confronted the dark forces and, throughout Luke-Acts, various political agents faced the dilemma of choosing sides. This conflict intensified with Jesus's engagements in Jerusalem.

Darrell Bock notes that in Luke-Acts "restoration encompasses a victory over transcendent forces, Satan, and evil."[28] While Bock describes these conflicts as "battles" with darkness, Darío López Rodriguez cautions against over-spiritualization. He insists that in Luke's Gospel socioeconomic marginalization "by those who wield political and economic power, constitutes—from the lens of the kingdom of God—a non-negotiable hermeneutical key for the missionary reflection."[29] Accordingly, this chapter has surveyed the ongoing conflict with dark supernatural forces in conjunction with socioeconomic and political implications. The discussion now shifts to the events in Jerusalem and how evil will respond.

---

28. Bock, *Theology of Luke Acts*, 399.

29. Bock, *Theology of Luke Acts*, 399; see also Rodriguez, *Liberating Mission of Jesus*, 125–26.

Chapter 2: Satan, Judas, and Betrayal: Prelude to Darkness (Luke 22:1–6 and Acts 1:15–20)

Judas thinks in the categories of the old economy, in terms of a zero-sum notion about money.[1]

—WALTER BRUEGGEMANN

Introduction and Background

LUKE'S PORTRAYAL OF JUDAS in Luke 22:1–6 and Acts 1:15–20 illustrate his association with the evil forces of wealth. Judas's treachery betrayed not only the social dynamic of Jesus's disciple group but also the essence of discipleship itself. The social, political, and economic factors of the setting illustrate that he became a symbol of the widespread exploitation within the Judean context. Furthermore, Judas's death symbolized the fate of the dark powers.

Jesus's entrance into Jerusalem and his immediate engagement within the temple were politically charged demonstrations protesting the economic malpractice of its rulers (Luke 19:28–40). This gesture prompted a series of public debates (honor challenges) initiated by the priests, lawyers, elders, and Sadducees (Luke 20:1–44). This "tense political backdrop"[2] built toward a climax, with the "political dilemma"[3] motivating a sense of

---

1. Brueggemann, *Money and Possessions*, 203.
2. Spencer, *Luke and Acts*, 251.
3. Ringe, *Luke*, 256.

urgency in which Satan and human operatives responded to Jesus. These events underlie the unfolding story of Judas.

Textual Analysis

Judas in Luke 22:1–6

Luke highlights the approaching Feast of Unleavened Bread and Passover. This pilgrimage festival swelled Jerusalem's population, stirring political and patriotic sentiments, recalling Israel's deliverance from Egyptian tyranny (Exod 11:1–10). The plagues inflicted upon the Egyptians disrupted various sociopolitical, religious, and economic routines. This culminated in God's victory in the "single most important historical and theological"[4] event of Jewish tradition. The Egyptian economy, based on excess production, relied on a strict work regimen that served Pharaoh's purposes by exploiting the enslaved populace.[5] Therefore, the backdrop to the historical occasion of Luke 22:1–6 includes God's liberation from Pharaoh's economic system. This creates a fitting signpost when greed and the dark powers again converge.[6]

The Passover required the chief priests to perform their public duties. Despite this, the imperfect active indicative tense of "began looking" (ζητέω, Luke 22:6 NET) ironically points out that their liturgical responsibilities seem subordinate to their ongoing objectives to organize Jesus's death (Luke 22:2).[7] Judith Lieu remarks on Luke's lack of explanation as to why Passover escalated the priestly sense of urgency.[8] Nevertheless, this occasion implicitly celebrates a liberation from the dark powers both past and present. Then Satan reappeared in the "final showdown,"[9] assisted not

---

4. Dallaire and Morris, "Joshua and Israel's Exodus," 20.

5. Brueggemann, *Sabbath as Resistance*, 2–5, not only highlights the severe work regiment Pharaoh imposed but also the activism of Torah, including the Sabbath-related laws in protest to Egypt's economic exploitation.

6. Just, *Luke 9:51—24:53*, 811, notes that the word ἤγγιζεν, located in Luke 22:1, together with the adjective ἐγγύς and verb ἐγγίζω, is frequently employed in Luke's inaugurated eschatology, indicating the event's significance.

7. L&N, "ἀναιρέω," 235, describes the meaning of the word ἀναιρέω as "to get rid of someone by execution, often with legal or quasi-legal procedures."

8. Lieu, *Gospel of Luke*, 176.

9. Danker, *Jesus and New Age*, 218.

only by Judas, but also the chief priests, as dark political and even imperial interests converge in this new exodus imagery.[10]

Gospel readers are alerted to the chief priests and scribes through Jesus's indication of their forthcoming rejection (Luke 9:22). Scribes were critical of Jesus from the beginning of his Galilean ministry, and they were frequently identified with the Pharisees.[11] Jesus's prediction was heightened by his public disputes with the leadership in Jerusalem. The judicial conspiracy to assassinate Jesus was delayed because the leadership feared the crowds.[12] Ultimately, under Roman patronage, the responsibilities of the chief priests included the maintenance of public order. Their concern regarding the crowds reflects the prominent risk of a protest or potential riot in response to Jesus's legal apprehension, as larger-scale, revolt-type of activity tended to jeopardize the priesthood's safety.[13]

Luke indicates a discrepancy between Jesus's public approval and his reception by the Jewish rulers. Jesus's economic message espoused a policy appealing to people who had been exploited by the elite, a group which included the mainstream peasant and marginalized populaces in Jewish Palestine. His message was also relevant to the diasporic pilgrims, since Jesus's rebuke of the temple's socioeconomic mishandling applied to levied temple taxes (Luke 19:45–48).[14] The temple and its rulers were inseparably identified with Roman occupation and Herodian politics.[15] Thus, Jesus's temple protest undermined the authority of the elite, signaling an attack upon the dark powers at Jewish ground zero.

This prompted a retaliatory counterattack. Satan's direct intervention occurred when he entered Judas. In contrast to the filling by the Holy Spirit, which produces prophetic speech in Luke-Acts,[16] Satan's possession inspired a negative voice of betrayal. In Lukan writings, Satan is the assumed accuser or adversary of Hebrew Scriptures, morphed into the personification of darkness, and known by various titles in Second Temple Judaism

---

10. Ahn, *Reign of God*, 149, 160–61.

11. Regarding negative association of scribes with Pharisees, see Luke 5:21, 30; 6:7; 11:53; and 15:2.

12. Luke utilizes Φοβέομαι, or "fear," in strategic ways, tending to indicate the internal disposition of persons in either a positive or negative reception to Jesus.

13. Josephus, *J.W.* 4.3–5; 6.4–5.

14. Oakman, *Jesus and the Peasants*, 191–97.

15. Horsley, *Jesus and Empire*, locs. 1111–12 of 2247.

16. See Luke 1:41–42, 67; 2:25–32; 4:1, 14–15, 18–19; Acts 2:4; 3:1; 4:8; 6:10; 7:55–56; 9:17–20; 10:44–46; 13:9–10; and 19:6.

as a primary culprit of evil.[17] Jesus previously commandeered Satan (Luke 10:18, 11:18, 13:16), prompting his strategic response.

Since Satan could enter one of Jesus's twelve primary disciples, Luke projects that the dark forces may penetrate any person or organization (Luke 4:5–6). Eduard Schweizer states that Judas's actions were "ascribed to Satan,"[18] and Charles Talbert remarks that "Satan manipulates Judas by his affection for money";[19] yet both understate the betrayer's culpability. Luke supplements Mark to elevate Judas's guilt to the extent that he is "more than a mere traitor, but a rival to God."[20]

Luke situates Judas as a pivotal character, enabling the conspiracy of the dark forces to materialize. The narrative intensified with his transferred allegiance to Satan, as Judas conspired with his new partners.[21] Among all Greek sources, παραδίδωμι (Luke 22:4) frequently amounts to an unjust act.[22] The chief priests were left rejoicing at Judas's resolution to their dilemma. Luke's usages of χαίρω (Luke 22:5) are more profound than simply being "glad" (NASB), "pleased" (NRSV), or even "delighted" (NIV). Rather, Luke uses χαίρω to express a fulfilling sense of missional accomplishment.[23] Hence, the prospects Judas delivers to the evil powers were deeply satisfying.

These dark culprits "agreed" (συντίθημι, 22:5) on a plan. This is a word Luke also uses to convey an unjust conspiracy to murder Paul in Jerusalem (Acts 23:20), consistent with other historical usages meaning "to frame, devise, or contrive."[24] David Garland contends (albeit with little argument) that Judas negotiates for his sum of money.[25] If so, his compensation was the result of greedy demand rather than natural reciprocity. Regardless, the powers elected to give him money, conveying a sense of bribery. The devil

---

17. Pagels, "Social History of Satan," 35–61.
18. Schweizer, *Good News*, 330.
19. Talbert, *Reading Luke*, 206.
20. Harvey, *Judas Iscariot*, 190–91, 237.
21. L&N, "στρατηγός," 481; in addition to its use in Luke 22:52 and Acts 4:1, 5:24, and 5:26, στρατηγός, or "officers," is also applied to legal authorities in Philippi (Acts 16:20, 22, 35, 36, 38).
22. Oropeza, *Footsteps of Judas*, 23, 43, 143.
23. Regarding Luke's use of χαίρω as a fulfilling sense of missional accomplishment, see Luke 1:14, 28; 6:23; 10:20; 13:17; 15:5, 32; 19:6, 37; 23:8; Acts 5:41; 8:39; 11:23; 13:48; 15:23; and 15:31. Fox, *Hermeneutics of Social Identity*, 232, notes χαίρω is often a response to "eschatological salvation," but here indicates that Judas "loves money more than Jesus."
24. MGS, s.v. "συντίθημι."
25. Garland, *Luke*, 1431.

had offered Jesus authority over earthly kingdoms, which he rejected (Luke 4:1–12). In turn, evil sought a more auspicious opportunity to disrupt the Jesus operation (Luke 4:6, 13). A dark reallocation of resources was extended to Judas with money (and influence, rather than direct political rule) as the exchange mechanism to derail Jesus's activities. In so doing, the dark forces, money, and greed between Judas and the powers converged.

The love of money is the antithesis of discipleship (Luke 16:14) and served as a potent tool for the dark influences.[26] Luke deviates from the Matthean (26:15) record, which attached a numeric value (thirty) to the volume of coins Judas received. Instead, Luke has multiple reasons for supplying an open-ended quantity, which ultimately makes the betrayal more extensive (to be argued in the following section). Nevertheless, upon making financial arrangements, Judas then awaited an opportunity. Previously, when the devil ceased his initial testing of Jesus, he awaited a more favorable time (Luke 4:13), and Satan's entrance of Judas captivated that potential.

The insider/outsider boundaries of the disciples were violated when Judas was possessed by darkness, generating a theoretical threat to the purity of Jesus's inner circle.[27] Judas later delivered Jesus with a kiss (Luke 22:47). The nature of his betrayal was more complex than simply locating and identifying Jesus, who had been openly visible in the temple (Luke 19:45—21:38). Because the chief priests feared public outcry, they opted for a secret arrest.

Nevertheless, the theory that Judas's primary usefulness was in leading the officers to retrieve Jesus on the Mount of Olives is uncompelling. This perspective would require the assumption that Jesus's entourage would have been able to outmaneuver a likely intelligence detail. A more satisfying theory is that Judas's treachery included testimony providing incriminating evidence to secure Jesus's legal indictment.[28] The judicial questions inquire of Jesus's self-identification as "Christ," "Son of God," and "king," which the text indicates as ample evidence for execution by the authorities (Luke 22:66–71; 23:1–5). From the Gospel's portrayal, these terms represent insider knowledge and are likely the basis of what Judas conveyed to

---

26. When Jesus dispatched disciples, he told them not to carry ἀργύριον (Luke 9:3, 10:4).

27. Pilch argues two primary elements of impurity are corrupt infiltration, observed when Satan enters Judas, who becomes a profaned member of the Jesus group. Moreover, inconsistencies are another source of impurity, and Jesus's disciple group became an example of this, having mixed composition. Pilch, "Purity," 147.

28. Stein, *Luke*, 536.

the rulers. Luke does not supply any of these terms as having been publicly ascribed to Jesus except in attestation from the dark powers (Luke 4:41, 8:28), with which Judas ultimately aligned.

The effectiveness of evil was not merely in drawing the chief priests, scribes, Sanhedrin, Herod, and Pilate into cooperation, but in targeting the Jesus group itself. The success at purchasing Judas inspired the ambitions of the dark powers toward Peter, attempting to further disrupt the Jesus group by sifting him as wheat (Luke 22:31). Peter thus experienced his own honor duel with evil (Luke 22:54–62),[29] and the "power of darkness" appeared to gain momentum at the time of Jesus's distress leading up to his arrest (Luke 22:53 NET).

The Sanhedrin's questioning of Jesus involved several figures, including some Pharisees, whom Luke already portrayed as greedy (Luke 16:14).[30] The body comprised Sadducees, "power brokers" benefiting from their elite status,[31] strongly supported by the wealthiest class.[32] Additionally, Caiaphas, the high priest and Sanhedrin member, led an institution known for greed (to be discussed on pages [XREF] 22 and 23). His lengthy tenure suggests he was politically astute and skillfully served Roman interests, even offering sacrifices for the emperor.[33] Notably, during Caiaphas's term, temple funds were scandalously misappropriated to fund an aqueduct—a scheme for which he was largely responsible.[34] The Jerusalem scribes, also ruling-class members, benefiting socioeconomically from their positions, joined in the conspiracy.[35] Judas then joined forces with these greedy, socioeconomic elitists in Jerusalem, attempting to undermine the Jesus group.

Judas's betrayal exceeded mere misdeeds toward Jesus—it involved a transition of alliance to the dark powers of wealth. Luke's narrative extends the Passover motif through Jesus's meal (Luke 22:7–20), symbolizing the

---

29. The testing of Jesus's disciples is also reflected in their response to the sacred moment of the Last Supper when they begin to argue over the greatest among them, a clear dismantling of the reversal conceptuality that Jesus has reinforced in the Gospel (Luke 22:24–27).

30. Luke 16:14; cf. Luke 5:27–39; 7:36–50; and 15:1–2, 11–32.

31. Saldarini, "Sanhedrin," 5:977. See also Strauss, "Sadducees," 824.

32. Josephus, *Ant.* 13.10.6.

33. Chilton, "Annas and Caiaphas," 8–9. See also Philo, *Embassy* 157, 317; Josephus, *J.W.* 2.197; and *Ag. Ap.* 2.77, regarding temple imperial sacrifices.

34. VanderKam, *From Joshua to Caiaphas*, locs. 7191–95 of 8802. See Josephus, *Ant.* 18.3.2; *J.W.* 2.9.4.

35. Horsley, *Scribes, Visionaries, and Politics*.

"exodus" he would fulfill in Jerusalem (Luke 9:31) to confront greed and the dark powers. The meal itself, with Jesus as its metaphoric substance, signified liberation. Unlike the Passover from Egypt, Jesus's exodus progressed geographically from Jerusalem to the "ends of the earth" (Acts 1:8).

Following the meal (Luke 22:14–23), the disciples disputed their honor status (Luke 22:24–31), and Jesus warned Peter of Satan's target (Luke 22:31–34). At the Mount of Olives, urgency intensified through Jesus's prayer and warnings in Gethsemane (Luke 22:39–46). There, Judas betrayed Jesus to the arresting party (Luke 22:47–53). Jesus was questioned by the high priest (Luke 22:54–65), examined by the Sanhedrin (Luke 22:66–71), and passed between Pilate (Luke 23:1–5) and Herod (Luke 23:6–12) before Pilate ultimately sentenced him to crucifixion (Luke 23:13–54). The resurrection marked Jesus's triumph over the dark powers, witnessed by the women at the tomb (Luke 24:1–12), travelers to Emmaus (Luke 24:13–35), and the eleven disciples (Luke 24:36–43). Acts records the commissioning "to the ends of the earth" (Acts 1:8), followed by Jesus's ascension (Luke 24:44–52; Acts 1:1–11).

The disciples initially remained in Jerusalem (Acts 1:12–14),[36] and Luke indicates a transition with the phrase "in those days" (ἐν ταῖς ἡμέραις, 1:15). This delineates the time frame between ascension and Pentecost. In that new setting, just as at Passover, the disciples awaited a festival. They were gathered in distinct space, but in an expanded number from twelve to one hundred twenty. This increased quantity functioned as a crucial narrative bridge demonstrating the failure of the dark powers to seize control of the Jesus group. Rather than the disciples being diminished due to internal conflict, they instead multiplied, a repeated characteristic of the earliest Jerusalem church in Acts (5:1–14; 6:1–7).

Judas in Acts 1:15–20

In that setting, Peter declared that the events associated with Judas "fulfilled" (πληρόω, Acts 1:16) Scripture; therefore, the role of the dark powers was in fact limited. Luke's usage of πληρόω is reserved for notable eschatological

---

36. The ascension also bears some thematic resemblance to the stories of both Joseph and Daniel, who are placed into their own metaphoric graves (Gen 37:18–24; Dan 6:1–28) yet ascend to imperial influence in Egypt and Persia respectively, a perspective reinforcing the lordship of Christ.

events,[37] and previously had only been used authoritatively by Jesus. Peter's elevated voice illuminated an apostolic contrast to Judas's negative speech and signified his victory over the dark powers that sought to sift him in a trial likely more intense than Judas's (Luke 22:31).

Peter described Judas as a "guide" (ὁδηγός, 1:16) for those who "arrested" (συλλαμβάνω, 1:16) Jesus. Identifying him as a ὁδηγός ascribes a strong degree of culpability to the betrayer as a primary vessel of the dark powers rather than a mere assistant.[38] Jesus's detention extended beyond a legal detainment; the term συλλαμβάνω conveys not only "arrested" but also "to take, seize, or take possession."[39] This idea signals the intent of dark forces to take control of persons and institutions by whatever means are necessary. This could be either through spiritual possession, penetration of the disciple group, negotiation (Luke 4:1–13; 22:1–6), or physical and judicial means, as with the apprehension of Jesus.

Peter noted that Judas was "numbered" among the disciples, originally sharing their same vocational allotment (Acts 1:17). The disciples were called to detach from material wealth and embrace an intangible inheritance (Luke 12:33; 18:28–30). However, Judas traded this apostolic calling for monetary gain, using it to "buy" (κτάομαι, Acts 1:18) a field. Luke's use of κτάομαι connects Judas's actions to Simon Magus's attempt to purchase apostolic power (Acts 8:20) and a Roman officer's bribe for citizenship (Acts 22:28). Each usage reflects a pursuit of honor through improper means. Luke's new temple theology draws from the Levitical model, where vocation substituted for land inheritance. This was exemplified in Barnabas, a Levite who sold his property for communal benefit (Acts 4:37). As priests of this new temple paradigm, the disciples were called to forsake land ownership and embrace ministry, a calling Judas ultimately rejected.

Luke deviates from Matthew, who states the chief priests purchased property with Judas's returned money (Matt 27:7). Alternatively, Luke's material argues not for a remorseful Judas, but a greedier one. Since Lukan writings do not clearly delineate between significant and humble estates, the size of Judas's asset is uncertain.[40] The expectation of Luke's readers is

---

37. See Luke 4:21, 9:31, 21:24, 22:16, and 24:44.
38. L&N, "ὁδηγός," 204; this word can indicate leadership.
39. MGS, s.v. "ὁδηγός."

40. Luke's terms for real estate vary but offer little detail on property size. He uses iterations of γῆ ("land, earth, ground, country") over fifty times, οὐσία ("property," Luke 15:12–13) two times, and ὑπάρχω ("possession") thirteen times, with three instances related to real estate (Acts 4:32, 34; 5:4). βίος appears twice for "estate" (Luke 15:13, 30), and

that antithetical disciples were associated with wealth. Such a viewpoint generates a literary and narrative presumption that Judas's purchase was sizeable, consistent with Luke's generalization of landowners.[41]

Theories attempting to reconcile Luke and Matthew's accounts regarding Judas are unconvincing,[42] and the competing accounts are not intended to be harmonized.[43] Matthew's mention of thirty pieces of silver, a modest sum equivalent to thirty days of wages, raises doubts about whether this amount alone could motivate treachery.[44] However, Luke's anonymously reported payment to Judas maintains an open-ended perspective suggesting a substantial quantity as the dark powers had powerful motivations to provide a compelling economic incentive for betrayal.

Judas's actions secured him a volume of economic well-being that not only made his treachery worthwhile but also identified him with the disdained rich of Lukan theology.[45] Judas, presumably part of the socioeconomic majority class living at subsistence level, attempted to disrupt the narrative momentum of Luke-Acts by defying its reversal motif. Luke's message, that "the first will be last" and "everyone who exalts himself will be humbled" (Luke 13:30; 14:11; 18:14 NET), promoted a social reordering that devalued wealth. In response, Judas attempted to inflate his economic standing by conspiring with the elite, illustrating the corrupting influence of wealth. Upon Judas's demise, Jerusalem designated a specific name for the location. Therefore, the land is understood as being in proximity to the city where Luke locates the earliest church.

However, the narrative flow of Acts is "to the ends of the earth" (Acts 1:8). Therefore, as the church disembarked and detached from the city, Judas, the anti-disciple, whose betrayal contrasted with Luke's theological and literary grain, also contrasted with the missional trajectories of the

---

ἀγρός ("field") ten times, but none of these instances specifies land size. χωρίον, used four times in Luke, can mean "land," "field," or "farm" (MGS, s.v. "χωρίον"); and it can extend to indicating an "estate" (*EDNT*, "χωρίον," 3:492). L&N, "χωρίον," 17, adds that χωρίον is often associated with "cultivation or pasture" (though further detail is lacking). Barrett, *Critical Exegetical Commentary—Acts*, 98, concurs that "χωρίον means an estate or farm (Mart. Pol. 7.1; cf. Xen. *Hell.* 2.4.1.)."

41. Regarding Luke's view of landowners, see Luke 12:13–21; 15:11–31; and 20:9–19.

42. Oropeza, *Footsteps of Judas*, 144.

43. Fitzmyer, *Acts of the Apostles*, 224.

44. France, *Luke*, 339–40.

45. For Luke's disdain of the rich, see Luke 1:53; 6:24; 12:13–21; 16:19–31; 18:18–30; and 21:4.

earliest church. He does this by attaching himself to that region through land ownership. Furthermore, near Jerusalem, the cost value of real estate was presumably higher, adding more intrigue to the sum negotiated by Judas. Location is integral, and being near the core of Jewish sociocultural, political, and religious life produced prime real estate for the area. This enabled its landholders to benefit from the economic prosperity associated with Jerusalem, which was largely promulgated by ongoing Herodian construction projects and three annual religious pilgrimage festivals.

The geographical purity map from the later Mishnaic tradition was ingrained into the disposition of first-century Judaism. The fabric of this worldview was that of all the places on earth, Israel was the holiest, yet the closer one moved toward Jerusalem, the holier the real estate.[46] These realities not only enforced Jerusalem as the societal core of purity but also enhanced the region's honor dynamics. Since obtaining a Jerusalem residence was equivalent to climbing the social ladder, possessing such sacred land would engender the envy of the greedy. The increasing land prices in Jerusalem contributed to the revolt of 66 CE, a trend rooted in policies already established in Jesus's time.[47] Likely written following Jerusalem's destruction, Luke connects Judas's actions to this economic dynamic, subtly linking him to the forces that would ultimately contribute to the city's demise.

Purity was both political and economic,[48] as Jerusalem's wealth was "derived in one form or another from its sanctity."[49] Judas's land acquisition near Jerusalem associated him with the greedy system perpetuated by the ruling elites. In Judea, the land was predominantly owned, managed, and influenced by the minority wealthy class.[50] Land control ultimately stemmed from Caesar's authority over all agrarian industry as "the social order of Rome became dominated . . . by land aristocracy."[51] The Herodian household, which accumulated high quantities of land in Judea, benefited from this structure.[52] The same was true for much of the upper priestly class (with whom Luke associates Judas's betrayal) who secured preferred land

---

46. See "Ten Degrees of Holiness," Mishnah, *Kelim* 1:6–9.
47. Goodman, *Rome and Jerusalem*, 390–91.
48. Borg, *Meeting Jesus Again*, 86.
49. Goodman, "Pilgrimage Economy of Jerusalem," 59.
50. Friesen, "Injustice or God's Will?," 17–36.
51. Oakman, *Jesus and the Peasants*, 14.
52. Horsley, *Jesus and Politics*, 111.

surrounding Jerusalem,[53] further enabling the region's commerce to be "controlled by wealthy priestly interests."[54] Luke was aware of this phenomenon, and throughout his "writings there is evidence of the great disparities in wealth, power, and privilege present in the Roman Empire," acknowledging "those who control large amounts of land."[55] The elitist land owners continued to accumulate property. Meanwhile, due to the ramifications of a debt policy whereby land was collateral in programs enabling the creditor to exploit the populace, the majority peasant class steadily saw their estate possession eradicated.[56]

These debt systems were enacted in Judea,[57] leading to a "widening gap between rich and poor as the economy of Judea was integrated into the wider Mediterranean world."[58] Debt-related land seizures were enabled by "demands for tribute, taxes, and tithes by multiple layers of rulers,"[59] which trajected to both Jerusalem and Rome, furthering a greedy financial connection between the two locations. This greedy characterization extended to the priesthood who served the Second Temple which was initially under Persian patronage as a mechanism for tax solicitation,[60] relating the historic priesthood to economic imperial interests in that era.[61] The temple essentially functioned as a banking operation,[62] which perpetuated notoriously greedy actions of the priestly elites, including the seizure of tithes by the armed temple guard.[63] The temple institution was involved in (and benefited from) both taxation, one of the primary culprits of economic

---

53. Freyne, "Galilee and Judaea," 50.
54. Oakman, *Jesus and the Peasants*, 66.
55. Oakman, *Jesus and the Peasants*, 143–45.
56. Goodman, *Ruling Class*, 53–54. See also, "First Jewish Revolt," 417–27.
57. Adams, *Social and Economic Life*, 78.
58. Goodman, *Ruling Class*, 51n44.
59. Horsley, *Jesus and Politics*, 90.
60. Schaper, "Jerusalem Temple as Instrument," 528–39.
61. Hays, *Temple and Tabernacle*, 162. There is also a history of bribery associated with the priesthood in the Second Temple period. Several Second Temple texts perpetuate a viewpoint of greedy priests: see Pss. Sol. 8:10–12; 1QpHab 1:13—2:10; 8:8–12; 2 Macc 4:7–10, 23–25.
62. Charlesworth, *Jesus and Temple*, 4.
63. Josephus, *Ant.* 20.206-7, 214. See also Borg, *Meeting Jesus Again*, 93, who contends that priests used their position to declare produce from peasant farmers as "unclean" if they suspected it had not been fully tithed on, limiting or possibly even excluding transactions on that crop.

exploitation, and the general debt system. This was because "high priestly families and others with access to storehouses or funds drew upon them to make loans at high interest to villagers who were struggling to feed their families after meeting their obligations for tribute, tithes, and offerings."[64] From the interest charged and/or from "foreclosure" on loans, they increased their own wealth and control of land."[65] If indeed "debt probably was most thoroughly exploited by those aligned with Rome,"[66] then Jerusalem, the temple, and Rome were not only interdependent but also intertwined with the dark powers of greed.

The vast amounts of land seized by the aristocracy forced the migration of many households from ancestral land.[67] Strikingly, the "limited good" conceptuality within the world of the text asserted that land was a completely distributed asset. In peasant locations, including Judea, it was a depleting resource becoming inaccessible to the common populace due to the apprehension by the elite.[68] The limited-good worldview assumes stark and immediate zero-sum implications; for Judas to secure property, someone must lose their land possession. In the view of the majority class living at or below subsistence and facing socioeconomic marginalization, a tarnished or unpopular person acquiring land often suggested that someone's ancestral property had unjustly been seized. Therefore, Judas's incorporation into the dark powers ultimately associated him with the greedy forces of economic manipulation, extortion, and exploitation that influenced the Judean setting and gained access to land. This reading is entirely plausible given Luke's wealth ethics and his deployment of positive and negative examples throughout his two volumes. Judas's purchase was financed by the "cost" (μισθός, 1:18) of his treachery, which reinforces that the economic exchange was not reciprocity or "reward" (NET, NRSV) but a negotiated expectation.

Judas was unable to enjoy life as a possible elitist near Jerusalem. Further unique material records that he fell headfirst. In a world that valued nobility in death,[69] the Lukan version renders a far less honorable outcome for the betrayer. In contrast, the suicide in the Matthean source delivers a gentler option, as that method was deemed appropriate under some

64. Horsley, *Jesus and Politics*, 111.
65. Horsley, *Jesus and Politics*, 111.
66. Oakman, *Jesus, Debt, Lord's Prayer*, 51.
67. Adams, *Social and Economic Life*, 13.
68. See Foster, "Peasant Society," 293–315. Meanwhile, others have appealed to biblical studies; see Neyrey, "Limited Good," 102–5.
69. Pilch, "Noble Death," 133–8.

circumstances.[70] Luke's narrative extends the most dishonorable attribution to the dark collaborators, and the shameful sequence of falling headfirst produces an apparent incision from the abdomen. The humiliation of an accidental fall was exacerbated with the head being the most visible and distinguishing portion of the body, highly associated with honor. Additionally, the descriptive features of personal identity prominently include several orifices (eyes, ears, mouth, and nose) located on the head. Jewish purity operated in high correlation to physical orifices, which served to surrogate the social body.[71] Simply put, threatened societies concern themselves with entry and exit points of the body politic, therefore the prioritization and treatment of physical orifices reflect the concerns of social openings. Judas, in an act of treachery, made penetrable the orifices of the disciple group, making it susceptible to Satan's entrance, further posing a threat to Peter.

Peter's speech enforced a reversal for the betraying disciple as his fate was compounded when he "burst open in the middle and all his intestines gushed out" (Acts 1:18 NET).[72] Judas's shameful demise was multiplied with the complexity of both a presumed head wound and an incision of his sternum, producing a massive (unnatural) physical orifice indicating considerable uncleanliness. This imagery evokes allusions to Jezebel (1 Kgs 21:23; 2 Kgs 9:10), Israel's dark queen who was judged for her greedy actions toward Naboth.[73]

Noble deaths were esteemed in ancient Judaism; 2 Maccabees contrasts honorable deaths with shameful ones. Eleazar and seven brothers chose virtuous deaths over compromising their purity (2 Macc 6:18—7:42). Meanwhile Antiochus Epiphanes, who instigated their martyrdom, suffered a shameful death from rotting flesh and worms (2 Macc 9:9). Similarly, in 3 Maccabees, King Ptolemy permitted undefiled Judeans to slay their polluted counterparts in the most shameful ways (3 Macc 7:14). Josephus later expressed a preference for execution over living with the shame of being captured by Rome.[74] Clearly, Judas was associated with the profane acts of treachery, compounded by the shameful mechanism of his demise.[75]

---

70. Seneca, *Ep. Mor.* 70; Tac. *Ann.* 15.62–64.

71. Douglas, *Purity and Danger*, 122–29.

72. In Luke 22:20, Jesus refers to his blood being ἐκχυννόμενον or "poured out."

73. The description of Judas's death is mirrored by that of Herod Agrippa I's death in Acts 12:20–24.

74. Josephus, *J.W.* 3:137.

75. Fitzmyer, *Acts of the Apostles*, 220, misses Luke's motivation and intentions when he states that "the way that Judas died is not important."

The details of Judas's death were well attested around Jerusalem (Acts 1:19). Collectivistic societies employed a "gossip network," a societal benchmark, making newsworthy material available within the dyadic settings.[76] The population surge between Passover and Pentecost would have enabled the shameful tale to extend across the Palestinian region, and in diasporic contexts, even "to the ends of the earth." Moreover, Luke chronicles the location as the "field of blood," supplying further echoes to Jezebel.[77]

Geographical identity was a crucial societal distinction; therefore, even the ground shared Judas's profanity through the perpetuated tradition of the betrayer's field. Blood functioned as a potent defilement, logically connected to corpse impurity, the greatest source of uncleanliness. When blood escaped the body, an orifice was presumed to have lost its integrity, or even worse, a new orifice was generated (flesh wound). Accordingly, the designated "field of blood" indicated extremely tainted qualities.[78] Peter quoted the psalmist: "May their camp become desolate" (69:25 MT, 68:26 LXX) and "may his days be few. May another take his job" (109:8). The apostle's voice relates these psalms specifically to Judas's status. The broader context of these quotations involves shameful rebuke, including hopes for the perpetrator to experience blindness (69:23), orphaned children, a widowed wife (109:9), and a destitute household (109:10, 12). They also include a wish for the traitor's genealogy to be eliminated (109:15) and his assets lost to creditors (109:11).

The psalmist's vivid description is that of exile contrasting the significant christological sign in Luke-Acts being the return from exile. Therefore, geographic exiles were incorporated into the movement through the narrative flow extending "to the ends of the earth" (Acts 1:8). However, Judas was exiled near Jerusalem itself. The value of his property declined, becoming desolate, functioning as a desert, as land beyond societal norms, where only exiles may congregate.[79] The irony was that Judas's estate, through its proximity to the geographical purity core, was formerly desirable but then became defiled space. This reallocation of purity illustrates Luke's reversal motif in the context of geography. Jerusalem is depicted in a progressively

---

76. Regarding the social necessity of the "gossip network," see Daniels, "Gossip in the NT," 204–13.

77. Holladay, *Acts: A Commentary*, 86–87, argues for parallels to Balaam, who was noteworthy regarding his greedy behavior while being an oracle.

78. See Thiessen, *Jesus and the Forces*, 15. Thiessen remarks on blood and corpses as primary pollutants (cf. Lev 12–15; Num 19).

79. Pilch, "Desert and Wilderness," 28. Luke 15:24 indicates exile as a form of death.

negative light throughout his writings, while in contrast, after Jerusalem later rejects Paul, Rome's anticipated receptivity to the gospel becomes a prime literary consideration.

It was by Judas's impure death that the disciple group was cleansed from his polluted actions of betrayal. Lukan theology asserts wealth and material ethics as the purity markers of the church;[80] thus, the grotesque shame of Judas's actions was prominently depicted in his humiliating and unclean death. The apostles are commissioned to be witnesses first in Jerusalem (Acts 1:8); ironically, Judas unwittingly became the initial witness according to Luke's description that the city's inhabitants were familiar with the betrayer's fate.[81]

Joseph Fitzmyer contends that Luke's passion narratives uniquely convey victory over Satan.[82] Likewise, Judas's fate further depicts that triumph as he represented the destiny of the dark powers and exploitative economic systems in Judea, and his purchased land became a signpost for Jesus's prophetic rebuke of Jerusalem. Moreover, Peter's ultimate success over Satan's sifting strengthened his apostolic role and encouraged the brethren during a critical moment,[83] restoring group integrity and solidarity. Additionally, Judas was demonstrated to be replaceable (Acts 1:21–26); therefore, his actions did not strategically compromise the function of the twelve. The human agents of darkness that attempted to strike a fatal blow to Jesus and his disciple group lost. Jesus is further empowered by his ascension, and Judas's negative speech is supplanted by apostolic voice beginning in Acts 1:15–20.[84]

Synthesis

This section argued that Judas as both a traitor and anti-disciple embodied roles counter to the undercurrent of Lukan theology, aligning with the wealthy elite disdained by Luke. Unlike Matthew's account, Luke portrays Judas not only conspiring with dark powers but emulating them through his land acquisition. The land, near Jerusalem—a hub of economic, religious,

---

80. Davies, "Purity, Spirit, and Reciprocity," 259.

81. Bauer, *Acts as Story*, 79.

82. Fitzmyer, *Gospel According to Luke*, 1367.

83. Parsons, *Acts*, 32.

84. Judas's demise thematically echoes the rich man in Jesus's parable of Luke 12:13–21.

and cultural significance—symbolized wealth and power, contrasting sharply with Luke's reversal ethics and the call to reject materialism.

Oakman notes that "in the late republic and early empire, political networks were established, maintained, or destroyed by the bestowing of political favors, loans of money, or other social goods."[85] The Herodians and the temple elites were both part of this Roman network that enabled the rich to become wealthier in a limited-good society that severely restricted economic possibilities for the subsistent majority. Judas insinuated himself into this dark partnership, becoming identified with and symbolizing this corruption. Additionally, the greed perpetuated by the ruling elite generated the sociopolitical atmosphere which ultimately led to the Jewish Revolt. Likewise, Judas's actions, in representative form, depicted the economic happenings in Jerusalem, leading to its destruction.

Furthermore, Judas's betrayal of insider/outsider dynamics threatened the purity of Jesus's disciple group and made the orifices penetrable by Satan. His tainted actions were met with judgment indicated by an unclean and shameful death, which represented the fate of the evil resistant forces. The Jerusalem gossip network circulated this news among the region, producing an unclean reputation regarding his defiled land, which became a symbol of exile. Although Judas suffered a polluted demise, the apostle Peter and Jesus's disciple group thrived, increasing in effectiveness and number. Judas's dishonorable death, Peter's steadfastness, and the early church's emergence each signaled a defeat of the dark powers.

---

85. Oakman, *Jesus and the Peasants*, 13.

Chapter 3: Ananias and Sapphira: Greed and the Spirit of Deception (Acts 5:1–11)

Throughout Acts human greed is always depicted as a most destructive force. It certainly was so for Judas (1:18) and for Ananias and Sapphira (5:1–11).[1]

—John B. Polhill

Introduction and Background

This chapter explores the dynamic interplay of Ananias and Sapphira's choices concerning their monetary donation. Examining the theological and social dimensions of this passage provides a deeper understanding of the necessity of full disclosure and proper allocation. Surrendering land and detaching from wealth diminished the couple's public honor. Though their social status in Jerusalem was at risk, they sought to gain credibility in the church by imitating Barnabas's generosity. In their attempt to secure a status comparable to Barnabas, they were willing to deceive the collective of believers.

In Acts, the church learned from this circumstance that one cannot offset or compensate for a loss of societal honor by soliciting power within the disciple group. Neither can one maintain a devotion to money while successfully integrating into the core of the Christian community. Consequently, these two characters risked jeopardizing the success and unity of the church, operating like Judas in an antithetical mode to discipleship, as the dark powers sought to undermine the trajectory of the Jesus group.

---

1. Polhill, *Acts*, 219.

Peter demonstrated Jesus's victory through the emerging church, establishing his apostolic authority as the primary witness at Pentecost (Acts 2:1–41). There, unified tongues signaled the reversal of Babel's confusion (Gen 11:1–9; Acts 2:1–13), the antecedent of the archetypal empire Babylon. Moreover, Peter provided an explanation of the events: first, the egalitarian reversal characteristic of Joel 2:28 (Acts 2:17–21); and second, Jesus's ascension. This evokes the psalmist: "The Lord said to my lord, 'Sit at my right hand until I make your enemies a footstool for your feet'" (Ps 110:1 MT, 109:1 LXX, NET). Thus, Jesus's continued victory over darkness is affirmed (Acts 2:34–36). The early church's response to these events was to form a sacrificial community, eschewing greed and dedicating themselves to communal life through asset liquidation and distribution to those in need (Acts 2:42–47).

The temple remained a focal point in the cosmic duel, highlighting the triumph of God in the continuous stand against darkness. This was demonstrated through the healing of a lame man (Acts 3:1–10), where, in contrast to Judas, Peter declared his lack of money (Acts 3:6). That episode enabled Peter to further witness to the resurrected Christ (Acts 3:11–26), resulting in his and John's arrest by the priests, the temple guard, and the Sadducees. This brief incarceration led to the addition of five thousand new disciples (Acts 4:1–4), far exceeding the three thousand at Pentecost and proving to be another victory over evil resistance.[2] The temple elite attempted to further stall apostolic momentum, but this only motivated Peter to deliver another authoritative speech (Acts 4:5–12).

The agents of darkness recognized the "boldness" (παρρησία) of the uneducated and common men and ordered them to cease their gospel

---

2. Some scholars have focused on the historicity of Luke's numerical figures; see, for example, Reinhardt, "Population Size of Jerusalem," 237–65; and Keener, "Plausibility of Luke's Growth," 140–63. In contrast, Witherington, *Acts of the Apostles*, 156, suggests that in Acts 2:41—and by implication in other cases—Luke's numbers may reflect historicity or merely indicate a large number without symbolic or literary design. More helpfully, Davis, "Rhetorical Use of Numbers," 40, highlights that Old Testament numbers often serve rhetorical or poetic purposes rather than literal or symbolic ones. According to Klein, "Chronicler's Code," Chronicles, as a prophetic historiography like Luke-Acts, creatively uses names, lists, and numbers as narrative devices. Reinforcing this, other scholars argue for the Chronicler's use of numerical exaggeration to engage readers; see Davies, "Mathematical Conundrum," 465–69; Fouts, "Incredible Numbers," 283–9; and "Defense of Hyperbolic Interpretation," 377–87. Luke's historiography, drawing from the same genre, likely incorporates nonliteral numbers to achieve his theological and narrative aims; see Klein, "How Many in Thousand," 281.

proclamation (Acts 4:13–18).³ The diminished effectiveness of the dark powers was evident, as Peter and John's direct refusal to comply resulted only in threats rather than mortal danger (Acts 4:19–22). The apostolic gathering reported and reflected on those events, drawing on Ps 2 in their response: "Why do the nations rage, and the peoples plot foolish things? The kings of the earth stood together, and the rulers assembled together, against the Lord and against his Christ" (Acts 4:25–26 NET).

Their adjacent commentary situated the passage christologically, delineating Herod, Israel's aristocracy, and even Pontius Pilate, representing the gentiles, as agents of evil resistance who conspired against Jesus (Acts 4:27). The unquoted portion of Ps 2 articulates God's reign over conquered nations through his son. A signpost for this emerging Christian movement was evident in their petition: "And now, Lord, pay attention to their threats, and grant to your servants to speak your message with great boldness" (παρρησία, Acts 4:29 NET).⁴ The Spirit of God affirmed their unity by shaking the building and enabling communal speech (Acts 4:31). This solidarity was further reflected in the practice of selling land to support the collective, as exemplified by Barnabas, a Levite (Acts 4:32–37).

Textual Analysis

Luke introduces two characters whose presence is confined to a single pericope: Ananias and his wife, Sapphira. Their literary placement quickly generates intrigue, as Luke frequently employs compound narratives and juxtaposed characters.⁵ Luke contrasts Ananias and Sapphira with Barnabas not only to highlight ideal versus corrupt ethics but also to underscore

---

3. The word παρρησία has an initial and primary "political" meaning within ancient Greek context. In the Hellenistic world it conveys an "openness to truth," equivalent to the modern idiom "speaking truth to power" and it is used in Acts as a mechanism to confront and defeat the dark forces. See *TLNT*, "παρρησία," 3:56.

4. Παρρησία or "speaking truth to power."

5. Bird, *Bird's-Eye View*, 152, notes, "Not to be forgotten is the chorus of faithful characters, major and minor, in Luke-Acts, who are often juxtaposed with bad or faulty characters," while Edwards, "Parallels and Patterns," 485, remarks on Luke's repetitious pairing of characters. Examples include the comparisons of Zechariah to Mary (Luke 1:18–38), Simeon to Anna (Luke 2:25–38), John the Baptist to Jesus (Luke 3:16–22), the centurion to the Jewish elders (Luke 7:1–10), the sinful woman to Simon the Pharisee (Luke 7:36–50), Martha to Mary (Luke 10:38–42), the good Samaritan to the priest/Levite (Luke 10:30–37), the Pharisee to the tax collector (Luke 18:9–14), the rich ruler to the poor widow (Luke 18:18–30; 21:1–4), and the rich man to Lazarus (Luke 16:19–31).

the ongoing conflict with dark forces.⁶ Barnabas's selfless support strengthened the early church and established him as a pivotal figure. In contrast, Ananias and Sapphira's deceitful imitation, aimed at elevating their status within the church, raised the threat of another potential traitor among the disciples. The significance of this section is further emphasized by its connection to Peter's testing by Satan, continuing to vindicate him as the battle with the evil powers persists.⁷

The evil forces, having failed to combat the apostolic group through political and judicial means, then sought to replicate the previous betrayal (that of Judas) by attacking the church from within. Within the first-century context, Sapphira was a name associated with wealthy women.⁸ Given that socioeconomic classes tended to marry within their own strata, the reader understands that both members of this couple were people of status.

Echoing the actions of Barnabas and the Jerusalem church (Acts 2:45; 4:34, 37), this couple "sold property" (πωλέω κτῆμα, Acts 5:1). Luke previously uses the word πωλέω when Jesus instructed followers to detach from possessions (Luke 12:33). This instruction was further exemplified in Jesus's directive to the wealthy ruler to sell his goods, distribute them to the poor, and inherit the kingdom of God (Luke 18:22).⁹ However, Ananias and Sapphira "kept back" (ἐνοσφίσατο, Acts 5:2) part of the proceeds. The word ἐνοσφίσατο often depicted fraudulent activity, including theft and embezzlement.¹⁰

The translation "he kept back" (NET) conveys the action, while the lexical possibilities indicate the motive. The word's usage in other sources "is directed against the common property that exists also for my sake, or that belongs to a community of which I am a member."¹¹ The term is used in 2 Macc 4:32 to describe theft when Menelaus stole golden vessels from

---

6. Smith, *Literary Construction*, loc. 2519 of 4291, acknowledges a strategic juxtaposition between these characters but does not explicitly remark on the larger feud with darkness.

7. Smith, *Literary Construction*, loc. 2519 of 4291.

8. Keener, *Acts*, NCBC, 205. Schnabel also describes Ananias and Sapphira as a well-to-do couple without substantiating his view. Schnabel, *Acts*, 478.

9. Three other locations include negative references largely associated with key eschatological events; see Luke 17:28, 19:45, and 22:36.

10. *EDNT*, "νοσφίζομαι," 2:478, gives the translation "embezzle"; see also *TLNT*, "νοσφίζομαι," 2:546–47.

11. Reimer, *Women in Acts*, 9.

the Jerusalem temple, and it is used comparably in other ancient writings.[12] Luke clarified that this action was carried out by Ananias with his wife's "knowledge" (Acts 5:2), thereby generating a duplicity of guilt. Their mistake was fully realized when their actions mirrored those of Barnabas, who had "brought" (φέρω, Acts 4:37, 5:2) and "placed" (τίθημι, Acts 4:37, 5:2) the proceeds at Peter's feet (NET).

Peter directly linked the actions of Ananias and Sapphira to Satan's influence, asking, "Why has Satan filled your heart?" (Acts 5:3 NET). Just as Satan "entered" (εἰσῆλθεν, Luke 22:3) Judas, so he also "filled" (πληρόω, Acts 5:3) the hearts of this couple. While Luke typically uses πλήθω ("to fill") to denote the Holy Spirit's influence, here he juxtaposed Satan's presence with the filling of Ananias and Sapphira. Conceptually, the parallel is clear: just as the Holy Spirit's filling inspires motive, action, and speech, Satan's influence compelled Judas, Ananias, and Sapphira toward greedy ambitions. Judas's greed drove him to secure money before purchasing land, while the couple in this pericope initially possessed land but deceitfully retained money from its sale.[13] The ironic link between the two situations underscores greed as a primary weapon of the dark forces.

Peter explicitly stated that Satan had led the couple to lie to the Holy Spirit, exposing their deceptive intent and greed. Moreover, Satan filled their "heart" (καρδία, Acts 5:3), the principal seat of thoughts, actions, and motivations, where they devised their wicked plan. This reference to Ananias and Sapphira's "heart" created a contrast with the condition of the early church community's heart, which Luke connects to shared table fellowship.

Acts 2:46 and 4:32 describe the group's commonality, including their meal sharing, as having sincerity of καρδία. In Luke-Acts, clean hearts are the source of purity.[14] Luke's description of the early church's corporate meals as having communally pure hearts contrasts with the overindulgent, disruptive, and unruly behavior heavily associated with Greco-Roman feasts.[15] The pure hearts of these Jerusalem disciples enabled them to be socially responsible and to solidify their community. Meanwhile, Ananias

---

12. Josephus, *Ant.* 4.274; 14.164; Epictetus, *Disc.* 2.20.35; Plut. *Pomp.* 4.1; Strabo, *Geogr.* 2.3.4–5.

13. As discussed previously regarding the account of Judas, the land aristocracy surrounding Jerusalem meant that Judas's asset seizure associated him with the greed of the elites perpetuated within that region. Similarly, Ananias and Sapphira are presumed wealthy since they are liquidating land within the proximity of Jerusalem.

14. Shellberg, *Cleansed Lepers, Cleansed Hearts*, 3–4.

15. Finger, *Widows and Meals*, locs. 2525–29 of 4280.

and Sapphira's hearts were occupied by Satan, who sought to destabilize the Jesus group. While Luke does not explicitly state that Ananias and Sapphira broke the unity of table fellowship, it is implicit since the early church shared group meals. Judas broke the bond of unity shared at the table, where he was exposed (Luke 22:21–22). This couple did likewise, a choice that circumvents the witness and lifestyle of the pure-hearted disciples in Jerusalem.[16]

Ananias and Sapphira were proven impure through their words. Luke-Acts places a heavy emphasis on speech in connection with the Spirit. Meanwhile, this couple's polluted words were incongruent with the Spirit's boldness that imbued the early church members in the face of opposition.[17] Unlike the disciples, who courageously testified truth to the socioeconomic and political forces, Ananias and Sapphira emulated those corrupt powers through their greed and attempted manipulation for control. Thus, their lie was indicative of a state of being, and their disingenuous discipleship was confirmed by their deceptive words.

The couple "sold" (πιπράσκω, Acts 5:4) their "possession" (ὑπάρχω, Acts 5:4). The former term, πιπράσκω, is used in Acts 2:45 and 4:34, and the latter, ὑπάρχω, is employed three times in Acts 4:32–37 to describe the positive examples of communal life. Ananias and Sapphira liquidated a "field" (χωρίον, Acts 5:4). This not only links the couple to the positive examples of the church—in which the same word is used (Acts 4:34)—but also connects them to Judas, who acquired a field (Acts 1:19).

Peter's question, "Before it was sold, did it not belong to you? And when it was sold, was the money not at your disposal?" (Acts 5:4 NET), prompts a variety of scholarly responses. Lear remarks that "the issue with Ananias and Sapphira's actions appears not to be that they did not give all of their possessions, but that they lied."[18] When comparing Acts 5:1–11 to 4:32–37, Noble observes, "If Ananias was truly free to not sell his property or, having sold it, to not hand over the proceeds, then it would seem that doing so was not a universal practice of the community, as the second summary clearly asserts."[19]

Meanwhile, Seccombe presents a mediating view: "The particular crime of Ananias and Sapphira was their collusion to defraud the

---

16. Lear, *What Shall We Do*, 136.
17. Lear, *What Shall We Do*, 136.
18. Lear, *What Shall We Do*, 135–36.
19. Noble, *Common Property*, 210.

community. Peter's question shows that they were not obliged to sell the piece of land for the benefit of the community."[20] This third view provides the most opportune interpretive possibilities, as Peter's accusation targets both the deception and embezzlement factors because of the public pledge. This position is enhanced through consideration of both historical and sociocultural factors.

John Polhill rightly asserts that "one does not embezzle one's own funds but those of another, in this instance those that rightfully belonged to the common Christian fund."[21] The question arises as to when Ananias and Sapphira's assets became communal property. The community ethics of the emerging church were noticeable, yet hardly proprietary; such practices were shared, at least ideally, across the Hellenistic and Jewish worlds. Examples include Plato's remarks on the absence of private property among the Athenian military and Ovid's poetic articulation of how communal living could eradicate wars.[22]

Furthermore, the early church practiced a form of kinship that finds parallels in Aristotle's and Euripides's observations of commonality and sharing within friendship models.[23] Seneca warned against greed, while Vergil contended against a "lust of possession."[24] Additionally, the requirements of the Qumran community demanded the surrender of property and wealth.[25] Clearly, the concepts of sharing and communal property had intellectual and, in some cases, practical precedence.

The funds brought to Peter by the married couple, in fact, belonged to the community. First, the bedrock of Jesus's message was the Isaianic new exodus accompanied by a Jubilee that appeared both spiritual and physical (Luke 4:14–21).[26] The Jubilee of Lev 25 reinforced a worldview in which all assets (land and possessions) belong to God and are merely allocated to human stewards. From this foundation, Luke's wealth and material ethics emerge, partly revealed by his reversal motif—that the wealthy are destined

---

20. Seccombe, *Poor and Possessions*, 291–92.

21. Polhill, *Acts*, 156.

22. Plato, *Resp.* 3:416D–417B; 4:420C–422B; 5:462A–466D; *Leg.* 679B–C; Ovid, *Metam.* 1.89–112, with a focus on 1.97–100.

23. Arist. *Eth. nic.* 8–9; Eur. *Andr.* 6–7.

24. Seneca, *Ep. Mor.* 90.38; Vergil, *Aen.* 8.319–27.

25. 4QSd 1:2, 1QS 5:2; 6:17–22.

26. Isa 40:3–5; 41:17–20; 42:14–17; 43:1–7, 16–21; 48:20–21; 49:8–13; 51:9–11; 52:10–12; 55:12–13.

for humility. Judas's effort to become elite represented a counter-trajectory to the reversal motif, circumventing it by acquiring assets and becoming associated with the powerful class. As with Judas, Ananias and Sapphira's greed demonstrated a greater allegiance to money than to Jesus's ethical principles.

This couple's choices also represented a counter-trajectory to the early church. They were faced with how to respond to Jesus's call to wealthy disciples. Earlier Lukan precedent provides at least two potential paths for the wealthy. First, the rich ruler was exhorted to liquidate all his assets for the benefit of the poor but failed to do so (Luke 18:18–30). Alternatively, Zacchaeus surrendered half of his assets with transparency and gave restitution at a 400 percent interest rate (Luke 19:1–10). Ananias and Sapphira were neither willing to offer total relinquishment nor transparency in their partial asset offering. Moreover, since generosity functioned as a vital weapon in the struggle against dark forces, Ananias and Sapphira were expected to comply with group consistency (major real estate liquidation with complete donation of funds). Their wealth status required noticeable participation.[27]

The couple failed to fulfill Jesus's call to wealthy disciples by refusing to engage in a genuine reversal. This is incongruent with the exemplary Barnabas, introduced immediately prior to Ananias and Sapphira, who operates as their literary character foil. Luke's audience would have initially been inclined to suspect a character like Barnabas, since he was a Levite possessing land and benefiting from unjust land ownership.[28] However, Barnabas fulfilled the call to reversal, fully relinquishing the land as a symbol of restorative justice, comparable to the actions of Zacchaeus (Luke 19:1–10). William Shepherd remarks that as "the example of Barnabas shows, the Spirit inspires a community of goods, not a community of greed."[29] In contrast, Ananias and Sapphira, symbols of Jerusalem's wealth, refused to fully participate in Luke's economic rebalancing.

Moreover, Ananias and Sapphira committed their offerings through their spoken pledge. The integrity of the emerging church was tied to the attributes of God. Luke emphasizes that the promises of God are kept; accordingly, the community members were also expected to maintain their

---

27. See Luke 1:53; 6:24; 8;14; 12:13–21; 14:7–14; 16:19–31; 19:1–10; Acts 2:42–47; and 4:32–37.

28. Regarding Levite ownership of land, see Num 18:20; Deut 10:9; 12:12; Josh 14:3–4; and 18:7.

29. Shepherd, *Narrative Function of Spirit*, 172.

word as agents of prophetic speech. Furthermore, the values and trust granted in collectivistic life depended upon honoring one's words. In first-century Jerusalem, there was hardly a concept of private life.[30] Given that nearly every aspect of the apostolic group was "in one accord" (Acts 1:14, 2:1, 4:24) it is expected that Ananias and Sapphira's words and actions were publicly conducted.

Additionally, the gossip network not only assured but required information to be shared so that persons could appropriately consider honor-shame dynamics adjacent to any news. As a result, testimony initially indicating a positive action of Ananias and Sapphira would have been transferred quickly throughout the church, which Luke indicates as constituting multiple thousands. While lying and deception were, in some cases, accepted practices for maintaining public honor, such behavior was deemed inappropriate within the collective setting that Luke describes as the earliest church in Jerusalem.[31] Therefore, Ananias and Sapphira's lies, in association with greed, constituted insulting words and fraudulent in-group actions like those of Judas, coupled with conveying inaccurate information concerning their internal honor.

Honor was fundamental in the world of Luke-Acts, as Xenophon states: "For indeed it seems to me, Hiero, that in this man differs from other animals—I mean, in this craving for honor."[32] As explored in 5.2.2, land ownership signified a greater honor status the nearer it was to Jerusalem. Based on the location of their holdings, Ananias and Sapphira benefited from a relatively high socioeconomic pedigree, even if they were not ruling elitists. Upon relinquishing sacred and valuable land, this couple stood not only to surrender monetary funds but also to diminish their honor and status among the Jerusalem populace. Given their apparent greed, it is likely they wanted to keep part of the proceeds to preserve either their public honor or economic comfort. Their actions underscore Jesus's warning, "How hard it is for the rich to enter the kingdom of God" (Luke 18:24 NET). Their attachment to wealth proved to be a barrier to fully embracing the Jerusalem church's model.

Their public honor was degraded through the sale and release of assets, causing them to appear more like peasants losing ancestral grounds

---

30. In this context, "There is an unwillingness to leave alone the lives of others or to have others leave alone one's own life." See Introduction to *HBSV*, xxxii.

31. Pilch, "God and Lying Spirits," 240.

32. Xen. *Hier.* 7.3.

than land aristocrats. This perception would circulate among Jerusalem's public gossip network. In a limited-good society fearful of expendability, this couple attempted to mitigate their social risk and compensate for their evaporating public perception outside the church by acquiring honor within the church. In other words, if they could not maintain public honor, they would settle for praise within the Jerusalem church.

The model this couple attempted to emulate was that of Barnabas, whose donation represented a key victory in the cosmic war against darkness. His reputation achieved significant honor within the disciple community, and he was instrumental in Saul's initial reception in Jerusalem (Acts 9:27). He was later a key figure in the church at Antioch (Acts 11:22–30) and was successfully commissioned for ministry (Acts 13:1–3). His full dedication makes him the third most frequently mentioned figure in Acts.

Ananias and Sapphira were motivated to compete for honor parallel to that of Barnabas. Therefore, they exhibited both social and economic greed. Their attempt to seize power, control, and influence as emerging pivotal figures placed the group's solidarity in jeopardy, representing the dark powers' effort to infiltrate the emerging church, just as Satan had infiltrated Judas. In ancient times, the wealthy were known for mocking the poor.[33] Ananias and Sapphira, through their wealth, deceit, and false witness, attempted to make fools of the apostolic community to which they belonged.

Peter, who ultimately triumphed when the dark powers sought to sift him, confronted these agents of evil. Luke describes both the response of the villains and the community. Ananias heard Peter's words and died.[34] The collective responded with "great fear" (μέγας φόβος, Acts 5:5). The concerns of misinformation cycling through the gossip network of the early church were tempered by their fear. This resulted in the accurate circulation of the news of both Peter's authority and Ananias and Sapphira's fate.

The group, presumably comprising many thousands of disciples, was alerted to the realized shame of the couple. Moreover, the church was warned of the ongoing feud with darkness, whereby Satan's activities appeared proximate to Jerusalem, inhabiting both Judas and the couple. Honorable deaths were desirable; yet, as with Judas, these deaths resulted in shameful gossip. As Judas's descriptive qualities were prominent, so also were the dual consequences with Ananias and Sapphira.

---

33. Petron. *Sat.* 26–78; Juv. *Sat.* 3, 5, 14; Mart. *Epig.*; Ar. *Plut.*; Plaut. *Com.*

34. The word πίπτω or "fell down" used regarding Ananias is reminiscent of Judas's γίνομαι (Acts 1:18).

Ananias's body was carried outside the location, wrapped, and buried. The quick burial was likely a pragmatic decision. Just as Judas's humiliating death resulted in land profanity, so, too, Ananias died shamefully. A likely concern was to prevent tangible contamination, not merely from corpse uncleanliness, the most prominent of Jewish purity concerns, but also to avoid tarnishing the gathering space of the new apostolic temple.[35] Thus, comparable to how Judas polluted the disciple group, yet the collective was purified by his unclean death, so also the Jerusalem church was cleansed from this couple's profaned acts through their shameful demise.

Several Old Testament events parallel this narrative. These include Nadab and Abihu's offering of a polluted sacrifice (Lev 10:1–8), Uzzah's defilement of the ark by touching it (2 Sam 6:1–7), and Hophni and Phinehas's tabernacle misdeeds (1 Sam 2:11–25). Each case involves a misappropriation of sacred duties, resulting in death as judgment. Similarly, Ananias and Sapphira's malpractice within Luke's new temple paradigm reflects priestly corruption. The community's swift burial of Ananias before Sapphira's arrival (Acts 5:7) likely aimed to contain impurity.

Peter questioned Sapphira about the "payment" (ἀποδίδωμι, Acts 5:8), a term also used in Acts 4:33, contrasting her actions negatively with Barnabas. The use of τοσοῦτος (Acts 5:8) obscures the exact amount, mirroring the anonymity of Judas's payment. Peter's question offered Sapphira a chance to repent but instead revealed her complicity. By accusing her of testing the Spirit, Peter framed their pursuit of status as an honor challenge not only against him but against God.

This "test" (πειράζω) recalls the attempts to tempt God during the exodus (Exod 17:2; Deut 6:16; Ps 78:18), which also underpinned Jesus's confrontation with the devil (Luke 4:1–13). Ananias and Sapphira's deception, like Judas's betrayal, involved a conspiracy driven by Satan, as Peter notes they "agreed" (συμφωνέω, Acts 5:9) on their plan. Their actions exposed vulnerability within the church, presenting themselves as insiders while acting as outsiders, challenging the community's integrity through greed and testing the Spirit.

Peter declared that the same feet would transport Sapphira (as they did Ananias) off the premises. The repeated mention of feet recalls the actions of the community (Acts 4:35), including Barnabas's genuine act of laying money at the apostles' feet (Acts 4:37). By contrast, Ananias's deceptive offering at Peter's feet (Acts 5:2) is underscored by literary irony when

---

35. Walton, *Acts 1—9:42*, 361.

Sapphira herself dies at Peter's feet (Acts 5:10). As news of their deaths spread swiftly through the gossip network, fear gripped the community of believers (Acts 5:5, 11), reinforcing the cautionary example of Judas's fate (Acts 1:19). Luke's introduction of the term "church" (ἐκκλησία, Acts 5:11) emphasizes the narrative progression, indicating that the collective stood firm following the Judas-like betrayal, marking another victory over darkness.

Two further Old Testament parallels to Acts 5:1–11 warrant attention. The first is Gehazi, Elisha's servant, who lied to secure Naaman's bounty refused by the prophet (2 Kgs 5:19–27). Gehazi's greed resulted in impurity—leprosy. In 2 Kgs 5, Elisha aided Naaman, a Syrian military commander with leprosy, a story central to Jesus's message at Nazareth (Luke 4:27). Naaman was reformed through healing, aligning with Luke's portrayal of Roman military officials as agents of societal change. Gehazi's greed contrasted with Elisha's altruism and threatened to distract Naaman from his transformation. Similarly, Ananias and Sapphira's selfish actions, driven by greed, endangered the church's mission to reach "the ends of the earth" (Acts 1:8).

The second crucial intertextual parallel connects Acts 5:1–11 with Achan's story during Joshua's conquest. Jericho's wealth was reserved for God's treasury (Josh 6:17–19), but Achan misappropriated (ἐνοσφίσατο) it (Josh 7:1), paralleling the description in Acts 5:2. Achan's theft was ultimately against God, defrauding Israel and causing their defeat at Ai, before divine judgment brought his death (Josh 7:22–26). Achan's actions undermined Israel's distinct covenant identity, betraying their call to remain separate from Canaan's inhabitants. Similarly, Ananias and Sapphira's conspiracy betrayed the church's collective testimony, exemplified by Barnabas. Just as Israel's conquest emphasized wealth ethics as markers of purity and identity, the church's mission to the "ends of the earth" upheld these values as weapons against the dark powers.

Synthesis

This section has argued the limitations of allocative freedom afforded to Ananias and Sapphira. First, Jesus's Jubilee ethics assert that all assets belong to God and are simply on loan to human stewards. Moreover, the Lukan reversal motif requires the greatest surrender by the wealthy, yet this couple was neither willing to sacrifice all their proceeds nor to be transparent regarding their limited communal designation. Furthermore, Ananias and Sapphira's declarations and actions presumably took place in a public space. Therefore, the integrity of their speech was predicated upon their fulfillment of their pledge to give the complete proceeds from the land sale. Among the early church members, this created the expectation that their honor status within the church would align comparably well with that of the trusted rising figure, Barnabas.

Given these factors, the only responsible choice this couple could have made was to surrender the land proceeds in their entirety. Instead, like Judas, they opted to forgo full participation in Luke's reversal motif of the wealthy becoming humble. They relinquished assets on their own terms, accompanied by Satan-infused lies. Regarding the land sale, on the surface, their betrayal seems different from that of Judas, since they sold land rather than acquiring it. However, just as Judas sought to increase his public status, this couple greedily sought an ecclesial honor status above their means as compensation for their loss of public standing through relinquishing personal wealth. They enviously attempted to gain the honor of an exemplary insider, Barnabas, but operated through deception and the influence of evil.

One danger imposed by Satan's influence on Ananias and Sapphira was the interference their actions could have caused within the early church's group unity and momentum. Had this couple assumed Barnabas-like roles, their greedy motivations would have ultimately made them negative witnesses (contra Peter). As with Judas, their deaths were shamefully remarkable, generating gossip attesting to their evil characteristics rather than to any honorable acts among the disciples.

Some question the severity of this couple's death when compared to the seemingly idle judgment against the leaders who later kill Stephen.[36] However, the impure connotation of being Satan-indwelled, and how that state threatened the social orifices of the church, risked the integrity of the economic practices and spiritual purity of the Jesus group. It also presented a gateway for the dark forces to continue attacking the apostolic community. Therefore, such insider violations required a stark response.

Garland rightly observes that "persecution has failed,"[37] both against Jesus (with the resurrection) and the early disciples. Peter's trial scenes demonstrate that, rather than silencing the apostles (as with Jesus's crucifixion),

---

36. Bence, *Acts in Wesleyan Tradition*, 70.
37. Garland, *Acts*, 52.

the temple elite were rendered ineffective and made a mockery of (Acts 3–4). Consequently, the dark powers sought another gateway into the disciple community. In doing so, disingenuous participants were revealed, and the evil forces were unable to inflict any unmanageable harm.

The missional success was further exemplified in the following scene. There, the people "carried" (ἐκφέρω, Acts 5:15) the sick to Peter, in contrast to the earlier instance where the church ἐκφέρω the corpses of failed disciples away from him (Acts 5:6, 9, 10). Luke's use of the root word ἐκφέρω, which appears only four times—all within Acts 5:6–15—links these scenes. In a counterpoint to the initial disruption by the dark powers evident in the carrying out of corpses in Acts 5:1–11, the temple scene in Acts 5:12–16 depicts more believers coming to faith. These people are carried to the apostles to witness their authority over unclean spirits.

In response to Peter's success, the Sanhedrin once again arrested and questioned the apostles, but they continued to affirm the priority of their allegiance to God over obedience to human authorities (Acts 5:17–32). This same body of leaders that orchestrated Jesus's death once again sought execution; however, Gamaliel intervened, declaring that if the movement was of God, it was unstoppable. This statement resonates throughout the remainder of Luke's second volume (Acts 5:33–42).

With that failure to disrupt the church's momentum, the dark forces grew increasingly impotent. Satan proved unsuccessful in seizing and manipulating additional traitors for judicial or infiltrative purposes and experienced a significant setback when an insider among the Sanhedrin, Gamaliel, thwarted extreme action through his caution. Even as the Sanhedrin resolved to beat the apostles, its influence was limited, as the punishment resulted only in apostolic joy. The early church members continued their temple activities in defiance of the incapacitated ruling elite (Acts 5:40–42).

The following scene provides further evidence of the triumph over darkness when the potential for greed again threatens to disrupt the early church (Acts 6:1–7). Although an accusation was made regarding the mishandling of resources reserved for the needy and possibly marginalized widows, the church leadership responded quickly, deliberately, and effectively, combating the potential for greed to take root.[38] Simply put,

---

38. Earlier scholarly works have contended that Acts 6:1–7 evidence tension that eventually leads to a disuniting of the Jerusalem congregation along the lines of Hellenistic influence; for example, Conzelmann, *Theology of St. Luke*; and Hengel, "Studies of Early Christianity." However, Hill, *Hellenists and Hebrews*, later argued those supposed

in contrast to Judas, Ananias, and Sapphira, Satan's influence was either absent or unmentioned in this controversy. No insider betrayal occurs, and no one suffers a shameful death. This demonstrated progress, as the church navigates smoothly through this conflict, having overcome and moved past the tests of greed. In fact, the church likely grew because of that effective ministry to widows.[39] The narrative then shifts toward expansion beyond Jerusalem, a fitting occurrence after the church successfully passed its greed-related testing.

---

divisions to be overstated. More recently, commentators like Gaventa maintain that this section displays a rectified problem; see Gaventa, *Acts*, 116. Meanwhile, Maloney and Reimer, *Acts of the Apostles*, 209, observe this as gender-inclusive problem-solving; while Pervo rightly understands that the motif continues that the church faces a crisis that is ultimately remedied, leading to further success. The pericope conforms to a typical Lukan narrative pattern in which threats to the stability of the community are resolved through appropriate action. See Pervo, *Acts*, 152–53.

39. Walton, *Acts 1—9:42*, 419.

Chapter 4: Simon Magus in Samaria: The Temptation to Bribe Divine Power (Acts 8:4–25)

If we fault Simon for anything it should be for his intoxication with and addiction to power.[1]

—Willie James Jennings

Introduction and Background

THE CHURCH'S ADVANCEMENT AGAINST greed and darkness is displayed as it effectively quells a potential crisis involving food distribution to widows. The church's handling of this issue lacks any imagery akin to Ananias and Sapphira's deaths (Acts 6:1–7). Stephen's brief but critical role was another indication of successful ministry; his speech and actions prompted accusations and a trial before the high priest (Acts 6:8—7:53). While Stephen's stoning seemingly served the interests of dark forces, it simultaneously advanced two critical aspects of the gospel mission. First, it prompted the church's dispersal from Jerusalem, setting in motion the fulfillment of Jesus's vision to the "ends of the earth." Second, that persecution introduced Saul of Tarsus, who, despite his initial role as a fierce opponent (Acts 7:58; 8:1–3), later became the primary catalyst for the gospel's expansion to Rome.

Persecution "scattered" (διεσπάρησαν, Acts 8:1) the believers. Yet paradoxically, while the Babylonian diaspora served the interests of imperial power, this dispersion ultimately set the church on a collision course with

---

1. Jennings, *Acts*, 79.

the oppressive forces of darkness embodied by Rome. Luke emphasizes the narrative shift with Philip "preaching the word" (Acts 8:4) and the Samaritan response to his "proclaiming the Christ" (Acts 8:5).

Textual Analysis

Although the Samaritan region was less than fifty miles (or a three-day journey) from Jerusalem, historic tensions between its residents and the Jews divided the areas. Luke often provides specific locations in his writings; yet on this occasion, many English translations render Philip's destination as "a city in Samaria" (NIV). This use of the indefinite article creates ambiguity. However, the manuscript Papyrus 74 includes a definite article.[2] This is translated in the NRSV as "the city of Samaria" and in the NET as "the main city of Samaria" (Acts 8:5), both supporting the capital as the location.

Though known as Sebaste in the first century, the region's capital was called Samaria in the Old Testament, famously associated with Ahab, Jezebel, and Elijah—an important intertext for Luke. Sebaste's blend of Torah memory and first-century Hellenism marked the city as an ideal transitional ground between Judaism and paganism.[3] The pagan influence was apparent in the presence of Simon, of whom "all the people, from the least to the greatest, paid close attention to" (Acts 8:10 NET). Evidently, as an empowered patron, he received honor from influential, high-profile figures, likely including prominent leaders residing in the capital.

The recipients of Philip's message are described as being "of one accord" (ὁμοθυμαδόν, Acts 8:6). This echoes both the unity at Pentecost (Acts 1:14, 2:46) and the communal life of the church in Jerusalem (Acts 2:46, 4:24, 5:12). Luke highlights that the crowd "heard" (ἀκούειν, Acts 8:6) Philip, further recalling the auditory emphasis at Pentecost (Acts 2:6, 8, 11, 22, 33, 37). The "signs" (σημεῖα, Acts 8:6, 13) accompanying Philip's ministry indicate divine acts. Luke uses these to emphasize (1) christological markers (e.g., Luke 2:12, 34; 11:16, 29–30; 23:8), (2) apocalyptic imagery (e.g., Luke 21:7, 11, 25), and (3) the pneumatological and ecclesial age inaugurated through the apostles (e.g., Acts 2:19, 22; 2:43; 4:16, 22, 30; 5:12; 6:8).

Although Luke demonstrates a deep interest in the Davidic dimensions of Christology, particularly in Peter's preaching in Jerusalem (Acts 1:1; 2:25, 29, 34; 4:25), this emphasis held counter relevance to Samaritan

---

2. MSS (P74, ℵ, A, B, 1175).
3. Klauck, *Magic and Paganism*, loc. 240 of 2074.

tradition. Instead, the Samaritan context resonated with the Mosaic new exodus motif. Consequently, the primary "sign" in Samaria points to the prophetic figure of the new Moses (Deut 18:15), referenced in Peter's speech in Jerusalem (Acts 3:22), and actualized in Philip's confrontation with dark powers. Moses demonstrated the superior power of God over the dark powers of Egypt with signs (Exod 4:9, 17, 28, 30; 7:3; 10:1–2). Likewise, Philip was given power over the unclean or impure spirits. Jesus commanded these otherwise anonymous spirits (Luke 4:33, 36; 6:17–19; 8:29–39; 9:42; 11:24), signs that Peter attests in his preaching (Acts 5:16).

Pinpointing the precise meaning of "unclean" or "impure" spirits is challenging. However, Luke likely draws on Second Temple Jewish thought, where such spirits were viewed as invasive forces that polluted individuals.[4] This interpretation aligns with texts from the period that describe these spirits as entities breaching human boundaries, introducing both physical and spiritual uncleanliness.[5] This concept parallels observations on Jewish purity, specifically regarding physical orifices as representatives of social openings. When either the physical or social body becomes permeable, it introduces vulnerabilities, increasing exposure to potential impurities and defilement.[6]

Upon expulsion, these spirits made a dramatic and unwilling response, "crying with loud shrieks" (βοάω φωνῇ μεγάλῃ, Acts 8:7 NET). Such exertions are comparable to the pattern in Jesus's Galilean ministry (Luke 4:33; 8:28). These acts of release (along with Philip's healings) in part comprise the Isaianic new exodus and Jubilee experience, which Jesus identified as the bedrock of his ministry (Luke 4:18–19). Philip was received with "significant joy" (πολλὴ χαρά, Acts 8:8), a consistent response directed toward Jesus, but the first of its kind in Acts. Previously, the dark forces were compelled to counterattack in response to both Jesus's activity and the success of the early church in Jerusalem; a similar resistance was encountered in Samaria. Luke introduces Simon, a practitioner of magic (μαγεύων, Acts 8:9), another named character of resistance who counters the theological grain of Acts.

In the Greco-Roman world, magic was about power, a means by which largely powerless people, subjected to uncontrollable variables, accessed resources.[7] Philo clarified between forms of magic based on social percep-

---

4. Heiser, *Demons*, 196.
5. Witmer, *Jesus, Galilean Exorcist*, 153–54; see also Wahlen, *Jesus and Impurity*, 32.
6. Douglas, *Purity and Danger*, 122–29.
7. Pilch, "Snakes and Magic," 44–45.

tions, generally of the practitioner.⁸ "Good" magic was viewed as a tool of noble persons, including royalty and philosophers. Meanwhile, negative magic was associated with women, slaves, and others of low social esteem. In some contexts, negative magic was a mechanism for selfish gain while its positive counterpart benefited community life.⁹ Indeed, a variety of ancient writers remarked that magicians should practice for public benefit without soliciting money.¹⁰ Klauck notes, "The predicate 'divine,' or even 'god,' is bestowed on prominent individuals, mostly wonder-workers, doctors, philosophers, rulers and kings, since these were seen as immediate bearers and mediators of divine powers."¹¹ For example, Empedocles himself was honored as more than a mortal but as a god, with people seeking divination and healings from his magic.¹² Philo contended that magic should only be handled by the socially reputable, most appropriately the elite; otherwise, it would be mismanaged.¹³ The Jewish religious worldview shaping the narrative of Acts assumes a prohibition against magic.¹⁴ Ancient Near Eastern records, Second Temple traditions, and later Jewish Talmudic writings consistently associate magic not only with rituals or symbolic acts but also with the influence of spiritual forces, including demonic beings.¹⁵

The impact of Simon's magic was substantial, having "amazed" (ἐξίστημι, Acts 8:11) the populace—a reaction commonly elicited by Jesus (Luke 2:47; 8:56; 24:22) and his apostles (Acts 2:7, 12). The Samaritans declare Simon as "great" (μέγας, Acts 8:9, 10). This descriptor is also applied to Philip's work (Acts 8:6), as the people "pay close attention" (προσεῖχον, Acts 8:10) to both figures, positioning Simon and Philip as character foils. Simon captured the admiration of all, from the "least" (μικρός, Acts 8:10) to the "greatest" (μέγας, Acts 8:10), indicating the diverse socioeconomic groups united in their regard for him. Notably, they attributed to Simon

---

8. Philo, *Spec. Laws* 3.100.

9. Pervo, *Acts*, 207–8. Philo, *Spec. Laws* 3.100.

10. Barrett, *Critical Exegetical Commentary—Acts*, 414. Herm. Mand. 11.12; cf. Plato, *Leg.* 909a–b; Philo, *Spec. Laws* 3.93–95; Lucian, *Alex*, 4–5; Juv. *Sat.* 6.546; Philostr. *Vit. Apoll.* 8.7; Soph. *Oed. tyr.* 387–89.

11. Klauck, *Magic and Paganism*, locs. 254–57 of 2074.

12. DK 31B112.

13. Philo, *Spec. Laws* 3.93–95.

14. Regarding prohibitions against magic, see Lev 19:31; 20:6; Deut 18:10–11; Judg 8:27; 1 Sam 23:6, 9; 28:7–19; 30:7–8; 2 Kgs 5:9–14; 21:6; Isa 8:19.

15. Walton and Walton, *Demons and Spirits*, 118, 123. See also Reed, *Demons, Angels, and Writing*, 196.

"the power of God" (ἡ Δύναμις τοῦ θεοῦ, Acts 8:10). In Luke-Acts, "power" (δύναμις) is a recurring concept symbolizing Jesus's authority,[16] the Holy Spirit's presence (Luke 22:49; Acts 1:8), and apostolic ministry (Acts 4:7, 33; 6:8; 8:13; 19:11).[17] Its only association with dark forces is through Simon Magus, suggesting an ironic contrast. Whereas Jesus and the apostles used divine power to liberate individuals from evil spirits and illness, Simon's influence coexisted with these forces. This is evident in the persistence of unclean spirits in the city until Philip's arrival, which highlights Simon's ineffective or compromised power.

Pervo asserts that "the great power of God" (Acts 8:10 NET) was a formal title. He notes that an altar located in Saittai of Lydia bears the translated inscription, "[There is] one god in heaven, the great Heavenly Men, great power of the immortal god."[18] He locates another example among words painted in Sebaste from 300 CE, translated as "[There is] one god, the ruler of all, the great Maiden [Kore], the invincible one."[19] These findings indicate the potential precedent of an individual being regarded as a visible form of God. Papyrus 74 provides stronger evidence from textual tradition, with the manuscript recording[20] "I am the Great Power of God" in relation to Simon.[21] In Sebaste, the Greeks synthesized the pantheon of deities into a single God, and by the second century, early Christian interpreters viewed Simon as having claimed to be the "avatar" or "incarnation" of that God.[22] This is consistent with many examples in classical literature of those who performed public services self-presenting as a god (or direct representative).[23]

In preparing his audience for the forthcoming reversal, Luke repeated the statement that the people "paid close attention" and were "amazed" (ἐξίστημι, Acts 8:11 NET) by Simon for a "long time" (Acts 8:11). This was

16. Regarding the power of Jesus, see Luke 4:14, 36; 5:17; 6:19; 8:46; Acts 2:22; and 10:38.

17. Jesus dispatched power to his disciples (Luke 9:1, 10:19) and is at times used apocalyptically (Luke 21:26–27; 22:69).

18. Pervo, *Acts*, 209. The inscription reads: "εἷς θεὸς ἐν οὐρανοῖς, μέγας Μὴν Οὐράνιος, μεγάλη δύναμις τοῦ ἀθανάτου θεοῦ."

19. Pervo, *Acts*, 209. The inscription reads: "εἷς θεὸς ὁ πάντων δεσπότης μεγάλη κόρη ἡ ἀνείκητος."

20. MSS (P74, ℵ, A, B, C, D, E, 33, 1739).

21. Fitzmyer, *Acts of the Apostles*, 404.

22. Keener, *NT*, 342.

23. Klauck, *Magic and Paganism*, locs. 255–57 of 2074.

interrupted when, despite their affections for the magician, the Samaritans believed Philip's preaching concerning the kingdom of God and the name of Jesus the Christ. Simon had amazed the Samaritans, and in turn, all parties were amazed by Philip. Likewise, the magician was called "great" even by the "great" citizens, yet Philip demonstrated "great power" (μέγας δύναμις, Acts 8:13). Moreover, Simon believed, was baptized, and remained close to Philip. The parallel between these two figures quickly ceded to Simon's (and the Samaritans') subordination to Philip. There are some allusions to Elijah and the prophets of Baal in 1 Kgs 18; yet more striking are the connections to the exodus, when Egypt's magicians were unable to match Moses's power (Exod 9:11). Within this cosmic duel, "Philip's message about the name of Jesus and the kingdom was a message of supernatural war. The name of Jesus releases people from Satan's authority."[24]

Given the advancements in Samaria and the anticipated backlash from dark forces, it was necessary that the apostles sent Peter and John to investigate. Both apostles were actively engaged in earlier spiritual conflicts in Jerusalem, making them particularly suited to assess and support the developing work in Samaria. Luke supplies a pragmatic purpose for Peter and John's arrival, simply stating that the Holy Spirit had not fallen among the Samaritans. For narrative and theological purposes, it is significant for Peter, as the principal leader, to be present when Luke depicts a mirror to Pentecost. Peter, the proven veteran in the cosmic duel against darkness, was a paramount presence ensuring that nothing placed the movement in jeopardy (Judas, Ananias, and Sapphira).

Peter and John enabled Spirit accessibility with the laying on of hands, a seldom-occurring formula in Luke-Acts used in some key moments, including the liberation from Satan (Luke 4:40; 13:13; Acts 6:6; 9:12, 17; 13:3; 19:6). In a setting with various components competing for power, Simon was proven inferior to Philip and more so to Peter and John. In Luke-Acts, speech is a hallmark of Holy Spirit activity. However, Simon's interest was not in what he heard, but in what he saw, particularly the presumed interpersonal transferability of power through hand gestures.[25]

Simon observed the supreme power at work, which resulted in a personal testing for him, similar to the devil's offer to Jesus (Luke 4:1–13) and the tests faced by Judas, Ananias, and Sapphira. Moreover, with the dark

---

24. Schreiner, *Acts*, 319.

25. Transference of power by the laying on of hands was a common method in the social world of the text; see Malina, "Hands/Feet," 84.

powers seized and expelled, Simon's power was weakened (if not abolished). This explains his aggressive response, since in a limited-good environment, once his magic was rendered ineffective, his access to power was forever depleted while being socially tarnished by expendability.

Simon, unable to counter Philip, Peter, and John with competitive force, attempted to reorganize whatever potential remained for him as a patron of power. Therefore, this magician "offered them money" (Acts 8:18), attempting to purchase the gift from the apostles. Greed-driven bribery recurs—first with Judas (Luke 22:1–6) and again when Satan fills Ananias's heart. He and his wife, drawn by their own assets pledged to the community, essentially fall prey to a dark temptation (Acts 5:1–11). Bribery was a tool employed by those with excess funds, attempting to illegitimately gain access to control.[26] Simon, who had fleeced the Samaritan community and accumulated honor and money, was compelled to retain his status.

Interestingly, while Barnabas and Ananias both laid money at Peter's feet as a symbol of sacrifice and subordination, Simon offered finances for the power (ἐξουσία, Acts 8:19) of apostolic hands. However, like Ananias and Sapphira, he disingenuously attempted to secure inappropriate ecclesial honor status. Simon's behavior was consistent with that of those in his profession who charged for their services, bartered for influence, and even purchased priesthood roles in cults.[27] All of these activities defied Luke's wealth ethics and posed a risk to the infant church in Samaria.

The awkwardness of the exchange is that "Simon's offer is to purchase the ability to give the Spirit rather than to purchase the Spirit himself."[28] He attempts "a model of control of spirits similar to that followed by priests of pagan idols" which "may reflect his previous magical practice."[29] He does this with the intention "to make money by charging people who wish to receive the Holy Spirit from him."[30] This display is consistent with the greed exhibited by many magicians.[31]

The hunger for power, honor, money, and authority was a weapon of darkness that attempted to disrupt Jesus's disciple group. This occurred at a

---

26. Arist. *Pol.* 5.8, 1316a; Cic. *Off.* 2.21.73; Cic. *Verr.* 2.3.69; Tac. *Ann.* 2.38; Plut. *Mor.* 535C; Plut. *Alc.* 22; Juv. *Sat.* 3.41–43.

27. Derrett, "Simon Magus," 52–68.

28. Walton, *Acts 1—9:42*, 520.

29. Walton, *Acts 1—9:42*, 520–21.

30. Walton, *Acts 1—9:42*, 520–21.

31. Walton, *Acts 1—9:42*, 521.

critical moment in Jerusalem when the disciples argued over who would be "regarded as the greatest" (Luke 22:24). Jesus responded:

> The kings of the Gentiles lord it over them, and those in authority over them are called "benefactors." Not so with you; instead the one who is greatest among you must become like the youngest, and the leader like the one who serves. For who is greater, the one who is seated at the table, or the one who serves? Is it not the one who is seated at the table? But I am among you as one who serves. (Luke 22:25–27 NET)

Passing the test of these temptations imparted true power and honor status in the early church. Jesus exhibited this power and authority over dark forces (Luke 4:32, 36; 5:24; 20:2, 8), with some recognizable parallel to a Roman officer's command over subordinate soldiers (Luke 7:8). This same authority was bestowed upon the apostles (Luke 9:1, 10:19).

Simon sought to circumvent the path to authority espoused by Jesus. Instead of becoming one who humbly serves others, he craved immediate access to apostolic power to serve self. Likewise, Ananias and Sapphira initially had money under their authority (Acts 5:4). Although they desired to gain an impression mirroring Barnabas, they were unwilling to surrender it and therefore could never become like the Levite. Additionally, Barnabas's emergence in the church was observed through a progression of multiple narratives before he was finally trusted to be dispatched with authority. Bauer rightly contends that "in Luke-Acts money represents the power of this world."[32] Accordingly, Simon used the weapon of darkness—money—to attempt to counterfeit the kingdom of God.

Peter's response highlights Simon's use of money (ἀργύριον, Acts 8:20), echoing the funds given to Judas (Luke 22:5). This recalls Jesus's instruction to his disciples to carry none (Luke 9:3), a principle Peter himself upheld (Acts 3:6). Later, Paul would similarly affirm that he coveted no one's ἀργύριον (Acts 20:33). Moreover, the term χρῆμα (Acts 8:18) is also used to denote Simon's attempted wealth transference. This word appears in connection to Barnabas (Acts 4:37), highlighting the contrast between these characters. Selfless relinquishment—the antithesis of bribery—was the appropriate mechanism for relationship in the household of God, as "apostolic ministry . . . carries a degree of detachment from materialism and possessions."[33]

---

32. Bauer, *Acts as Story*, 139.
33. Cho and Park, *Acts*, 178.

Peter declared that Simon's money could share his "fate" (ἀπώλειαν, Acts 8:20), a term implying eternal consequences. Most translations render it as "perish" (NIV), though the LEB reads, "May your silver be destroyed along with you!" These variations aim to capture the weight of Peter's rebuke, which reflects his judgment that Simon attempted to "acquire" (κτάομαι, Acts 8:20) apostolic power—the same word used for Judas's acquisition of a field. The attempted purchase was of God's "gift" (δωρεά, Acts 8:20). This word is consistently used by Luke in reference to the Holy Spirit (Acts 2:38, 10:45, 11:17), which clearly could not be secured with wealth as if it were a magician's formula. Moreover, bribery, an unjust weapon, was an extremely negative and offensive form of social currency in the church. Peter's declaration that the money should be destroyed was not mere rhetoric; as the greed-inducing dark powers faced destruction, so should their money, their vessel of power and control.

Peter denied Simon a "share" (κλῆρος, Acts 8:21). Judas exchanged his κλῆρος for land, transitioning from an insider to an outsider. Likewise, Simon is indicated as being beyond the margins of the church. Like Ananias and Sapphira (Acts 5:3–4) and in contrast to other testimonies from Jerusalem (Acts 2:37, 46; 4:32), Simon's "heart" (καρδία, Acts 8:21) was corrupt. Yet the magician's life was spared because he was exterior to the group and unable to betray it. Simon was given the invitation to "repent" (μετανόησον) from "evil" (κακίας) and pray to the Lord for mercy (Acts 8:22).

His state was underscored by Peter's use of the terms "gall" (χολὴν, Acts 8:23) and "bitterness" (πικρίας, Acts 8:23), echoing the warning in Deut 29:18 against idolatry. The rebuke intensified as Simon was further described as bound by "chains" (σύνδεσμον, Acts 8:23) of "unrighteousness" (ἀδικίας, Acts 8:23). This phrase draws on Isa 58:6–7 (LXX), when the prophet envisioned God breaking chains of injustice through acts of generosity—a stark contrast to the magician's self-serving attempt at bribery. Moreover, the ἀδικία motive is reminiscent of Judas's act (Acts 1:18).

Even under the extensive weight of Peter's blistering censure, Simon still miscalculated the apostolic function. Rather than praying on behalf of himself, as instructed, he petitioned for Peter's intercession. A further exodus allusion is present in the account of Pharaoh requesting Moses to pray on his behalf. However, Pharaoh never repented but only hardened his heart (Exod 8:8, 15, 28, 32; 9:28, 35; 10:17, 20),[34] strengthening the case for Simon's continued outsider status. As Pervo states, "Christianity has

---

34. Parsons, *Acts*, 118.

nothing in common with magic," so there appears to be no commonality with this character.[35]

Simon's intense desire to acquire power analogous to that of Peter indicates his belief in the absolute necessity of obtaining divine gifts. This included the desire to grant pardon for wickedness through a brokerage relationship with the powers. The magician himself was in such a partnership with evil, granting him many socioeconomic benefits—reciprocity that was the dominant form of exchange from the Samaritans. Ultimately, Simon's final response was motivated by a desire to avoid the punitive realities of Peter's curse rather than by a genuine desire for an appropriate relationship with God and the apostles.

Samaria, as a geographic bridge to the "ends of the earth," momentarily became ground zero in the war against evil. Perhaps "Satan will do everything he can to stop the reuniting of the north and south."[36] Additionally, the Samaritans were receptive to the prophet like Moses, who is referenced in the following terms:

> There must never be found among you anyone ... who practices divination, an omen reader, a soothsayer, a sorcerer, one who casts spells, one who conjures up spirits, a practitioner of the occult, or a necromancer.
> The Lord your God will raise up for you a prophet like me from among you—from your fellow Israelites; you must listen to him. (Deut 18:10–11, 15)

From this sequence, it is evident that Moses was not only the liberator from Pharaoh's economic exploitation but also an advocate against activities associated with magic. This demonstrates that the new exodus cannot coexist with the dark powers; therefore, the two sides were destined for conflict.

Like Empedocles, Simon's local honor was elevated to a god-like status.[37] In a time when elitist power brokers controlled magic,[38] this practitioner positioned himself in a prime location of influence, where the imperial cult had a dedicated temple.[39] Given Rome's disdain for magic, Luke's early readers may have questioned how the narrative description of Simon might

---

35. Pervo, *Acts*, 214.
36. Schreiner, *Acts*, 316.
37. DK 31B112.
38. Philo, *Spec. Laws* 3.100.
39. In Greek, Sebastos is Augustus; see Richardson, *Herod: King of the Jews*, locs. 210–11 of 5600.

SIMON MAGUS IN SAMARIA

coincide with imperial representation. To this, Justin Martyr addressed the Roman Emperor Antoninus Pius in the 150s CE (perhaps within a generation of Acts' production), stating that Simon was from the Samaritan village of Gitto (proximate to Justin's home). He also asserts that his magic was empowered by devils, and that upon reaching the imperial capital, Simon was celebrated as a god by some Romans.[40]

While these claims cannot be verified, neither can their historicity be disproven.[41] Regardless of their accuracy, there is strong evidence that the early church circulated stories regarding Simon, connecting him to Rome. While speculative, if Luke's readers in Rome were familiar with the Simon Magus tradition, the logical sequence suggests that Simon could have been expelled from Samaria by the Holy Spirit only to reemerge in Rome. Therefore, the textual, narrative, and theological indications leave room to consider Simon and Rome in a sort of dark collaboration. Nevertheless, the power and influence Simon held over the Samaritans resembled the control the empire exercised over the governance, religion, and economics of occupied lands.

Synthesis

After Ananias and Sapphira, Luke no longer refers to Satan directly. Instead, this narrative describes the concluding instance in which the operatives of darkness attempt to infiltrate the church or test it with money. Philip's arrival in Samaria disrupted the dark forces, and Simon, the broker of evil and a community patron, found his powers impotent. The unclean spirits expelled by Philip depicted an occupying external presence that attached itself to a weaker body to exhaust and manipulate its resources. Similarly, Simon, a more visible presence representing the dark powers, was likely guilty of comparable exploitation, profiting economically and benefiting from high social honor in exchange for community favors.

Desperate and greedy to preserve his honor, regain his profit opportunities, and rejuvenate his power, Simon employed the tactic of the insatiably manipulative when he attempted to convince Peter to empower him with apostolic gifts. Unlike Barnabas, who surrendered assets at the apostles' feet (Acts 4:37–38) without a demand for reciprocity, the antagonists Ananias and Sapphira (Acts 5:1–11) and then Simon offered money with ulterior

40. Justin Martyr, *1 Apol.* 26.
41. Ferreiro, "Fall of Simon Magus."

motives. Simon was far from becoming a true disciple, offering to relinquish wealth in an attempt at bribery to preserve his local influence.

The church's arrival signaled an end to the exploitation by the dark powers in Samaria, enacted both by Simon and the unclean spirits. This, in turn, was a portent of the evil forces's impending defeat when the gospel reaches Rome. This imperial power controlled the wealth, materials, and assets of each conquered location as if it were an unclean entity occupying a social body. Alternately, it could be considered a "Simon," a physical presence holding power over the populace across multiple demographics.

Philip departed Samaria and met an Ethiopian eunuch, a political influencer and chief treasurer to Queen Candace (Acts 8:26-40). This powerful official, functioning like an economist, responded to Philip's message and became a representative of Africa in the gospel's expansion. The defeat of darkness continued as Saul of Tarsus encountered Jesus on the road to Damascus, shifting allegiances to become a key figure in God's kingdom (Acts 9:1-22). Despite opposition and a narrow escape from Damascus, Barnabas advocated for Saul's acceptance in Jerusalem (Acts 9:23-31).

Meanwhile, Peter's ministry confronted death and evil through healings and raising the dead (Acts 9:32-43). His pivotal encounter with Cornelius, a Roman noted for his generosity, marked that centurion as an ideal gentile convert. This not only signaled the church's target of Roman officials, but also Rome as the narrative destination (Acts 10:1-48).[42] Peter defended his actions in Jerusalem, leading to the church's celebration of ethnic inclusion (Acts 11:1-18). Barnabas later joined the growing disciple community in Antioch, bringing Saul with him (Acts 11:19-26).

---

42. Kochenash, *Roman Self-Representation*, 101.

Chapter 5: The Death of Herod Agrippa I: Divine Justice and the Fall of Hubris (Acts 11:27—12:24)

Chronically challenged when it came to raising money and therefore constantly in quest of funds, he was as gifted as his grandfather when spending was involved. . . .[1] [I]n Rome proper, no Herodian had ever been in a more powerful position than Agrippa I.[2]

—BRUCE CHILTON

Introduction

THE DISCIPLES RECEIVED THEIR initial identification as Christians at Antioch, highlighting the ongoing victorious progression of the church as it extended beyond Palestine (Acts 11:26). These Christians in Antioch passed the purity test of greed versus financial surrender by demonstrating generosity in sending resources to assist members of the Judean churches in weathering an impending famine. Their aid was delivered by Barnabas and Saul (Acts 11:19–26).

---

1. Chilton, *Herods*, 180.
2. Chilton, *Herods*, 191.

Textual Analysis

Famine in Acts 11:27–30

Prior to introducing Herod Agrippa I, Luke leads with an impending famine prophesied by Agabus, evoking the Elijah and Elisha motif, particularly Elijah's duel with state-sponsored idolatry (Acts 11:28).[3] Luke associates Agrippa I's death in 44 CE with events adjacent to the famine. Historical evidence indicates that famines bookended Agrippa's death. The first occurred in 41 to 42 CE in Rome and the latter around 44 to 48 CE, as the systemic effects food crises in Judea, Syria, Greece, and Egypt prompted a drastic rise in grain prices.[4] Food shortages had severe consequences in a world where Rome controlled agriculture, and the populace received little benefit from any surplus, even during productive years.[5] The economic fallout of food shortages was critical, further exacerbating the disparity between the wealthy and the majority subsistent classes.[6] Philostratus described such a situation in Aspendus where the wealthy had stockpiled the harvests for exports, making it inaccessible to locals.[7] Malnutrition and vitamin-deficiency complications depleted immune systems, increasing the risk of disease and disrupting fertility schedules, all of which had crippling socioeconomic ramifications.

The opening phrase of Acts 12:1, Κατ' ἐκεῖνον δὲ τὸν καιρὸν, is translated by Fitzmyer as "at that critical moment." This links the vulnerable conditions of Agabus's fulfilled prophecy to Luke's introduction of Agrippa I, whom he designates as Herod.[8] Luke uses this misnomer to prompt his readers to view Agrippa I as part of the Herodian dynasty's collective evil.[9]

In the ancient world, a populace unsettled by the socioeconomic repercussions of famine often responded with actions ranging from banditry to outright revolutionary activity.[10] Political tensions intensified during times of shortage, even in the imperial capital. Emperor Claudius,

---

3. See 1 Kgs 18.
4. Witherington, *Acts of the Apostles*, 373. Schnabel, *Acts*, 919–20.
5. Carter, *Roman Empire and NT*, 110.
6. Malina and Rohrbaugh, *Social Science Commentary*, loc. 6867 of 7128.
7. Philostr. *Vit. Apoll.* 1.15.
8. Fitzmyer, *Acts of the Apostles*, 486.
9. The chapter refers to Agrippa I as Herod or Agrippa, while Herod the Great (Agrippa's grandfather) and Herod Antipas are designated accordingly.
10. Josephus, *Ant.* 20.101.

attempting to pacify his discontented constituents, repealed taxes in Rome during this period to inject some economic stimulus into his immediate region.[11] Client kings felt pressure from both ends, needing to manage the discontented poor while simultaneously extending tribute to their superiors. At such a time, Agrippa I, desiring political capital, sought to maximize favor by targeting the early Christian group as a public enemy in Jerusalem, hoping to boost his popularity during a fragile economic crisis.[12]

Herod sought to "oppress" or "ruin" (κακῶσαί, 12:1) the church.[13] Luke employs variations of the root word κακόω five times in total (Acts 7:6, 19; 12:1; 14:2; 18:10), with the first two instances describing Pharaoh's actions toward Israel in the exodus account (Acts 7:6, 19). In Acts 12:1, the term reappears as Agrippa I assumes the role of a surrogate Pharaoh, enacting persecution against God's people. Meanwhile, as a counterpoint to Agrippa I's actions during the famine, the believers in Judea received financial support from sources beyond the region, sent by way of the disciples in Antioch (Acts 11:27–30). This literary alignment juxtaposes the economic ethics of the church during a time of need against a public economic system through which Rome continued to extract money and resources from the region. Agrippa's antagonism against the church culminated in his initial primary target, James, the brother of John, who was executed by the king (Acts 12:2).

Agrippa I's Persecution in Acts 12:1–19

James, while subordinate to Peter and John in terms of Luke's literary attention, was nevertheless a core apostle in Jerusalem. Although Luke does not explicitly provide the reasoning behind James's execution, Willimon draws upon Acts 4:25–26, following the arrest and trial of Peter and John, where the Christ followers ask God for strength. In this passage, the apostles quote Ps 2, identifying contemporary public rulers including Herod (Antipas):[14] "The kings of the earth stood together, and the rulers assembled together, against the Lord and against his Christ. For indeed both Herod and Pontius

---

11. Graham, "Imperial Responses," 26–52. Cassius Dio, *Hist.* 60.11.1, notes that in 42 CE, a grain shortage caused unrest among the population. Suet. *Claud.* 18, describes a more severe famine in 51 CE, during which Emperor Claudius personally financed provisions and worked tirelessly to avert disaster.
12. Chilton, *Herods*, 193.
13. MGS, s.v. "κακόω."
14. Willimon, *Acts*, 111.

Pilate, with the Gentiles and the people of Israel, assembled together in this city against your holy servant Jesus" (Acts 4:26–27).

Thus, early in Acts, Luke identified the ruling powers, including the Herodian dynasty, as opponents of Jesus. The apostolic petition was, "And now, Lord, pay attention to their threats, and grant to your servants to speak your message with great boldness (παρρησία)" (Acts 4:29).[15] Willimon asserts that the reference to political "boldness" (παρρησία) was likely directed at Agrippa. Luke previously suggests an aggressive attitude on the part of James as Jesus begins his journey toward Jerusalem:[16] "The [Samaritan] villagers refused to welcome him, because he was determined to go to Jerusalem. Now when his disciples James and John saw this, they said, 'Lord, do you want us to call fire to come down from heaven and consume them?'" (Luke 9:52–54). James's stance was comparable to that of John the Baptist, who rebuked Herod Antipas for unjust acts (Luke 3:18–19), resulting in John's beheading—a fate James also shared.[17] John the Baptist advocated for food sharing, generosity, and economic restraint on the part of the Herodian guard (Luke 3:10–14). It is reasonable to infer that James likewise criticized Agrippa I's economic policies during a time of famine, a pressing public issue in Jerusalem. James's presumed political rebuke of Agrippa I likely led to his execution by beheading, a punishment typically reserved for political crimes, particularly revolutionary acts.[18]

The occasion in Acts 12 was Passover (12:3), an event that again serves as a narrative benchmark, recalling both Israel's liberation from the dark forces of Egyptian tyranny and Judas's betrayal of Jesus (Luke 22:1–6). As a historical figure known for craving approval, Agrippa sought to replicate his success in martyring James by arresting and planning the execution of Peter (Acts 12:3). Peter's incarceration and miraculous rescue from prison are peripheral to this study's conclusions (Acts 12:4–17). However, in this account, Luke continues the theme of triumph over darkness, demonstrated through Peter's escape. Agrippa, in turn, appeared foolishly incompetent and ordered the execution of the guards (Acts 12:18–19). Yet, as with Judas, Ananias, Sapphira, and Simon Magus, the reader is not left in suspense regarding the fate of the villain; justice is delivered as Luke dramatically recounts Agrippa's shameful demise.

15. Παρρησία or "Speaking truth to power."
16. Chilton, *Herods*, 193–99.
17. Chilton, *Herods*, 195–96.
18. Barrett, *Critical Exegetical Commentary—Acts*, 574–75.

Agrippa I's Trade War in Acts 12:19–20

The king travelled to Caesarea to address a political and economic issue. Acts 12:20 describes the king's relations with the Tyrians and Sidonians in negative terms. The verb θυμομαχέω, a hapax legomenon meaning "to fight with animosity, desperation, or obstinacy," illustrates the intense feud between Agrippa and his northern neighbors.[19] Tyre and Sidon, the counterparties to the quarrel, were two prominent Phoenician port cities on the Mediterranean. Although these cities had historically played significant economic roles, their influence had diminished by the Roman period, though they remained important on a local level.[20]

Jewish history intersected with these two cities on several occasions. For example, Rome granted Simon the Hasmonean limited influence in the region.[21] Later, Tyre faced conflict with portions of Galilee but was resisted by Jonathan.[22] Bronze tablets placed in Tyre by Julius Caesar declared that Hyrcanus was a Roman ally.[23] Additionally, Herod the Great contended with Marion of Tyre in 40 BCE over Galilean territory and travelled to Tyre to employ its people for various tasks, extending construction projects into the city, including temples.[24] These port cities were competitive with Caesarea yet were ecologically disadvantaged, relying on grain imports from Jewish Palestine due to their terrain being limited to sea and mountains.[25]

The Old Testament frequently references Tyre and Sidon, noting their role in providing supplies for the construction of Jerusalem's first and second temples, as well as the king's palaces.[26] However, these cities were also the subject of prophetic rebuke.[27] Additionally, Solomon took a wife from Sidon and incorporated the goddess Astarte into his worship practices (1

---

19. MGS, s.v. "θυμομαχέω."
20. Sala, "Sidon," *LBD*; and Ferry, "Tyre," *LBD*.
21. 1 Macc 11:59; Josephus, *Ant.* 13.146.
22. Edwards, "Tyre (Place)," 6: 691.
23. Josephus, *Ant.* 14.197–98.
24. Josephus, *Ant.* 14.298–99; *J.W.* 1.231–38, 275, 422, 543.
25. Kistemaker and Hendriksen, *Exposition of Acts*, 445.
26. Regarding Tyre and Sidon's role in contributing to construction in Jerusalem, see 2 Sam 5:11; 1 Kgs 5:1, 6; 7:13–14; 1 Chr 14:1; 2 Chr 2:3; Ezra 3:7; and Neh 13:16.
27. Regarding prophetic rebuke of Tyre and Sidon in the Old Testament, see Isa 23:2–17; Jer 47:4; Ezek 26:1–15; 27:1–32; 28:1–22; 29:18–20; 32:30; Joel 3:4; Amos 1:9–10; and Zech 9:2–3.

Kgs 11:1–33). Later, Queen Jezebel, a central figure in Israel's idolatry, was the daughter of King Ethbaal of Sidon (1 Kgs 16:31).

Nevertheless, Luke presents an intriguingly positive view of Tyre and Sidon. Jesus speculates on a greater potential receptivity to his ministry in these cities (Luke 10:13–14), a possibility realized when Paul found comfort in these locations, in contrast to his unsettling experiences in Jerusalem (Acts 21:3, 7; 27:3). Moreover, Jesus's message of Jubilee at Nazareth (Luke 4:14–21) included a commentary comparing his ministry to Elijah, who, during a time of famine, served the widow in Sidon (Luke 4:25–26; 1 Kgs 17:1–24). Ironically, people from these two cities attended Jesus's Sermon on the Plain, listening to his reversal ethics contrasting the fates of the hungry and the well fed (Luke 6:20–25). In Acts 12, they were victims of a trade war instigated by the powerful Agrippa I, who "cuts off food supplies from the people."[28] Operating under Roman agrarian policy, individuals like Agrippa I reaped personal economic benefits from agricultural production, especially after the export quota to Rome was met. Furthermore, the trade war may have been motivated by Agrippa's need for Judean approval, particularly after his failed attempt to kill Peter.

The grain trade between the Herodian dynasty and Tyre and Sidon appears to have been long-standing.[29] The people of Tyre and Sidon had an "environmental interdependence" on Agrippa's kingdom,[30] relying on grain imports not merely as an economic concern but as a matter of survival. Considering this alongside Luke's themes on wealth ethics, Agrippa's actions were ethically apostate. He defied the principles of sharing food as taught by John the Baptist, whom his uncle martyred (Luke 3:11), and he represents the cursed rich and well fed in the Sermon on the Plain (Luke 6:24–25). Additionally, Agrippa resembles the wealthy fool who selfishly hoarded his produce (Luke 12:13–21) and failed to love his neighbors, as exemplified by the Samaritan (Luke 10:25–37).

Christina Petterson notes that few scholars (only two in her assessment) make the connection between Agrippa's actions and the famine prophesied by Agabus (Acts 11:28–30).[31] Agrippa's engagement in a poorly timed trade war exploited the desperation of vulnerable people, exacerbating the effects of the famine in the region. Agrippa's policy centered on

---

28. Parsons, *Acts*, 178.
29. Oakman, *Political Aims of Jesus*, 75–76.
30. Trainor, *Acts*, 90–91.
31. Petterson, *Acts of Empire*, 51.

dominance. Famines provided an opportune time to reinforce class distinctions, power structures, and economic control.³² This royal dominance promulgated by Agrippa was the likely reason the offering from Antioch was sent to Judean churches rather than to Jerusalem proper.³³ Similarly, Galen (129 to 216 CE) highlights the dichotomy of agricultural command, whereby urban elites benefited disproportionately, leaving the rural peasants who produced the crops with insufficient resources.³⁴ Luke reflects a similar distinction as he often juxtaposes the city and the countryside,³⁵ conveying a general suspicion of Jerusalem in his writings. Agrippa I, in particular, utilized Judah's old capital to a greater degree than either his predecessors or his successor, further entrenching his identity with that location.³⁶

In Acts 12:20, Blastus, the king's "chamberlain" (NIV),³⁷ though occupying a traditionally domestic role responsible for Agrippa's household affairs,³⁸ emerged as a crucial player in brokering negotiations. The people of Tyre and Sidon convinced Blastus to assist them in seeking peace, possibly even bribing him to intervene. This appears to have been necessary given Herod's stubborn demeanor and exertion of control over trade.³⁹ Never known to "suffer from modesty,"⁴⁰ Agrippa continued to leverage his power by summoning representatives from Tyre and Sidon to Caesarea. This was a Roman-styled competitive port city that served as a fitting backdrop to bolster the king's image as a "child of Rome."⁴¹

The irony lies in the fact that Caesarea's grounds were originally established as a Phoenician shipping colony by Sidon's King Strato II. This detail may have influenced Herod's choice of this location, subtly signaling his rise to prominence against the backdrop of Tyre and Sidon's decline.⁴² In Caesarea, Agrippa I made a dramatic appearance, taking the "judgment

---

32. Gapp, "Universal Famine," 258–65.
33. Spencer, *Acts*, 128.
34. Galen, *De alim.* 1.1–7.
35. Oakman, "Countryside in Luke-Acts," 151–80.
36. Hadas-Lebel, "Caligula, Agrippa," 87.
37. For the chamberlain's role, see Epictetus, *Disc.* 1.19.17–23; 3.33.15; and 4.7.1–19.
38. L&N, "κοιτών," 85.
39. Xen. *Mem.* 3.11.1.; Barrett, *Critical Exegetical Commentary—Acts*, 589.
40. Chilton, *Herods*, 179.
41. Chilton, *Herods*, 177.
42. Arterbury, "Caesarea Maritima," 86–88.

seat" to deliver a speech. The gathered crowd responded with shouts (ἐπιφωνέω, Acts 12:22), deifying him by proclaiming, "The voice of a god, and not a man" (Acts 12:22 NET). Kellum clarifies that Luke's use of "Θεοῦ" suggests Herod was called a god rather than a conduit for God.[43]

Agrippa I's Demise

Agrippa I, a "Romanophile" eager for power and admiration, closely emulated the ambitions and cultic practices of his mentor, the "megalomaniac"[44] Caligula. Known for declaring, "A man ought either to be frugal or be Caesar,"[45] Caligula was affirmed by the Roman Senate "partly out of fear and partly with sincerity."[46] He became the first Roman emperor to demand divine worship during his lifetime, using this cult to amass greater wealth.[47]

Caligula promoted his own deity by wearing divine attire, erecting temples, and installing cult images in his honor.[48] Though tales of his excess—such as housing a horse in marble quarters and engaging in incestuous acts—may have been exaggerated, they reflected a public consensus regarding his insatiable greed and self-idolization.[49] As Caligula's protégé, Agrippa also proclaimed his own greatness,[50] eliminated rivals, including family members who had supported him,[51] and minted coins bearing his image—an idolatrous act.[52] His demands for public celebration and glorification led to disturbances and riots,[53] and, like Caligula, he became known for his royal attire.[54]

In both Luke's and Josephus's accounts, Agrippa's desire for idolatrous reverence ultimately led to his demise. Agrippa's acceptance of praise

---

43. Kellum, *Acts*, 148.
44. Richardson, "Herod (Family)," 584.
45. Strauss, *Ten Caesars*, 106.
46. Cassius Dio, *Hist.* 59.26.3–5.
47. Suet. *Cal.* 22.2–3; Cassius Dio, *Hist.* 59.27.3.
48. Jones, "Roman Imperial Cult," 5:806; Suet. *Cal.* 22.2–3.
49. Strauss, *Ten Caesars*, 106.
50. Chilton, *Herods*, 192.
51. Chilton, *Herods*, 181. See also Rogerson, *Chronicle of OT Kings*, 195.
52. Chilton, *Herods*, 197, 182–83.
53. Richardson, "Herod (Family)," 584.
54. Josephus, *Ant.* 19.8.2; Suet. *Cal.* 19.1–3; 32.1; Cassius Dio, *Hist.* 59.17.

exceeded even Roman norms, as Caesar expected humility from client kings.[55] "The voice of a god and not a man" echoes descriptions of Nero, the likely Caesar when Paul reached Rome, whose divine association is similarly depicted in Luke's portrayal of Agrippa I.[56] Tacitus, Cassius Dio, Philostratus, and Suetonius each discuss how the populace excessively celebrated Nero's divine voice, both night and day.[57] Moreover, Nero considered Thrasea Paetus disloyal, as he had never acknowledged his sacred voice.[58]

Building on Agrippa's historical connection to Caligula and Luke's parallels to Nero's divine voice, Caesarea's significance is further underscored by its temple dedicated to Augustus, the "savior of the world." Additionally, Josephus notes that Agrippa was in Caesarea for a festival honoring his Roman patrons, highlighting the city's role as a center of imperial allegiance.[59] Another point of intersection lies in the narrative's imagery. Agrippa, known for his affinity for regal attire—evidenced by his guards being adorned in gold and silver—wore a gleaming silver robe in Caesarea.[60] Josephus vividly describes how the silver fabric shimmered under the sun in a dazzling display that was likely calculated and rehearsed.[61] This spectacle reflected the influence of Agrippa I's mentor, Caligula, renowned for his elaborate dress.[62] Similarly, his patron Claudius was known to wear golden robes,[63] while Nero—whom Luke subtly connects to Agrippa—favored impressive attire.[64] In this scene, Agrippa I, though only a client king, is fashioned in the image of the Caesars, who were deified as gods. This act of self-presentation takes

---

55. Keener, *NT*, 357.

56. Rowe notes the complexity in assessing New Testament documents, especially the imperial cult, particularly of Acts in relationship to the time the writer wished to convey (an earlier period) to his contemporary time frame, likely late first or early second century. See Rowe, "Luke-Acts and Imperial Cult," 5.

57. Tac. *Ann.* 14.15; Cassius Dio, *Hist.* 62.20.5; Suet. *Nero* 20; Philostr. *Vit. Apoll.* 5.7.

58. Tac. *Ann.* 16.22.

59. Josephus, *Ant.* 19.8.2.

60. Philo, *Flacc.* 26–35; Chilton, *Herods*, 177.

61. Chilton, *Herods*, 199. Josephus, *J.W.* 1.414–15; *Ant.* 15.339; 16.136–44. It is likely that Luke either depended on Josephus as a source, or at least shared documentation or access to earlier oral tradition with the Jewish historian. See Mason, *Josephus and NT*, 251–96.

62. Suet. *Cal.* 19.1–3; 32.1; Cassius Dio, *Hist.* 59.17. Caligula even had a gold chain given to Agrippa; see Chilton, *Herods*, 183.

63. Tac. *Ann.* 12.51.

64. Suet. *Nero* 25.1; Cassius Dio, *Hist.* 52.20.3.

place in the shadow of the Caesarean temple, a prominent landmark built by the Herodian dynasty to honor the imperial cult.

This extravagant display and celebration stood in stark contrast to the reality of the common people of Tyre, Sidon, and Judea during a time of famine, a disparity Luke likely intended his audience to recognize. The clothing, the location, and the voice all contribute to a sense of pageantry in the purposeful self-representation of the divine. Klauck describes the Lukan presentation of Agrippa I in divine terms:

> [Agrippa I] is praised because the crowd believe that they can sense the divine power and the divine being in his person. He promises peace, he bestows benefactions, he behaves kindly and mercifully, just like a real god. Here we encounter once again the phenomenon of a "divine man" in the setting of the classical cult of rulers.[65]

During a time when the people of Tyre and Sidon were suffering and requesting peace "because their country's food supply was provided by the king's country" (12:20 NET), Agrippa's opulent Roman-style games in Caesarea made a mockery of their plight. This occurred against the backdrop of historically attested famines in Judea, when the widespread peasant populace was still reeling from the effects of previous food shortages and ongoing recovery efforts. His extravagance stood in stark contrast to the pending needs of others.

To further magnify the offensive injustice of Agrippa I's lavish greed and self-deification, the king's lifelong financial mismanagement is well-recorded. Agrippa spent nearly his entire adult life in debt, rarely being solvent,[66] squandering wealth he did accumulate through "lavish hospitality and entertainment" to win the favor of emperors Caligula and Claudius, whom he emulated.[67] For a time, Agrippa I, who was raised in Rome, lost his successful standing[68] and returned to Judea as a "freeloader,"[69] yet still did not relinquish a lifestyle beyond his means.[70] Later, he gave his ten-year-old daughter in marriage to a wealthy family in hopes of securing his

---

65. Klauck, *Magic and Paganism*, locs. 649–53 of 2074.

66. Chilton, *Herods*, 176.

67. Josephus, *Ant.* 18.6.1–2, 106–8, 143–49, 166–67, 237; *J.W.* 2.181; and Philo, *Flacc.* 25. See also Chilton, *Herods*, 176.

68. Goodman, *Rome and Jerusalem*, 78–79.

69. Chilton, *Herods*, 170; Josephus, *Ant.* 18.237.

70. Josephus, *J.W.* 2.181; *Ant.* 18.106–8; Philo, *Flacc.* 25.

financial stability.⁷¹ Agrippa's character personified the greed, wealth, and self-deification of imperial power.

Agrippa's dramatic display was mirrored by an equally dramatic demise. In Luke's account, Agrippa was struck down "immediately" (παραχρῆμα) by the angel of the Lord for failing to redirect the people's deific praise (Acts 12:21–23). The term παραχρῆμα, frequently employed by Luke, underscores divine intervention, as seen in the cases of Ananias (Acts 5:10) and Elymas (Acts 13:11), enhancing the narrative's urgency and signaling divine judgment. Similarly, the use of ἐκψύχω for Agrippa's death aligns his fate with that of Ananias and Sapphira (Acts 5:5, 10), connecting these events thematically.

Luke intensifies the gravity of Agrippa's punishment by describing his death as being "eaten by worms" from within, symbolizing both moral decay and divine retribution. This depiction contrasts with Josephus's account, which attributes Agrippa's death to severe stomach pain over five days following his acceptance of divine honors inspired by his shimmering attire.⁷² While Josephus emphasizes Agrippa's suffering, Luke highlights the immediacy and severity of God's judgment, magnifying the theological implications of his arrogance.

Agrippa I died because he allowed himself to be identified as a god instead of giving glory to God (Acts 12:23). This was immediately followed by the statement, "But the word of God kept on increasing and multiplying" (Acts 12:24 NET), a clear indication of the victory of God and the downfall of evil powers. As with Judas, Ananias, and Sapphira—other characters who previously represented greed and exploitation near Jerusalem—the king experiences a shameful death that spreads through the gossip network of his context. Agrippa I's death is comparable to the demise of Judas (Acts 1:17–19), Antiochus IV Epiphanes (2 Macc 9:5–28), and other villains.⁷³

Agrippa I was also connected to antiheroes of the Old Testament tradition. These include various allusions: Pharaoh, who ordered the execution of young Hebrew males while maintaining exploitative economic practices (Exod 1:15–22); Balaam, the greedy oracle who attempted to derail Israel's trajectory (Num 22:22); Haman, who sought to eliminate the

---

71. Josephus, *Ant.* 19.277; Chilton, *Herods*, 179.

72. Josephus, *Ant.* 19.8.2.

73. Josephus, *Ant.* 17.6.5, 168–79 (death of Herod the Great); Hdt. *Hist.* 4.205 (death of Pheretime); Paus. *Descr.* 9.7.2 (death of Cassander); Josephus, *J.W.* 1.656 (death of Herod the Great); Lucian, *Alex.* 59 (death of Alexander the false prophet).

Jewish presence in Persia (2 Kgs 5:1–27); and Nebuchadnezzar, an imperial leader who boasted in his greatness (Dan 4:28–37).[74]

Luke subtly connects Agrippa I and Solomon, both criticized for greed and economic exploitation. His references to Solomon cast suspicion, notably through literary associations with the deviant prophet Jonah (Luke 11:29–32), the parable of the wealthy fool (Luke 12:13–21),[75] and Stephen's critique of Solomon's temple (Acts 7:47).[76] Luke's omission of Solomon in Jesus's genealogy, substituting Nathan instead (Luke 3:31), further hints at a critical view, emphasizing Solomon's failure to follow Deuteronomic guidelines against royal greed.[77]

Solomon's dealings with Tyre's King Hiram underscore this critique. Though Hiram initially aided David's palace construction (2 Sam 5:11) and provided essential resources for Solomon's temple, engaging in lucrative trade deals (1 Kgs 5:1–18; 7:40–45), Solomon failed to reciprocate adequately, suggesting possible greed (1 Kgs 9:11–27; 10:22). Despite this, Solomon still required more gold from Hiram (1 Kgs 9:11–13). Luke's historical references and negative framing of Solomon, particularly his treatment of Tyre, resonate with Agrippa I's exploitation of the people of Tyre, hinting at a replay of greedy monarchs.[78]

Agrippa I, by receiving praise, was depicted as an object of worship, surpassing the responses made to Peter (Acts 10:25–26) and Paul (Acts 14:11–15; 28:6). Ramsay MacMullen remarks, "It is a very good exercise, at least from a historian's point of view, to imagine oneself a devout pagan

---

74. Schreiner, *Acts*, 401.

75. The wealthy fool accumulated and hoarded excess while conducting a construction campaign (Luke 12:13–21). Immediately afterward Jesus juxtaposes this parabolic character while evoking Solomon as a negative example (Luke 12:27).

76. Two other remarks in Acts (3:6 and 5:11) occurring at Solomon's Portico come immediately after Peter declares he has no silver or gold (contrasting Israel's third king) and directly following Ananias and Sapphira's greedy monetary mishandling.

77. Luke also has a great interest in Deuteronomy, which includes the restrictions on wealth, marrying foreign wives, and relying on Egyptian trade (Deut 17:14–20), each of which Solomon violated. Luke also has a new temple or tabernacle theology in tension with Solomon's temple ideology. Moreover, Luke favors the Northern Kingdom (Galilee and Samaria) as well as diasporic communities, which may contribute to his suspicious view of Solomon.

78. Curiously, Solomon's inadequate reciprocity and solicitation for more gold is placed in the text adjacent to a reiteration of the commandment against idolatry, which he violated (1 Kgs 9:3–9).

while reading various Christian writings."[79] Following MacMullen's method of imaginative reading, Luke's recipients in the broader Mediterranean context, including Theophilus—presumably a Roman elite—likely observed a distinct connection to Roman imperial worship within this pericope. The concept of "Roman imperial theology" frames Rome's founders as figures rooted in ancient Greek mythology, with the empire's rise seen as the fulfillment of sacred writings, ultimately embodied by Caesar Augustus.[80] The imperial cult was "one of the most powerful forces toward the unification of the Roman world,"[81] while its many "temples, images, rituals, personnel, and theological claims" honored the emperor with sacrifices, vows, offerings, and prayers.[82] Caesar worship accelerated to benefit living heads of state under Caligula, Claudius, and Nero, likely the reigning emperor when Paul reached Rome.[83] By the second century CE, Roman emperors were labelled "the god of the Romans."[84] Luke, writing not too distant from the turn of the second century, likely had ample motivation for a cryptic polemic against such practices.

Agrippa I's death took place in a city devoted to Rome, with a prominent temple erected for Caesar worship, during a festival that echoed imperial cultic acts.[85] In addition, Agrippa I's trade war closely resembled Roman economic policy,[86] and the king was cultically dressed in remarkable attire that prompted deific acclamation. This adulation was driven by his public, seemingly divine, speech, a connection to reports of Nero's divine voice. As Lynn Allan Kauppi observes, "For a Greco-Roman audience, Agrippa was the central focus of the ruler cult ritual. He has proved his political dominance."[87]

The rise of the Roman imperial cult had significant implications for the church, presenting an increasing problem at the time of Luke's writing. The danger was that failure to participate in imperial cult worship

---

79. MacMullen, *Christianizing the Roman Empire*, 111. This project employs the phrase "MacMullen's imaginative reading" to denote the application of his exercise.

80. Crossan, "Roman Imperial Theology," 59.

81. Goodman, *Rome and Jerusalem*, 66.

82. Carter, *Roman Empire and NT*, 7.

83. Jones, "Roman Imperial Cult," 5:807.

84. Winter, *Divine Honors*, 10. See also Tert. *Apol.* 24.9.

85. Winter, *Divine Honors*, 11, 24.

86. Carter, *Roman Empire and NT*, 110, says, "Food was about [Roman] power."

87. Kauppi, *Foreign but Familiar Gods*, 54.

could result in a verdict of "disloyalty and subversion,"[88] as emperors (e.g., Caligula) proclaimed that "there should be one lord, one king."[89] Historians have established that the rise of imperial cultic practices was remarkably substantial, and sociologically, their impact exceeded even the rise of Christianity in the first two centuries CE.[90] Such a dynamic inevitably placed the church and the imperial cultic practices at odds and destined for confrontation. Due to the inherent risk, Luke "cannot write openly"[91] against the cult. Nevertheless, in his prophetic imagination, he employed Agrippa's demise as a "type-scene to represent the destiny of the empire and of anyone who shows allegiance to those who call themselves divine and rulers of this world. In this regard, again, Luke is absolute: God."[92] Kellum questions the purpose of including Agrippa's death,[93] but this study highlights a recurring theme: villains are brought to justice, reinforcing the inevitability of victory over darkness as the narrative moves toward Rome. Agrippa I serves as a surrogate for the cosmic battle between God and the dark powers of greed and empire.

Ronald Allen notes a chiastic parallel between Acts 12:20–26 and the parable of the rich man and Lazarus (Luke 16:19–31).[94] Both stories include the vulnerable hungry, death, and an eschatological reversal. The extravagant living within the gated protection clearly indicates a man of elite standing, yet the reference to purple makes it more intriguing of royalty. Agrippa I's death personifies the rebuke of wealthy rulers and the systems enabling them to exploit and leave others hungry while benefiting themselves. This recalls Mary's introductory words in the Gospel, that God "has brought down the mighty from their thrones" (Luke 1:52 NET). This intratextual connection underscores that no organization is exempt from this reversal, including Rome itself. This is a weighty priority that demands consideration, especially given the narrative conclusion of Luke's second volume.

---

88. Carter, *Roman Empire and NT*, 54.
89. Suet. *Cal.* 2.204.
90. Winter, *Divine Honors*, 10.
91. Muñoz-Larrondo, *Postcolonial Reading of Acts*, 69.
92. Muñoz-Larrondo, *Postcolonial Reading of Acts*, 69.
93. Kellum, *Acts*, 147.
94. Allen, *Acts of the Apostles*, 112–13.

Synthesis

Regarding the connection between Acts 12 and the conclusion of Acts, Parsons notes a tremendous literary and rhetorical phenomenon:

> The rhetorical practice of inflection or *klisis* (inflecting the subject in the various Greek cases; see comments on Acts 9:1–30) may also indicate a major shift in action.... In light of this comment another interesting pattern emerges in Acts 12. God (*theos*) is inflected in the accusative case (12:5), genitive case (12:22), dative case (12:23), and genitive case again (12:24). In one instance, God (*theos*) is used to refer to "a god," and not Yahweh God (12:22). Strikingly we find a similar phenomenon in Acts chapter 28. God (*theos*) is inflected again only in the oblique cases: accusative (28:6); dative (28:15); genitive (28:23); and genitive again (28:31). Again, *theos* is used once to refer to "a god" and not the God (28:6). Furthermore, it is God in chapter 12, and not Herod or Peter, and God in chapter 28, and not Paul, who is so inflected and thus presumably the subject of each respective passage. Furthermore, "God" occurs in the last verse of each chapter. Not only is this observation significant for the interpretation of each passage, but it may provide further textual and rhetorical evidence for the overall structure of Acts. If our analysis of the inflection is correct, then the audience would have been prepared for such a major shift by the rhetorical markers left not only by the device of the chain-link interlock, but also by the oblique inflection of God.[95]

Parsons identifies that, with this linguistic device, a "major shift" occurs and notes the literary connection between Acts 12 and Acts 28.[96] However, he makes this connection without offering any theoretical insight into its significance or explaining its representation in Acts 12.

One primary connection between Acts 12 and 28 is the relationship of Agrippa I to Roman imperial power and culture, which included emperor worship. The reemergence of the linguistic device (*klisis*) in Acts 28, when Paul was preaching in Rome, depicts the true God juxtaposed with false deities—and Caesar, by implication. The potential of Parsons's analysis lies in the suggestion that Luke's audience should view God as the main protagonist of Acts in a story that now shifts direction. Agrippa I's destruction foreshadows the defeat of the dark powers on a larger scale at the end of

---

95. Parsons, *Acts*, 166.
96. Parsons, *Acts*, 166.

Luke's narrative. From this observation, this study now considers the cosmic battle played out in Acts' conclusion.

Acts 12 contains numerous new exodus parallels, including the famine (Gen 41:28–32), Agrippa's murderous resistance (Exod 1:15–22), Peter's miraculous rescue (Exod 14), and judgment upon the agitator (Exod 12:29; 14:28). Additional parallels are evident in the increase and multiplication of the church (Exod 1:7), and, finally, Saul and Barnabas being sent out into the land, like Caleb and the other scouts (Num 13:1–2).[97] The implication of these connections is that the Hebrews were delivered from imperial power toward conquest. Utilizing this imagery, Luke envisions a continuous exodus "to the ends of the earth" (Acts 1:8), symbolizing a victory over the dark powers, eventually culminating in Rome. Caesarea served as a miniature model of this expectation, allowing Luke to express his intentions subtly. The city, named in honor of the Caesar, was home to Cornelius, an imperial agent turned disciple, and a deified king described as a "Romanophile" who met judgment.[98]

Speech is a resounding motif in Luke's writings, and Agrippa's deified voice stands in contrast to the prophetic boldness of the apostles. Moreover, Agrippa is also juxtaposed with Jesus and Peter. Jesus rejected the devil's political offer of power (Luke 4:1–13), while Peter triumphed over a theoretical threat from the dark forces when he rejected deified treatment, by a Roman operative nonetheless (Acts 10). True power in Luke-Acts is associated with the preeminence of the Holy Spirit. However, Agrippa attempted to display his power through persecution, unjust economics, and undue worship, in contrast to Jesus's remarks: "The kings of the Gentiles lord it over them; and those in authority over them are called benefactors. But not so with you; rather the greatest among you must become like the youngest, and the leader like one who serves" (Luke 22:25–26). Pervo provides a fitting analysis of this reading:

> The initial and concluding references to the offering from Antioch frame the account with Christian benefaction, strongly contrasted to the supposed "benefactions" of tyrannical despots, who, having concocted a dispute, resolve it by accepting bribes and then rejoice to be hailed as saviors and benefactors.[99]

---

97. Schreiner, *Acts*, 399–400.
98. Richardson, "Herod (Family)," 584.
99. Pervo, *Luke's Story of Paul*, 43.

This observation provides an apt postmortem for Agrippa I, who self-identified as "the great king,"[100] a description resonating with Simon Magus, referred to as "the power of God that is called Great" (Acts 8:10). Meanwhile, the church was characterized by acting in "great fear" (Acts 5:5, 11) while affirming Jesus as "great" (Luke 1:32).

---

100. Chilton, *Herods*, 192.

Chapter 6: Bar-Jesus/Elymas in Paphos: Confronting the Powers of Deception (Acts 13:4–12)

> Bar-Jesus advised and practiced divinations in order to gain economic and social benefits; however, what Barnabas and Paul did was for earning nothing material but for helping the proconsul to be saved.[1]
>
> —Youngmo Cho and Hyung Dae Park

Introduction

Following Agrippa's death, the narrative shift in Acts moves distinctly beyond Jerusalem, with the church in Antioch functioning in a primary role in that Saul and Barnabas were commissioned for ministry (Acts 13:1–3). Barnabas, an antithetical character to Judas, Ananias, Sapphira, and Simon the magician, is repeatedly evoked as an ideal Lukan character, representing the correct gospel response of relinquishing wealth. Additionally, Barnabas is instrumental in Saul's reception in Jerusalem (Acts 9:26–31) and in the transport of money from Antioch to support Judean congregations during the famine (Acts 11:27–30). Accordingly, Barnabas's literary role is integral in the transition from the Petrine-emphasized ministry of the Palestinian region to the Pauline-dominated latter section of Acts.

---

1. Cho and Park, *Acts*, 10.

Textual Analysis

This duo, Paul and Barnabas, initially target Cyprus as their destination (Acts 13:4), a strategic shipping hub that flourished economically.[2] They first arrive in Salamis (Acts 13:5), a significant city with a long-standing Jewish community and multiple synagogues, many of whose members served as merchants in the port region. However, this community would later suffer during the failed Jewish uprising of 116 CE.[3] Saul and Barnabas "announced the word of God" there (Acts 13:5). They preach across the entire island and eventually reach Paphos (Acts 13:6),[4] marking approximately 112 miles from Salamis. At a pace of fifteen to twenty miles per day, this journey would have required six or seven days of travel,[5] aside from Sabbath rest and time spent engaging with communities. Paphos, rebuilt by Augustus following a devastating earthquake in 15 BCE, had become a center of government and the residence of the proconsul, renowned for its impressive buildings and extensive pagan history.[6]

A newly introduced character described as a Jewish magician personifies wickedness, presumably empowered by darkness and greedy by trade (Acts 13:6). There was esteem for Jewish magicians, noted to be "among the best in the Roman Empire."[7] This magician's ethnicity is certain, as is his apostasy, engaging in the "practices of foreign nations."[8] He is further described as a "false prophet" (ψευδοπροφήτης, Acts 13:6), compounding his disreputable status with a term used in the LXX to denote profiteering through deception.[9] The pseudo-prophet's name is Βαριησοῦς (Bar-Jesus, Acts 13:6), literally "son of Jesus," ironically appearing as a "devilish alternative to the true savior."[10]

---

2. Keener, *NT*, 358.

3. Keener, *NT*, 358. See also Kistemaker and Hendriksen, *Exposition of Acts*, 459–60.

4. The goddess Artemis was "fused" into the Phoenician Astarte. See Fitzmyer, *Acts of the Apostles*, 657.

5. Sullivan and Ferris, "Travel in Biblical Times," *LBD*.

6. Kistemaker and Hendriksen, *Exposition of Acts*, 460–61. The former location was of religious importance for the region, historically identified with the cults of the Syrian goddess Paphian, associated with the Greek goddess Aphrodite, and the city also had an impressive temple dedicated to Zeus. See also Bruce, *Book of the Acts*, 248; and Arnold, *Acts*, 118.

7. Keener, *NT*, 358.

8. Schreiner, *Acts*, 427.

9. Jer 6:13; 33:7–8, 11, 16 [26:7–8, 11, 16 LXX]; 34:9 [27:9 LXX]; 35:1 [28:1 LXX]; 36:1, 8 [29:1, 8 LXX]; Zech 13:2.

10. Peterson, *Acts of the Apostles*, 380.

This character is connected to Sergius Paulus, a proconsul and the executive Roman agent in the region, whom Luke describes as an "intelligent" (συνετός, Acts 13:7) man.[11] Yet, truth is sometimes concealed from the συνετῶν (Luke 10:21). Whatever favorable aspects Sergius Paulus possesses, his patronage of Bar-Jesus casts him in immediate suspicion of collusion with or subjugation to the magician's dark powers.

As evidenced throughout history, Roman leaders frequently utilized magicians and oracles. For instance, Caesar Augustus relied on sorcery and divination;[12] Tiberius incorporated the astrologer Claudius Thrasyllus into his household;[13] and Claudius, Nero, and Vespasian each employed the astrologer Balbillus.[14] Bar-Jesus possibly made himself indispensable to Sergius Paulus by offering dream interpretation, astrological forecasts, divinations, and possibly curses to aid the governor's work.[15] Skilled magicians and prophets could influence policy, bolstered by the strong reputation of Jewish magicians across the Mediterranean.[16]

Philo notes that magic was vital for political leadership,[17] while Jewish magical traditions fascinated figures such as Pliny the Elder.[18] Josephus records that Solomon's exorcism methods were replicated by a Jew named Eleazar, who impressed Vespasian.[19] Josephus also mentions Felix, a Roman official in Judea, being associated with a Jewish magician from Cyprus.[20] In fact, Richard Longenecker suggests that Luke might intentionally link Bar-Jesus (Elymas) to Atomos, who aided Felix in marrying Drusilla, the wife of Aziz.[21] Later, Marcus Aurelius associated with an Egyptian priest named Arnouphis, known for his powers.[22]

---

11. *LBD*, s.v. "Sergius Paulus"; "It is difficult to identify this Sergius Paulus with any extrabiblical figure."
12. Suet. *Aug.* 94–98.
13. See Nock, "Paul and the Magus," 308–30; cf. Suet. *Tib.* 14, 62.
14. Holden, *History of Horoscopic Astrology*, 29.
15. Pervo, *Acts*, 325.
16. Keener, *NT*, 358.
17. Philo, *Spec. Laws* 3.100.
18. Pliny, *Nat.* 30.2.11.
19. Josephus, *Ant.* 8.42–49.
20. Josephus, *Ant.* 20.142.
21. Longenecker, "Acts," 914. See Josephus, *Ant.* 20.142.
22. Cassius Dio, *Hist.* 71.8.4.

Prophets, like magicians, also gained political influence. Lucian noted that Abonoteichus, though inauthentic, was esteemed by many, including Rutilianus.[23] Josephus advanced his career by presenting himself as an oracle, claiming that prophets were uniquely qualified to write history.[24] While Sergius Paulus might have valued a "Jewish perspective" in his advisory,[25] Bar-Jesus is unlikely to have been viewed as a representative of the Jewish community in Cyprus.

Saul and Barnabas garner considerable attention as news circulated through the gossip network as they unsettled the dark forces. While Luke does not directly indicate trouble or suspicion, a wise proconsul would have been prudent to have investigated any movement gaining traction. Remarkably, this official summons them, "requesting to hear the word of God" (Acts 13:7). At this point, Luke refers to Bar-Jesus as "Elymas the magician" (Acts 13:8), more likely a pseudonym with uncertain etymology rather than a proper translation.[26] Elymas opposes Saul and Barnabas, asserting his influence over the proconsul, whom he intends to "deter away from faith" (Acts 13:8). The imperfect verb tense implies that until Elymas was dealt with, the gospel's transmission to Sergius Paulus would face ongoing interruption by the dark powers.

Paul,[27] "filled" with the Holy Spirit (Acts 13:9),[28] declares Elymas to be "full" (πλήρης, Acts 13:10)[29] of fraudulence, using the terms δόλος and ῥᾳδιουργία.[30] Paul also identifies Bar-Jesus (son of Jesus) as a "son of the devil" (υἱός διάβολος, Acts 13:10), linking him directly to the dark powers. In Luke's Gospel, the devil—largely synonymous with Satan in Second

---

23. Lucian, *Alex.* 30. Other examples include Tiberius (Suet. *Tib.* 14.4; [cf. Juv. *Sat.* 10.93–94]); Nero (Suet. *Nero* 36.1); Otho (Suet. *Otho* 4.1; 6.1); Vespasian (Suet. *Vesp.* 25); Domitian (Suet. *Dom.* 15.3). Even Marcus Aurelius enjoyed the services of Arnuphis, an Egyptian magician; see Cassius Dio, *Hist.* 71.8.4.

24. Pervo, *Acts*, 325. Josephus, *J.W.* 3.399–408.

25. Keener, *NT*, 358.

26. Wright, *Acts for Everyone*, 43.

27. Saul is now referred to as Paul for the remainder of Acts; therefore, this study likewise adjusts the name of this character from this point on. While the author does not explicitly state the purpose for the transition, most likely he fittingly incorporates the character's name of Roman citizenship as the narrative directs to the imperial capital.

28. Used by Luke in five other instances (Luke 1:41, 67; Acts 2:4; 4:8, 31), each accompanied by speech.

29. Πλήρης of fraudulence is antithetical of being πλήρης of Spirit (Luke 4:1; Acts 6:4, 5, 8; 7:44; 11:24).

30. See MGS, s.v. "δόλος" and "ῥᾳδιουργία."

Temple Judaism—represents the embodiment of evil.³¹ This evil included political and military oppression, a view shaped by Israel's history of imperial subjugation from Babylon to Rome.³²

The link between the devil and Elymas's effort to disrupt Paul's proclamation finds its parallel in other parts of the Lukan corpus. For example, the devil tests Jesus in the wilderness by offering him power over earthly kingdoms (Luke 4:1–13). Later, the devil appears in the parable of the sower, hindering the growth of the "word" (Luke 8:12). Peter's address to Cornelius, the first Roman representative in Acts, emphasizes Jesus's ministry as liberation from the devil's power (Acts 10:38). This context of liberation frames Elymas's opposition as part of a broader conflict with dark forces.

Paul further condemns Elymas as an "enemy of all righteousness" (διάβολος πᾶς δικαιοσύνη, Acts 13:10), aligning with additional historical conceptions of the devil as the adversary. Jesus similarly identifies dark forces when granting authority to his disciples and reflecting on Satan's fall like lightning (Luke 10:18). Psalm 110:1 (LXX), a key christological reference in Luke-Acts (Luke 20:42–43), as proclaimed by Peter (Acts 2:35) declares, "The Lord said to my lord, 'Sit at my right hand, until I make your enemies (ἐχθρούς) a footstool for your feet.'" These enemies, partially subdued at Jesus's ascension, included those who opposed him in Galilee and Jerusalem as well as adversaries from Jerusalem to "the ends of the earth" (Acts 1:8). Elymas represents one such opponent within this broader conflict.

Paul's description of Elymas as an enemy (ἐχθρός) of righteousness (δικαιοσύνη) parallels Zechariah's Benedictus, in which both terms are used with politically charged significance:³³

> [W]e should be saved from our enemies [ἐχθρούς], and from the hand of all who hate us. He has done this to show mercy to our ancestors, and to remember his holy covenant—the oath that he swore to our ancestor Abraham. This oath grants that we, being rescued from the hand of our enemies [ἐχθρούς], may serve him without fear, in holiness and righteousness [δικαιοσύνη] before him for as long as we live. (Luke 1:71–75 NET)

---

31. Bass, "Devil," *LBD*.

32. Watson, "Devil," 2:183–84.

33. Horsley, *Liberation of Christmas*, 116–17, refers to these verses as having political connotations in a Roman and paganistic world who resists the movements of God and likens it to a new exodus.

This anthem, even with anti-imperial undertones, presents δικαιοσύνη as a state of social salvation and stability, culminating in the declaration that God will "give light to those who sit in darkness" (Luke 1:79 NET). Luke later employs δικαιοσύνη in Peter's statement: "I now truly understand that God does not show favoritism in dealing with people, but in every nation the person who fears him and does what is right [δικαιοσύνην] is welcomed before him" (Acts 10:34–35 NET).

Moreover, Paul's Areopagus speech declares God's command for repentance in preparation for judgment based on δικαιοσύνη (Acts 17:30–31). For Zechariah, δικαιοσύνη is closely linked to liberation from ἐχθροί, including all forms of darkness. In Acts, this connection is highlighted when idolaters—or even a Roman representative (an enemy)—are welcomed into the household of God based on δικαιοσύνη (Acts 10:35). This same standard will be used to judge the pagan world, including Rome (Acts 17:31). In describing Elymas, Luke's rare pairing of ἐχθροί and δικαιοσύνη highlights the reign of God in Christ, the ongoing conflict with evil, and the expectation that earthly kingdoms, forces of darkness, and idolatry will be judged and subdued. This is a fitting designation as the gospel begins to cross the Mediterranean toward Rome. Sergius Paulus becomes the first noted convert in this season of expansion—though not without resistance from evil forces, driven in part by greed. Remarkably, δικαιοσύνη reappears when the Roman procurator Felix seeks a bribe from Paul (Acts 24:26). Paul's discourse on self-control, judgment, and δικαιοσύνη (Acts 24:25) intimidates the imperial agent, offering a hopeful preview of Paul's ultimate engagement with Rome.

Paul's referral to Elymas as the "son of the devil" as a personification of darkness is an example of the "art of insult," a common way of engaging in honor duels.[34] It is also a vivid portrayal of Elymas as the offspring of evil. This apt descriptor is evidenced in his pseudo-prophetic sorcery and his attempt to blockade the gospel. Elymas's evil nature is further characterized by his greed-motivated resistance. As the dark powers in Samaria are expelled, Simon the magician's role was disrupted, leaving him vulnerable to expendability, losing both his social honor and profit capabilities.

With the gospel gaining momentum in Cyprus, the evil forces are similarly agitated, and Elymas is positioned to become either ineffective because of the Holy Spirit's emergence or exiled if Sergius Paulus becomes a disciple. For Elymas, the best scenario would be the proconsul's rejection

---

34. Pilch, "Art of Insult," 158.

of the gospel. Otherwise, as a false prophet magician, even if he retained his powers, Elymas would presumably have to relocate, be deprived of an influential role, and subject himself to reintegration at a new destination. These factors necessitate a stronger effort than in Samaria of resistance by the evil powers.

Elymas is prioritized not as an individual but as a representative of evil[35]—a narrative type of the powers of the status quo maneuvering to maintain their societal control and influence over the proconsul. Just as the cosmic duel rages and evil loses ground with Cornelius's gospel reception, Sergius Paulus serves as a test case for reform. His story resembles Zacchaeus's (Luke 19:1–10), a figure torn between Roman interests and Christian discipleship. The reader anticipates a degree of ethical repositioning in his transformation. Therefore, Elymas's role is critical to the dark powers, comparable to the importance of Judas and others, as instruments to disrupt ecclesial momentum.

Elymas seeks to "prevent" (Acts 13:8) Sergius Paulus from coming to faith. Meanwhile, Paul accuses him of "making crooked the paths of the Lord" (Acts 13:8 NET), a direct contrast to John the Baptist's role in preparing the way (ὁδός) in Luke 3:4-6. This reference alludes to Second Isaiah (Isa 40:3–4), which offers hope for exiles and portrays God subduing the nations (Isa 40:2, 10). When John prepared the way for Jesus, repentance and cleansing involved ethical reforms in property and finances (Luke 3:10–14).

The ὁδός symbolizes Sergius Paulus's path to salvation and serves as a metaphorical gateway for Roman leadership. Luke later uses "The Way" as a term for the Christian movement as it advances toward Rome (Acts 19:19, 23; 22:4; 24:14, 22; 25:3; 26:13). This image is fitting, given Rome's famed transit network, which generated the well-known phrase "All roads lead to Rome." John the Baptist's Isaianic language (Isa 40:3–4) signals preparation for an emperor's arrival.[36] Its usage in this passage suggests that Christ's procession is imminent, alerting the dark powers that the gospel's advance across the Mediterranean marks the start of a spiritual offensive against imperial forces.

Paul declares that the "hand of the Lord" (Acts 13:11) has come upon Elymas, resulting in immediate (παραχρῆμα, Acts 13:11) blindness and a mist of darkness (σκότος, Acts 13:11). Luke's use of παραχρῆμα conveys a

---

35. Garrett, *Demise of the Devil*, 85.
36. Pilch, *Cultural World of Jesus*, 164.

context of judgment for both Sapphira and Herod Agrippa I (Acts 5:10, 12:23). Meanwhile σκότος contrasts with God's light (Luke 1:79, 11:35) and references "the hour for the power of darkness" during Jesus's arrest (Luke 22:53). It also alludes to the darkening at his death (Luke 23:44) and Paul's mission to turn people from darkness and Satan's power (Acts 26:18). Ironically, the "hand of the Lord" (χείρ κύριος) that opposes Elymas leaves him needing to be led by the hand (Acts 13:11).

This imagery recalls the Egyptian plagues (Exod 7:4–5, 17; 9:3; 13:3; 15:6), particularly those of darkness, symbolizing God's victory over Pharaoh and his magicians.[37] It also evokes Elijah's confrontation with Baal's priests on Mount Carmel, where the prophet challenges the dark forces of idolatry and the corrupt rule of Ahab and Jezebel (1 Kgs 18:15–45). Additionally, Deut 28:28–29 links blindness to judgment on idolatry. As with Judas, Ananias, Sapphira, Simon, and Agrippa I, Elymas is a villain serving the opposition who faces divine resistance and judgment.

Sergius Paulus, initially a presumed idolater and participant in the Roman imperial cult, then believes (πιστεύω, Acts 13:12). In Acts, Simon in Samaria is the first individual noted to ἐπίστευσεν (Acts 8:13), though the evidence demonstrates his inauthentic and greedy motivations. In contrast, the proconsul πιστεύω without any undermining testimony regarding his reception. Moreover, Sergius Paulus is "astonished" (ἐκπλήσσω, Acts 13:12), a term frequently used in positive responses to Jesus (Luke 2:48, 4:32, 9:43). Unlike Simon the magician, the proconsul is not merely captivated by the sign but by the teaching (διδαχή, Acts 13:12), echoing Capernaum's favorable reception (Luke 4:32).

These indications, along with Luke's interest in Roman governmental leaders, particularly following Cornelius, support a perception that for Luke, Sergius Paulus is a concrete and perhaps ideal example of Paul and Barnabas's ministry. This provides hope that in the imperial capital, darkness will be defeated (as with Elymas), and leaders will be receptive to the gospel (as with Sergius Paulus).[38]

---

37. Pinter, *Acts*, 303.

38. Keener notes comparison to 2 Kgs 6:18 when Syria attacked Israel, but Elisha interceded, and God blinds their army yet exhorts the king to show kindness to the Syrians by offering hospitality. Keener, *NT*, 358.

Synthesis

Elymas's role as a magician and false prophet categorizes him as an "agent of darkness,"[39] clearly evident in his resistance to Paul and Barnabas's ministry. Paul's attestation "son of the devil" conveys not only Elymas's alignment with imperial patronage but also his familial relationship to evil. Furthermore, like Judas, Ananias, Sapphira, Simon Magus, and Agrippa I, Elymas seeks power to enhance his honor and control sociopolitical and economic factors. He secures financial means and public influence by aligning with Sergius Paulus. Accordingly, "Luke has no love for those who have illicit, and probably profitable, dealings with the supernatural."[40]

Elymas has sought the status of the authentic prophets from his Jewish tradition, a position far superior to the ethics he promotes. Therefore, his envious nature was shameful.[41] Moreover, he attempts to preserve his social relationship with the proconsul, whereby the limited-good conceptuality makes him jealously afraid of expendability, another significant casualty of his social world.[42] If expelled from his duties, he would be unlikely to find a comparable political and economic standing elsewhere.

Again, physical orifices coincided with purity, and Bar-Jesus's blinded eyes represent an insulting form of punishment, likely correlating to the "evil eye," a prominent phenomenon among Hellenistic societies of this period.[43] Such dispositions were believed to transmit harmful qualities of greed,[44] a characteristic likely to produce greater fear from magicians.

As the gospel moves into the broader Mediterranean context, the dark powers are compelled to intensify their resistance. However, in Cyprus, the dark agent who "had given himself over to the evil powers"[45] is quickly subdued. Meanwhile, the other agent of power, Sergius Paulus, is receptive—a positive occurrence involving a key leader outside the Palestinian context, indicating momentum among the imperial demographic. Pervo rightly observes the "victory over Satan" in this passage but reduces the proconsul's

---

39. Parsons, *Acts*, 189.
40. Barrett, *Critical Exegetical Commentary—Acts*, 617.
41. Seeman and Malina, "Envy," 51–53.
42. Malina, *Windows on the World*, 122, 130–31.
43. Elliott, *Greece and Rome*, 271.
44. Plut. *Quaest. conv.* 680F–681E.
45. Osborne, *Luke Verse by Verse*, 238.

function to being apologetic in nature.[46] Thomas Martin, meanwhile, views Sergius Paulus as adding to the "legitimacy" of an "aristocratic Roman convert"[47] to encourage the church regarding its expanded demographics. Both positions understate the narrative function, nor do these theories fully address Elymas's motivations to resist the discipling of "an agent of a power (Rome) that can be repressive."[48]

Even one influential new disciple—though the text does not assume Sergius Paulus was alone—drawn to the "teaching" (which likely included Lukan socioeconomic ethics) could face tension with imperial policy. As the proconsul embraced the great reversal, he would likely find himself at intellectual or practical odds with Rome. Simply put, the ethics of the empire contrasted with those of the church. Yet, a reader such as Theophilus might wonder whether Sergius Paulus (or even Cornelius) would betray Christian ethics and face a fate comparable to that of Judas, Ananias, and Sapphira. In such a way, the Holy Spirit now seemingly has command over an imperial agent.

In all likelihood, "most first-century pagans, probably including the most excellent Theophilus, would undoubtedly have identified two magicians in this pericope, Bar-Jesus and Paul."[49] However, the challenge lies in the fact that there was "no period in the history of the empire in which the magician was not considered an enemy of society," often being punished by death.[50] Moreover, Pliny notes that all of Rome feared the possible effects of spells,[51] though exceptions were made in cases where the practitioner was under elite Roman patronage, as Elymas was. Using MacMullen's imaginative reading, Paul's curse upon Elymas is evidence of a power superior to that of the magician under Roman patronage. The church emerges as a broker of an extreme force that targets Roman agents offensively. This exchange of loyalties is an effective countermeasure to the previous dark collusion of Judas, Ananias, and Sapphira.

Cicero states that it was "punishable" for a Roman citizen (like Sergius Paulus) to convert to Judaism.[52] This, along with other factors, challenges

---

46. Pervo, *Acts*, 327.
47. Martin, "Paulus, Sergius (Person)," 5:205–6.
48. Allen, *Acts of the Apostles*, 115.
49. Walz, "Cursing Paul: Magical Contests," 168.
50. MacMullen, *Enemies of Roman Order*, 125–26.
51. Pliny, *Nat.* 28.4.228.
52. Cic. *Leg.* 2.8.19. See also Rapske, *Paul in Roman Custody*, 118.

the idea that Theophilus, a Roman elitist, would have seen this document as an apologetic. Such stark implications explain the use of the imperfect verb tense to describe Elymas's resistance. The dark forces properly assess the urgency of Paul's ministry and are determined to heavily oppose it or otherwise surrender more ground to the advancing kingdom of God.

From Cyprus, Paul and Barnabas travel to Pisidian Antioch, where their message proves highly effective among gentiles. However, some Jews, motivated by greed, resist their ministry, akin to the stance of Elymas (Acts 13:13–52). In Iconium, Jews again interfere, inciting leaders and plotting to stone them (Acts 14:1–7). As in other locations, dark powers work through certain Jews to influence public leaders, creating a consistent narrative thread in Acts.

The conflict continues in Asia Minor when Paul and Barnabas arrive in Lystra (14:6–18), where they are recognized as Zeus and Hermes. The priest of Zeus's temple attempts to offer sacrifices to them, highlighting how the Jesus movement ironically finds acceptance at the pagan temple, in contrast to rejection by the Jerusalem temple elite. Paul and Barnabas resist the temptation of power, echoing Jesus's triumph over similar tests (Luke 4:1–13). Despite their success among gentiles, idolatry and paganism remain tools of evil forces. Jews from Iconium arrive in Lystra to disrupt the apostolic momentum, even as their mission continues to thrive among gentiles in Syria.

Chapter 7: The Spirit of Python and the Philippian Encounter: Economic Exploitation and Spiritual Resistance (Acts 16:11–40)

The slave-girl's unusual exorcism in the "name of Jesus Christ" demonstrates the opposition of two powers. The text connects demons and unjust economic profit as at work together in the commercialization and exploitation of the slave-girl by her kurioi-masters.[1]

—Rubén Muñoz-Larrondo

Introduction

THE SUCCESS OF PAUL and Barnabas's ministry among gentiles prompts the Jerusalem Council to determine the terms of ethnic incorporation into the church (Acts 15:1–35). However, as one division is resolved, another sensitive matter emerges when Paul and Barnabas dispute over the handling of John Mark (Acts 15:36–42). The result is Barnabas's commissioning with John Mark, while Paul is accompanied by Silas, enabling each party to cover more ground and presumably further the victory over darkness. The disciple community in Derbe and Lystra continues to grow (Acts 16:5), yet Paul is prevented by the Holy Spirit and Jesus from continuing in Asia.

Paul receives a vision of a Macedonian man who solicits him to carry the gospel across new boundaries. The "we" narratives begin adjacent to

---

1. Muñoz-Larrondo, *Postcolonial Reading of Acts*, 287.

Paul's travel to Troas, adding intrigue as the writer introduces first-person accounts at this critical point.[2] From Troas, the "we" sail to Samothrace in the north Aegean, known for its "Great Gods," popularized in Hellenistic times.[3] An aware reader would recognize the intensity of the occasion as Paul penetrates more deeply into the circles of darkness. They arrive in Neapolis on the northern coast of the Aegean Sea, a significant port for Philippi, which lies ten miles inland.

Textual Analysis

Paul's arrival in Philippi, founded by Mark Antony in 42 BCE to locate Roman military veterans (later augmented by Octavian around 31 BCE), marks an important transition. The community operates under self-rule with rights comparable to an Italian city, fostering a sense of "superiority" in comparison to its regional counterparts.[4] Luke identifies Philippi as a leading city and a Roman colony, provoking Witherington to ask, "Why did the author go out of his way to introduce Philippi thus, when he never formally describes the technical status of any other city?"[5] Luke's audience was likely aware of these qualities, yet his reminder serves to activate that memory, functioning as a literary signpost as Paul transitions closer to Rome. This crossing of East/West boundaries is significant, as it was near Philippi where Octavian (Augustus) and Mark Antony defeated Brutus and Cassius, the assassins of Julius Caesar.

Philippi was the "wealthiest and most honored city" of the district.[6] Its mineral deposits generated great revenue, with gold being a primary product.[7] Paul is in Philippi for multiple days and meets Lydia, a dealer in the "ancient luxury" of purple, from Thyatira, a location known for purple manufacturing.[8] As with many industries, there were distinctions between the labor class producing the purple and those to whom it was distributed. Plutarch remarked that the upper classes adored the purple but despised

---

2. Campbell, *"We" Passages*, 87–90.
3. Barrett, *Critical Exegetical Commentary—Acts*, 777–78.
4. Witherington, *Acts of the Apostles*, 490.
5. Witherington, *Acts of the Apostles*, 490.
6. Keener, *NT*, 369.
7. Spencer, "Philippi," 1048. Cf. Strabo, *Geogr.* 8.34; Pliny, *Nat.* 37.15.57.
8. Fitzmyer, *Acts of the Apostles*, 585. See also Josephus, *J.W.* 6.8.3; CIG 3496–98 (I Nicator in 281 BCE).

the laborers involved.⁹ Those handling purple dye were generally alienated; however, Lydia appears far from a slave or laborer handling the material. Instead, she is a merchant or seller (πορφυρόπωλις, Acts 16:14)¹⁰ who, at the least, brokered transactions of the product in its finished form. Lydia likely resided "somewhere between the two extremes" of elitism and subsistent living,¹¹ with strong financial means compared with the vast majority in the Mediterranean context.¹² This positioning makes her a useful Lukan character, as a person with resources to extend generosity.¹³

Lydia not only benefited from a strong Philippian economy, supported by the colony's large wealthy migrant community,¹⁴ but she also respected God. Upon meeting Paul (and his companions), her "heart" (καρδία, Acts 16:14) is opened (διανοίγω, Acts 16:14). This state of her heart is consistent with the affirmations of the early church; she is described as single-hearted, standing in contrast to the corrupt hearts of Ananias, Sapphira, and Simon Magus.¹⁵ Lydia is receptive, and her household is baptized, a designation likely indicating that she was a widow,¹⁶ a status that, under Roman law, enabled women under certain circumstances to engage in commerce.¹⁷

Lydia's opened heart is further illustrated by her extended hospitality to Paul and his fellow travelers, presenting herself as an excellent disciple in new territory—being female, a merchant, and hospitable. Her response serves as an optimistic witness as the movement heads westward, eventually toward Rome. Her sacrificial generosity distinguishes her from the villains of this study. Unlike Simon and Elymas, she is no "charlatan or opportunist," while also supplying the venue for the "first house church in Europe."¹⁸

---

9. Plut. *Per.* 1.3–4.

10. *CGL*, "πορφυρό-πωλις," 2:1173. See also MGS, s.v. "πορφυρόπωλις."

11. Thompson, *Acts: Wesleyan Tradition*, 279.

12. Keener, *Acts: Exegetical Commentary*, 3:2398.

13. Based on historical potentials and Lukan artistic initiative, the reader is to suspect that Lydia fits on the "PS4" of Steven Friesen's Poverty Scale, beneath PS 1–3 of governing elites, but better off than many other merchants given that she deals purple in such a vicinity. See Friesen, "Poverty in Pauline Studies," 367–71.

14. Burnett, *Paul and Imperial Honors*, 112, 163.

15. It was illegal to convert to Judaism, therefore this is the initial subversive act in this Roman microcosm. Cic. *Leg.* 2.8.19 and Rapske, *Paul in Roman Custody*, 118.

16. Keener, *NT*, 370.

17. Bruce, *Book of the Acts*, 311.

18. Osborne, *Acts Verse by Verse*, 297–98.

In Philippi, Paul encounters a female slave empowered by a Python (πύθωνα, 16:16)[19] spirit that generated significant (πολύς, 16:16) profit (ἐργασία, 16:16) for her owners through oracles. Plutarch, a Delphian priest, records a spirit associated with this name functioning as a ventriloquist, externally controlling the speaker.[20] Often depicted as a serpent or dragon, this spirit guarded Apollo's temple and acted as his oracle on Mount Parnassus. Pausanias identifies this oracle as the cornerstone of Dionysus cults, which flourished in various regions, including Athens, Corinth, and Sparta.[21] The term evolved to signify a "spirit of divination," "prophecy," or general "ventriloquism."[22]

One tradition maintained that these female oracles were impregnated by a deity. While not universally accepted, this rumor drew sharp criticism from Plutarch, who at least recognized the popularity of the claims in his response. Additionally, these oracles frequently directed messages—both positive and negative—toward political figures.[23] Clearly, Jewish tradition condemned this type of activity, associating it with darkness (Lev 19:31; Deut 18:10–11; 1 Sam 28:8; Isa 8:19; Ezek 12:24).

For a fee, this slave would discuss the future or provide wisdom and counsel to the community and its leaders,[24] sometimes assisting in securing personal or collective safety or success in engaging a counterpart.[25] The Delphic oracles were highly sexualized,[26] and the lexical usage of παιδίσκη suggests a possible sexual function.[27] Regardless, slaves "were sexual objects" for their owners' exploitation, even if they were not explicitly prostituted.[28] Regardless, the dark spirit inhabiting this slave girl generates substantial economic production.[29] Eckhard Schnabel notes that she hosts a "demon,"

---

19. The syntax can read a pythonic (pythonian) spirit, or spirit named Python.

20. Plut. *Def. Orac.* 9 (*Mor.* 414E).

21. Pausanias notes this oracle as the foundation of Dionysus cults in various locations, including Athens (*Descr.* 1.2.5), Corinth (*Descr.* 2.27), Sicyon (*Descr.* 2.7.6), Sparta, and Patrae (*Descr.* 7.19.6–10).

22. Strabo, *Geogr.* 9.3.12; Plut. *Def. Orac.* 8 (*Mor.* 414E).

23. Pervo, *Acts*, 405–6.

24. Bruce, *Book of the Acts*, 312.

25. Schnabel, *Acts*, 1007–8.

26. Beard, *Confronting the Classics*, 31.

27. Barrett, *Critical Exegetical Commentary—Acts*, 784–85.

28. Cobb, *Slavery, Gender, Truth, Power*, 30.

29. Lucian, *Alex.* 9–13.

with Keener clarifying it as "a powerful demon," a signpost that the dark powers are at work.[30]

This girl follows Paul and his group, declaring them representatives of "the Most High God" and proclaiming a way (ὁδός, Acts 16:17) of salvation (σωτηρία, Acts 16:17). In Luke's Gospel, demons and unclean spirits often pronounce truth regarding Jesus; however, the phrase "Most High God" is unclear, possibly involving elements of mockery or paganistic undertones. Zeus was considered by many to be the supreme god of the Greek pantheon,[31] yet the oracle of Delphi was "notoriously ambiguous" in speech.[32] Ironically, Caesar Augustus, the founder of this colony, was identified as Zeus and Jupiter (his Roman counterpart) by his subjects.[33] A Hellenistic audience might find the spirit's claims uncertain. However, in Jewish tradition, the allusion to Balaam (Num 22–25)—a greedy hireling paid to curse Israel but who instead blesses—is the strongest indicator of this oracle's impact. Regardless of her intentions, she ultimately draws positive attention to Paul and Silas for multiple days. This topic will be explored further later in this study.

Paul is disturbed (διαπονέομαι, Acts 16:18), a word sometimes translated as "annoyed" (NET). In the New Testament, it appears elsewhere only in Acts 4:2, where temple leaders are unsettled by apostolic preaching. Paul turns and, rather than addressing the girl—the victim of exploitation—he directs his voice to the dark forces empowering her, expelling them in the name of Jesus Christ. This demonstrates superior power, as the spirit quickly departs from her. Bock asks, "Why was Paul bothered at the girl's proclamation?" and answers by reducing the response to Paul growing tired of mockery.[34] However, Paul's actions are not divorced from the same liberative substance as Jesus's concern for a woman "bound to Satan" whom he had delivered (Luke 13:16). Moreover, operating as a quasi-Balaam, with a voice directing pagans to a "way" of the "Most High God" has enabled her to function in a pseudo-evangelistic role, possibly leaving Paul conflicted for days (Acts 16:16).

---

30. Keener, *NT*, 371. See also Schnabel, *Acts*, 1197.
31. Pind. *Nem.* 1.60; 11.2.
32. Hdt. *Hist.* 1.53; Aeschylus, *Prom.* 661–62; Plut. *Garr.* 17; Paus. *Descr.* 8.11.10–12.
33. Decree of Halicarnassus, an inscription in modern Turkey, and Ovid, *Trist.* 5.2.
34. Bock, "Acts," 1183.

As a slave, the girl was "a commodity, only a body in use, and a site of penetration."[35] However, Epictetus remarks that true freedom is to be beyond the control and power of another.[36] Accordingly, while Paul is unable to provide judicial liberation from her slavery, he still offers spiritual freedom from the entity that has invaded her body. This scene, within the entire narrative, partly serves as an indictment of Roman exploitation, including slavery.

However, in a limited-good world, a benefit to one (the slave girl) implies a zero-sum effect upon another—in this case, her owners. These individuals are business oriented, receiving "great profit," yet, in contrast to Lydia and more consistent with the other villains in this study, they are examples of anti-disciples. In Luke-Acts, "ownership and discipleship are never easily aligned."[37] Moreover, as Peter declared Simon's currency should face destruction (Acts 8:20), so Paul destroys the revenue in Philippi. Based on Lucian's *Alexander the False Prophet*, a similarly situated oracle could charge "one drachma and two obols" per inquiry. This could amount to seventy to eighty thousand drachmas annually,[38] a remarkable sum for a single individual, enabling her owners to reside among the elite.

When the spirit of divination is expelled, so too was the profit (ἐξέρχομαι, Acts 16:19). Jealousy—protecting one's assets in this case—was considered a virtue in the ancient world. Meanwhile, due in part to the limited-good mindset, upward mobility was unusual and often suspect, as reflected in the case of Caius Furius Chresimus, a freed slave.[39] Others became envious of his success in producing agrarian goods at a greater per capita rate than his neighbors and accused him of sorcery. This example also highlights the potential perception of Paul's superior magic in Philippi, as a person capable of thwarting the profiteering of a well-to-do operation.

Moreover, among Roman values, the property rights of citizens were paramount,[40] leading to immediate action when those rights were perceived to be threatened. Josephus records the events leading to Tiberius's expulsion of Jews from Rome, when a group of Jewish men deceives a wealthy woman into sending purple and gold to the Jerusalem temple, then steals

---

35. Jennings, *Acts*, 159.
36. Epictetus, *Disc.* 4.1–15.
37. Jennings, *Acts*, 162.
38. Green, "Finding Will of God," 213.
39. Pliny, *Nat.* 18.8.41.
40. Bruce, *Book of the Acts*, 314.

her property.⁴¹ Curiously, in Philippi—a region known for gold mining—a presumably higher-status woman in the purple trade, Lydia, provides a housing base for Paul and his companions. These same companions disrupt a segment of commercial exchange, eliminating a resource that was apparently in high demand and extremely profitable, enabled by a strong foothold of the dark powers in Philippi.

In Philippi, "diversity was tolerated by Roman political leadership."⁴² However, disrupting the economic flow was a substantially intolerable matter, generating an enraged mob.⁴³ Paul and Silas are apprehended and taken before the magistrates (στρατηγός, Acts 16:20), a term often designating military commanders and a preferred "dignified title" for local Philippian rulers.⁴⁴ The accusation is ἐκταράσσω (Acts 16:20), which here implies more than corporate "confusion" but rather societal "unrest"⁴⁵ within a municipality. This serious charge essentially equates to undermining the Pax Romana (Roman order). The crowd's "self-assertion" as Roman is paramount as this "self-identification" underscores their view of being "guardians" of the imperial way.⁴⁶ Such a designation was consistent with colonial thinking, as the outpost served as a hub to proselytize or evangelize surrounding regions.

The claim of his opponents is that Paul promulgates a new "ethos" (ἔθος, Acts 16:21) that was οὐ ἡμεῖς παραδέχομαι οὐδέ ποιέω εἰμί Ῥωμαῖος, paraphrased as "alien to the Roman way of life" (Acts 16:21). There is an intrinsic "political" and "unpatriotic" nature to this accusation, especially in a key Roman location of power.⁴⁷ Edwards suggests that the charges "ignored the economic" culpability of Paul's actions.⁴⁸ However, Luke intends for readers to assess the financial obstruction and the political charge levied against Paul as one and the same, with Roman patriotism and economic policy being intertwined in a single "ethos." Moreover, offenses such as "treason, fomenting war or rebellion, participation in civil disturbance, the practice of philosophy, astrology or magical arts," as well as "theft,

---

41. Josephus, *Ant.* 18.82–83.
42. Reed and Wild, "Philippi," 795.
43. Pervo, *Acts*, 406.
44. Fitzmyer, *Acts of the Apostles*, 587–88.
45. CGL, "ἐκταράσσω," 1:458.
46. Muñoz-Larrondo, *Postcolonial Reading of Acts*, 293.
47. Streett, *Caesar and Sacrament*, 115.
48. Peterson, *Acts of the Apostles*, 462.

brigandage, piracy and sacrilege,"[49] were all punishable by imprisonment. Many were economically linked, and some could arguably apply to Paul.

Luke does not provide Paul's specific teachings at this locale. Up to this point, Paul has baptized Lydia's household who respond with generosity, consistent with John the Baptist's ethics of baptism (Luke 3:10–14). Then Paul exorcises a dark force from an enslaved girl. The people rise in the defense of greed, profit, and the social exploitation of slavery, essentially defending the dark powers and expressing discontent that the evil forces are being threatened. Paul's ethos is not his teaching (in this case) but his practiced liberation ethics, which they reject, being servants of the status quo.

The reader assumes that initially both Cornelius (whom Luke represents as being generous) and Sergius Paulus, both Roman representatives, also (at one time) have embraced the ethos of Roman patriotism. Yet in Philippi, a microcosm of Rome,[50] a spiritual battle ensues. Those who seek to preserve the imperial ethos find that it is incompatible with the kingdom of God.

The crowd is incited by anti-imperial accusations, and they συνεφίστημι (Acts 16:22), a word sometimes used for "revolt."[51] This disturbance is conducted under the oversight of the magistrates, who "had considerable power and wide discretion in its exercise," often with little accountability.[52] These leaders shame Paul and Silas by removing their clothing and permitting their beating with rods without any investigation or opportunity for Paul to speak. The leaders either have acquiesced to the mob mentality or are themselves complicit in the public outcry.

Moreover, in this community of Roman pride and elitism, they deny Paul his legal rights as a citizen of the empire, leaving him no opportunity to assert his social standing. This will ultimately become an embarrassment for a place so devoted to Roman law and order, as they have acted outside of imperial ordinances. Their disorderly conduct betrays the identity they so highly esteem.

Paul has interrupted the "great" (πολύς, Acts 16:16) profit, and he is served a "great" (πολύς, Acts 16:23) beating. Under prioritized security, he is incarcerated with Silas and placed in restraints, a method typically used for the most inferior social classes.[53] However, as Peter and the disciples had

49. Rapske, *Paul in Roman Custody*, 37, 44.
50. Aulus Gellius, *Noct. att.* 16.13, 9. Note how colonies maintain the appearances of the imperial capital.
51. MGS, s.v. "συνεφίστημι."
52. Rapske, *Paul in Roman Custody*, 67–68.
53. Rapske, *Paul in Roman Custody*, 125–27.

THE SPIRIT OF PYTHON AND THE PHILIPPIAN ENCOUNTER

embraced their worthiness to suffer in Jerusalem (Acts 5:40–41), Paul and Silas seem similarly content as they remain occupied in prayer and song.

The prison is shaken (σαλεύω, Acts 16:26) by a great earthquake, recalling Acts 4:31. There, Peter and the apostles reflect on the political powers aligned against them and affirm God superiority and his king's reign in Ps 2. They petition in prayer: "And now, Lord, pay attention to their threats, and grant to your servants to speak your message with great courage (παρρησία)."[54] The Spirit responds by shaking (σαλεύω) the building (Acts 4:23–31) preparing them for a greater political speech.

The earthquake in Philippi weakens the security mechanisms, appearing to free the inmates. In panic, the guard, fearing execution for allowing prisoners to escape, opts for suicide. Luke's design "mocks those who are in power," beginning with the prison attendant. Although enlisted to guard others, he finds himself in danger from his superiors and from his own hand, while his high-priority prisoners remain calm. This prompts the paradoxical question: "Who in the narrative is in need of salvation?"[55]

The guard's question about how to be "saved" (σῴζω, Acts 16:30) is ironically curious. The only other voice in Philippi to speak of God's salvation (σωτηρία, Acts 16:17) is the spirit of divination, a message which the oracle repeats for days. The reader is left to infer that the dark powers, while attempting to draw negative attention to Paul and likely threatening his safety in Philippi, has become, like Balaam, a mechanism for gospel proclamation. The jailer has likely heard word of this expression because it circulated from the oracle. Moreover, in a satire of mockery, in a Roman city whose founder, Caesar Augustus—a deified emperor—was widely acclaimed as the world's savior, this Roman representative (the jailer) inquires with Paul about salvation.

The text continues to depict allegiance to Christ through another household baptism (16:32–34), a "subversive act" that demonstrates gospel victory.[56] This individual conversion of someone of local rank, perhaps paralleling Cornelius, represents the institutions of Roman ethos; yet, like Lydia, this person displays the ethics of generosity accompanying baptism. The conversion itself is not only subversive, but also illegal,[57] as is the jailer's

---

54. Παρρησία or "Speaking truth to power."
55. Muñoz-Larrondo, *Postcolonial Reading of Acts*, 301.
56. Streett, *Caesar and Sacrament*, 116–17.
57. Cic. *Leg.* 2.8.19. See Rapske, *Paul in Roman Custody*, 118.

generous hospitality shown to the incarcerated Paul and Silas.[58] All of this further highlights the transfer of allegiance by this Roman agent.

The following day, the magistrates free Paul and Silas, desiring to send them away in εἰρήνη (Acts 16:26), a term indicating "political peace."[59] Apparently, overnight, the confusion has settled, and the leaders elect to rectify their unjust actions by releasing the duo while implementing a public order effectively expelling them from the city. Paul senses their vulnerability and relays that these rulers have permitted him to be treated unethically, given his Roman citizenship, thereby violating their own ethos.

Paul's accusatory language intensifies as he effectively, and ironically, places the magistrates on trial. He addresses the fact that the Philippian misdeeds have been covered up suspiciously, which amounts to an abuse of power. He strongly requests that the leaders make a public appearance. Overcome by fear (φοβέομαι, Acts 16:38), the magistrates shift their tone.[60] These legal figures have been made a mockery of, and they respond to Paul with caution, indicating the weakening of their establishment in the cosmic war against God. They begin to employ more conciliatory language,[61] begging (παρακαλέω, Acts 16:39) Paul to leave. He complies with their request on his terms, visiting Lydia before departing. As an honor challenge, the mob's actions are an attempt to dishonor Paul and Silas. However, their patient response serves as a riposte to the magistrates, shaming both the leaders and the community, while exposing the failures of their judicial process.[62]

The vantage point of MacMullen's imaginative reading of this passage dramatically and intensely enhances the narrative. The backdrop includes a vision redirecting Paul to Europe, and the first-person usage signals a unique literary signpost. Both of these elements serve as precursors to the concluding section of Acts in which Paul travels to Rome, when the "we" sections reappear.

Philippi "stood on the main road you would take if you were travelling between Rome and almost anywhere in Turkey or further east."[63] Luke records Paul's travels through multiple colonial settings, yet this is the only

---

58. Rapske, *Paul in Roman Custody*, 390–92.

59. Foerster, "Εἰρήνη, Εἰρηνεύω, Εἰρηνικός, Εἰρηνοποιός, Εἰρηνοποιέω," *TDNT* 2:410.

60. Muñoz-Larrondo, *Postcolonial Reading of Acts*, 297–98.

61. This word in Acts 16:39 is a word used by Luke to mean to "urge" or "beg"; see Luke 7:4; 8:31, 32, 41; 15:28; Acts 2:40; 9:38; 13:42; and 16:9, 15.

62. Pervo, *Acts*, 414.

63. Wright, *Acts for Everyone*, 105–6.

time a colony is explicitly designated in the entire New Testament. Pinter assesses that Luke "seems to be pointing out something distinctive about the status of Philippi."[64] Pervo clarifies that "the political status of Philippi will be important for both the outcome of this particular story and as a symbol of the place of the church in the Roman Empire."[65] The dark powers have been disrupted at Philippi, as observed in the expulsion of the oracle, a powerful entity deeply embedded in Greek cultural history.

Fitzmyer rightly notes the representative qualities of this location, indicating "the triumph of Christianity over pagan Greco-Roman practices."[66] However, this statement fails to consider additional warnings against imperialism. This location of Roman pride and ethos evinces a mob lynching mentality that denies Paul the opportunity to assert his citizenship with proper examination. Instead, this military-minded, Roman-identifying populace defies all discipline, law, and order—a surprising element not only for Roman citizens but also for a municipality with deep military roots.

Paul's criticism is expressed through the motif of mockery, identified as a form of resistance by postcolonial thinkers.[67] His rebuke essentially conveys that Roman justice and imperial arrogance should learn from the wisdom of the Holy Spirit. This passage describes the Spirit's ability to "overcome social, cultural, demonic, political, and legal difficulties."[68] However, much scholarship fails to acknowledge the implications and representative qualities of Philippi and, in turn, to apply that assessment to the conclusion of Acts in Rome.

Philippi serves as Rome in miniature, offering a preview and moving the narrative trajectory closer to the imperial capital itself. The reader expects coherence, noting that Jesus and the later disciple community have confronted political and religious leadership at Jerusalem (and Caesarea). Similarly, societal control has been challenged in Samaria (Simon). Likewise, in Cyprus, a person who was a symbol of Roman patronage (Elymas) has been disempowered while Sergius Paulus was successfully recruited. Now, in Philippi, the economic and judicial leaders have been placed on notice. This sequence constructs the expectation that when the movement

---

64. Pinter, *Acts*, 377.
65. Pervo, *Acts*, 402.
66. Fitzmyer, *Acts of the Apostles*, 583.
67. Bhabha, *Location of Culture*, 86–87.
68. Schnabel, *Acts*, 1183.

reaches "the ends of the earth," the imperial capital itself will face a comparable challenge.

The Philippian divine honors for Caesar carried significant representative implications.[69] Clint Burnett challenges the traditional view that the imperial cult was centralized and uniform across the Roman world, arguing instead that its practices were localized and community dependent.[70] Burnett observes that "Philippi mirrored Roman imperial divine honors almost perfectly, with one exception that proves the rule, demonstrating the Roman character of these honors in the colony."[71] In Philippi, imperial cultic priests held the highest public offices, such as magistrates, embedding these honors deeply into the city's public life.[72] Notably, Philippi's practice of divine honors may have even surpassed that of Rome itself by incorporating rituals on behalf of Tiberius into their regimen.[73] They also integrated wealthy migrants, intertwining the political, religious, social, and economic fabric of the city.[74]

With politics, military history, imperial worship, and economics each overlapping in ancient Rome (and in Philippi), it is hardly surprising that greed plays a significant role in this text. The slave owners have benefited from their control of people through exploitation, manipulation, and monopolization. They are empowered by a Roman infrastructure that not only enables but also encourages such practices by modelling these characteristics throughout the ancient world. This is evident in Philippi, where the slave owners wield enough influence—derived from money and power—to prompt a mob response. This goes against Roman law and order, as well as the expected discipline of this military-rooted town,[75] even leveraging the

69. Diodorus Siculus, *Library of History*, 16.95.1, notes that Philip II, namesake for Philippi, was revered as a god by some, including himself for his imperial success. Accordingly, this location has lengthy historical ties to cultic type viewpoints.

70. Burnett, *Paul and Imperial Honors*.

71. Burnett, *Paul and Imperial Honors*, 126.

72. According to Burnett, *Paul and Imperial Honors*, 163, one might entertain the possibility of these slave owners and magistrates in Philippi as such priests.

73. Burnett notes that "the Roman Senate did not divinize Tiberius. Despite this fact, Philippi deviated from its mother city and established a postmortem priesthood for him." Burnett, *Paul and Imperial Honors*, 130.

74. Burnett, *Paul and Imperial Honors*, 112, 163.

75. Rapske, *Paul in Roman Custody*, 119, considers it possible that there was a constituency of retired soldiers in late first-century Philippi but more likely their descendants, which still amply denotes the character of the city. Moreover, he notes that being heirs to soldiers they are property holders, which further substantiates the greedy character of

magistrates, at least temporarily. Like Simon in Samaria, who uses money (bribery) to ensure compliance, so too in Philippi, economic status has trumped government, law, and even the military, reinforcing the authentic Roman ethos. As "power, influence, and bribery frequently played a part in the process,"[76] the magistrates could tamper with judicial outcomes.

Paul's crime is disrupting the mechanics of economic processes, which is inherently "unpatriotic."[77] The Roman Empire is characterized by a stark socioeconomic divide. An elite class, comprising roughly 2 to 3 percent of the population, monopolized the empire's wealth.[78] This privileged class derived its power primarily from extensive land ownership, enabling control over production, distribution, and consumption.

This economic system, deeply embedded within the empire's hierarchical and oligarchical structures, facilitated the transfer of wealth from the broader populace to the elite through mechanisms such as taxation, rent, and interest.[79] While the Roman economy experienced periods of prosperity, this was typically reserved for citizens rather than provincial members.[80] Ancient empires were fundamentally about power, encompassing "a whole network of interrelated powers,"[81] and Rome's economic structure was a manifestation of this principle. Most of the populace engaged in subsistence agriculture and manual labor, sustaining the opulent lifestyles of the few. This lustful and insatiable economic superpower fueled imperial conquest.

Tacitus notes the words of Calgacus, a Caledonian leader in 85 CE, who inspired his troops against Roman invasion:

> Robbers of the world, having by their universal plunder exhausted the land, they rifle the deep. If the enemy be rich, they are rapacious; if he be poor, they lust for dominion; neither the east nor the west has been able to satisfy them. Alone among men they covet with equal eagerness poverty and riches. To robbery, slaughter, plunder, they give the lying name of empire; they make a solitude and call it peace.[82]

---

the city, as they are in a rush to protect the rights to commerce.

76. Rapske, *Paul in Roman Custody*, 37.
77. Streett, *Caesar and Sacrament*, 115.
78. Carter, *Roman Empire and NT*, 101.
79. Carter, *Roman Empire and NT*, 101.
80. Blanton and Pickett, *Paul and Economics*, 19.
81. Horsley, *Jesus and the Powers*, 17.
82. Tac. *Agr.* 29–32.

It was not only outsiders but Roman insiders from the first century who attest to this type of economic foundation. Petronius vividly describes the flourishing status of Romans at the expense of conquered lands,[83] while Juvenal acknowledges how the empire exploited foreign regions.[84] Cicero viewed leisure as a distinguishing characteristic of the elite, while the majority were destined for ongoing subsistent living.[85] Suetonius noted that the emperor believed mechanical advancements should not be distributed to the common class to make work easier, as they would lose their sense of economic purpose and foundation.[86]

On a tablet in Pompeii, a slave owner was forced to offer slaves as loan collateral, highlighting the ravenous metabolism of greedy exploitation intrinsic in the Roman financial system, which reduced slaves to commodities.[87] Moreover, at Pompeii's market, a section was devoted to divine honors,[88] intertwining the politics of dark idolatry with the greedy commercialization of the empire—a system of "interrelated powers" that maintained Roman dominance.[89]

When such powers are so correlated, systemic reform becomes necessary. The inseparable components of greed, the dark powers, idolatry, imperial worship, and socioeconomic policy were all destined for confrontation, as each was embedded within the Roman ethos. This is why Luke's writings recognize that the narrative must end in the imperial capital—a plausible deduction using MacMullen's criteria for reading.

If the empire favored the elite, then Christianity appealed to the marginalized. By the second century, Celsus observes it to be a religion of women and slaves (socioeconomic victims).[90] Pliny remarks that the church opposed fraudulent (greedy) activity, while Trajan responds that they must worship the Roman gods (including the imperial cult).[91] Within the same century, Athenagoras noted that disciples have been accused of

---

83. Petron. *Sat.* 119:1–7.
84. Juv. *Sat.* 6.92–99.
85. Cic. *Off.* 1.69.
86. Suet. *Vesp.* 18.
87. Reasoner, *Roman Imperial Texts*, 192.
88. Reasoner, *Roman Imperial Texts*, 188.
89. Horsley, *Jesus and the Powers*, 17.
90. Origen, *Cels.* 3.59.
91. Pliny, *Ep.* 10.96–97.

atheism because they forwent idolatry (including the imperial cult).[92] The apostolic message in Acts, even in Philippi, establishes the witness observed by second-century writers: an appeal to the lower classes, a refrain from idolatry, and insistence on economic integrity.

Philippi, a location characterized by loyalty to the Roman ethos, was a place with an intriguing military history that further highlights the intersection of war with greedy economics, idolatry, and the dark powers. The Roman system largely benefited the elite, as "victory in war brought senators the greatest glory and wealth from plunder,"[93] and the empire "celebrated military achievement as the greatest service of the state."[94] Indeed, the wealthiest class benefited the most from war, with senators furthering their assets while assisting various family members, friends, and clients along the way. The rich substantiated their income through the business of war, whether by maintaining the needs of the military or taking part in the loot via tax collection of new provinces.[95]

Additional forms of profitable bounty occurred by converting prisoners of war—both army and civilian—into slaves,[96] compounding the relationship between military victory, slavery, and economics (all emerging factors in this text). The ideal in Rome was to engage in constant, continuous, and ongoing war, and none of the ruling class saw a problem with this, as it caused their financial estates to flourish.[97] Given these components, just as Caesar was worshipped by the imperial cult, military conflict was idolized and treated as sacred by many. Moreover, the populace at Philippi likely included many heirs of veterans[98]—families that benefited from military service through property ownership. Steven Friesen places them as a "PS4" on his "Poverty Scale," denoting a group with "moderate surplus," just beneath the ruling elites.[99]

Accordingly, Paul's tangible actions of freeing a slave with a possessive spirit eliminated her profit potential, while signaling a more implicit protest of slavery-related exploitation and financial greed. This action is not

---

92. Athenagoras, *Leg.*
93. Goldsworthy, *Pax Romana*, 47.
94. Goldsworthy, *Pax Romana*, 52–53.
95. Goldsworthy, *Pax Romana*, 51–52.
96. Goldsworthy, *Pax Romana*, 51–52.
97. Goldsworthy, *Pax Romana*, 52–53.
98. Rapske, *Paul in Roman Custody*, 119.
99. Friesen, "Poverty in Pauline Studies," 323–61.

simply a polemic against the dark powers and economic policy, but even a subtle critique of Roman military endeavors. Given this, it is unsurprising that the crowd—likely property-owning heirs of veteran families—takes offense at Paul. They attack him as if they were a conquering army and the apostle were a resistance fighter.

Jesus's remarks in Luke 11:17–23 are integral to understanding the function of exorcisms in the narrative of Acts. The "finger of God" that overpowered the Egyptians and enabled control over dark spirits demonstrates the arrival of God's kingdom (Luke 11:20). In Philippi, through the action of casting out a long-standing spirit associated with Delphi, the kingdom of God arrives at that strategic location. With the evil powers unseated, the "fully armed guard" ensuring the "possessions are safe" is rendered subordinate to the Holy Spirit's superior force (Luke 11:21–22). The violent responses from the protectors of Roman ethos mirror the crowd's reaction to the economic disruption when Jesus had cast out the Legion (Luke 8:26–39), another scene with stark Roman-style military imagery.[100]

Synthesis

The dark powers are present with the spirit of divination, while greed is clearly articulated by the slave owners, who induce a mob reaction to preserve the economic vibrancy of their city. This demonstrates that the cosmic battle intensifies wherever the gospel disrupts local financial structures. The victory over darkness is shown not only through the expulsion of the Python spirit but also in Lydia's integrity as a generous, wealthy convert. It is further seen in Paul's survival, the jailer's conversion, and confronting Philippi's judicial powers. The imperial presence is robust, ranging from the activity of the imperial cult in a city functioning as a microcosm of Rome, to hints pointing toward Caesar and the Roman capital. Upon Paul's arrival, he seeks to unseat the forces of darkness, a goal which coincides with economic repercussions as the cosmic war intensifies, offering the reader a preview of expectations.

Paul and Silas depart Philippi and stop in Thessalonica, another key patriotic city in the region, engaging the synagogue. This results in a divided response, with some persons of high status coming to faith (Acts 17:1–4). However, Luke makes note of "Jews" who resist the Pauline ministry and publicly accuse Jason, declaring that the apostolic group has "stirred up

100. See Gangel, *Acts*, 272.

trouble throughout the world," has acted "against Caesar's decrees," and has declared Jesus as an alternate king (Acts 17:5–9). In contrast, Paul's ministry in Berea is well received, even among persons of high status (Acts 17:10–15). Next, the apostolic group arrives in Athens (Acts 17:16–34), where the darkness of idolatry is addressed, and Paul proclaims that God will judge the world.

As the trajectory continues toward Rome, more essential clues become evident. The resistance to Pauline ministry in Thessalonica brings further anti-imperial charges that prompt social disruption. Moreover, in Athens, false worship is targeted—a resounding message as the gospel continues its journey through the Mediterranean context to Rome.

Chapter 8: The Cult of Artemis in Ephesus: The Struggle over Economic and Religious Allegiance (Acts 19:1–41)

Ephesus had recently become a major centre of the new and rapidly spreading imperial cult, the worship of Rome and the emperor himself. Artemis had been joined by a much more recent divinity, with a massive claim to religious as well as political and military power.[1]

—N. T. Wright

Introduction

PAUL DEPARTS ATHENS FOR Corinth, founding a church there while meeting strong resistance (Acts 18:1–11). While there, Paul receives another vision in which the Lord states, "Do not be afraid, but speak and do not be silent," a sign as he assumes more risks heading toward the critical narrative climax in Rome (Acts 18:9 NET). Paul is then taken before the proconsul Gallio of Achaia, again accused of breaking the law.[2] However, Luke highlights the favorable ruling made by Gallio, validating the vision not to be afraid and leaving the reader curious about these governmental protections as the narrative drifts toward the imperial capital. This result further demonstrates that the Spirit is at work, even among Roman imperial agents.

---

1. Wright, *Acts for Everyone*, 170.

2. The text does not provide certainty regarding the exact nature of the accusations made against Paul, whether violating Jewish or Roman laws (or both); see Keener, *Acts: Exegetical Commentary*, 3:2768.

Paul leaves Corinth and passes through Ephesus, Caesarea, Jerusalem, and Antioch (Acts 18:18–23).

Textual Analysis

Luke introduces Apollos in Ephesus, a skilled teacher whose knowledge was limited to John the Baptist's activities (Acts 18:24–28). This sets up a parallel in Ephesus to the Jerusalem Pentecost of Acts 2, as John the Baptist's ministry was an antecedent of the Spirit's outpouring (Luke 3:16; Acts 1:5). This subtle Pentecost parallel continues in Acts 19:1–7, when Paul is in Ephesus with about twelve disciples (an allusion to Jesus's group) who had only received John's baptism. Paul lays hands on them, and they receive the Holy Spirit, speaking in languages (γλῶσσα). The only other mentions of γλῶσσα in Acts occur at critical moments: Pentecost in Jerusalem (Acts 2:3, 4, 11, 26) and Cornelius's conversion (Acts 10:46). These instances signify gentile inclusion with universal overtones and serve as a literary device in Luke's narrative, which ultimately leads to Rome.

This Pentecostal parallel at Ephesus occurs in the capital of the Asian province, with a notable port that enabled it to become the greatest economic hub of its region.[3] As the Roman Empire's third-largest city, Ephesus had a diverse populace, including many Jews. The city grew significantly during Roman times, with its commercial rise peaking in the late first into the second century CE, the likely timeline of Luke's writing. Its prime location was also facilitated by the advanced system of roads,[4] making Ephesus highly accessible as an intersection of major transit paths. This factor assisted Paul's ministry to the rest of the province, as Demetrius later claimed (Acts 19:26).

Paul speaks "without fear" (Acts 19:8) for three months in the synagogue, engaging in convincing dialogue concerning the "kingdom of God." This is the first openly public Lukan use of this phrase outside of Palestine, likely a product of Paul's fearless rhetoric and the compelling literary occasion. The synagogue's response in Ephesus heightens the narrative. Even though some do not receive his message, no significant resistance appears even after two years of ministry. This is a stark contrast to the Jerusalem response at both ends of Acts. Paul speaks openly in the public hall of Tyrannus daily (Acts 19:9). From that strategic location within a pivotal

---

3. Strabo, *Geogr.* 14.1.24.
4. Murphy-O'Connor, *St. Paul's Ephesus*, 187.

transit city, Paul's message spreads across Asia Minor among both Jews and Greeks, surprisingly without noted interruption (Acts 19:10).

Along with the Ephesian reception, Paul exhibits unusual power, and the Holy Spirit's influence strengthens while the dark powers weaken. Luke describes the unique phenomenon, the transference of the Spirit's power through various clothes, garments, and materials, which operate as conduits comparable to Paul's hands. This description is reminiscent of the notable depiction in Luke of the transference of power when a woman is healed by touching Jesus's clothes (Luke 8:40–48). Indeed, the event in Acts exceeds the account in Luke, as Paul's fabrics were dispatched on behalf of those in need rather than remaining on his person. Moreover, these garments appeared effective in demonstrating authority over evil spirits remotely. Remarkably, the materials were likely portions of fabric that had been used to clean sweat, dirt, and debris, which would typically have been considered unclean, but were made pure through the Spirit's presence.[5] The Spirit's strength over darkness is demonstrated to be more powerful than ever.

The weakened dark forces are further evident in the account of seven Jewish exorcists (ἐξορκιστής, Acts 19:13), a word Luke employs uniquely to indicate them as travelling charlatans. Their precise identity is unknown, but readers find them suspicious when they are referred to as itinerant or wanderers (περιέρχομαι, Acts 19:13).[6] Luke utilizes various characters in transit, but reserves this word in his thoroughfare imagery, singling out its use in this instance to indicate their inauthentic attributes.

These exorcists have used ineffective measures, attempting to mirror Pauline authority. Perhaps they have falsely deduced that if napkins could carry superior power, then they could evoke Paul's name for a share of that power, creating a thematic allusion to the account of Simon Magus. However, Luke's rare description, in combination with the material ethics he espoused, leaves the implicit understanding that this group is not motivated by generosity for communal benefit. Instead, these itinerant exorcists are presumed to have solicited payment, manipulating Paul's and Jesus's names as charmers with a magical formula.

The evil spirit responds, "Jesus I know, and Paul I am familiar with, but who are you?" (Acts 19:15). Suddenly, the greedy exorcists meet resistance by the dark powers when the man with the evil spirit jumps on

---

5. L&N, "σουδάριον," 71.

6. The word is used in 1 Tim 5:13 as a negative to those who go from house to house seeking to abuse hospitality.

them and overpowers them in a violent response to a unique scenario. The failed exorcists escape naked and wounded—a shameful depiction of their incapability and unclothed status.

The defeat of the dark forces in this case is evident in their self-confusion, wherein the evil spirits ironically drive away the charlatans—a role previously reserved for the Spirit-enabled apostles. This recalls Jesus's words in Luke 11:14–23, spoken in the context of exorcisms: "Every kingdom divided against itself is destroyed, and a divided household falls. So if Satan too is divided against himself, how will his kingdom stand?" Jesus's words on the prospects of the powers of darkness turning on themselves, noting that Satan's kingdom would fall, are juxtaposed with a proclamation of his own success: "But if I cast out demons by the finger of God, then the kingdom of God has already overtaken you" (Luke 11:20 NET). In other words, the dark powers have begun turning on themselves.

While the kingdom of God is preached in Ephesus, the dark powers are rapidly crumbling. The expulsion of evil spirits through garments touched by Paul demonstrates the arrival of God's kingdom. Meanwhile, dark forces face internal opposition as greedy exorcists are resisted not by the apostles but by the evil spirits themselves. Through the gossip network, the failed exorcism becomes a witness comparable to the negative testimony of Judas's death near Jerusalem, proximate to Pentecost. Similarly, these events become known throughout Ephesus.

The people of the region were afraid (φόβος, Acts 19:17), an integral marker in Lukan writings (Luke 1:12, 65; 2:9; 5:26; 7:16; 8:37). This fear is also noted in connection with the Jerusalem church at Pentecost (Acts 2:43) and in the response to Ananias and Sapphira's greed being confronted (Acts 5:5, 11). In a limited-good framework, as dark powers lose their societal control, the greedy exorcists are exposed. The zero-sum implications are that the name of the Lord Jesus Christ becomes further magnified, amplified, and exalted (μεγαλύνω, Acts 19:17), resulting in many turning to faith.

Meanwhile, many people who believed were also coming forward (ἔρχομαι, Acts 19:18), with the imperfect tense implying a continuous process of confessing and reporting their magic practices. Many of these new disciples had at some point, possibly before conversion, experimented with sorcery. Unlike Simon Magus and Elymas, these individuals are described more gently—not as magicians but as practitioners of magic, indicating a distinction between their identity and their character. This suggests that dark powers are being threatened. This practice that was previously a sign of dark powers that opposed the church is now being eagerly relinquished by participants.

The softer description is likely due to their remarkably unparalleled act of repentance in burning their dark literature, which Luke values at fifty thousand silver pieces. The exact type of coin, however, is uncertain.[7] Elsewhere, Luke specifically uses *denarius* (Luke 20:24) and *drachma* (Luke 15:8), whereas here the term *silver* (ἀργύριον, Acts 19:19) is linguistically ambiguous. Based on inscriptions, it is widely evidenced that the denarius, rather than the drachma, was the predominant coin in Ephesus, in references generally tracing back to earlier Hellenistic times.[8] However, the value of each coin was relatively equal. In terms of purchasing power, fifty thousand drachmas—roughly equivalent to fifty thousand denarii—could support one hundred families for five hundred days.[9] This represented twice the annual budget of Ephesus's famed Library of Celsus, constructed in the early second century.[10]

For further context, in 100 CE, a Roman agent in London purchased a slave for six hundred denarii; thus, the Ephesian sacrifice could have bought eighty-three slaves at that rate.[11] In the early second century, fifty thousand sesterces—worth about 12,500 denarii—were endowed to the Collegium of Aesculapius and Hygeia outside Rome. The funds covered expenses for sixty members, including banquets paid through earned interest.[12] Moreover, mansions, villas, and farms valued at fifty thousand sesterces marked an individual as "quite wealthy,"[13] yet such properties were only worth a quarter of the fifty thousand denarii that the Ephesians burned. In 63 BCE, Appuleius transported five hundred thousand drachmas from the entire Asian province to Rome as tribute—a sum equivalent to about nine times the Ephesian sacrifice—underscoring the remarkable scale of their conversion.[14]

The Ephesian repentance is public—a demonstration or protest of darkness—that likely resulted in fire near or within the city to have grabbed

---

7. Barrett, *Critical Exegetical Commentary—Acts*, 913.
8. Ehling, "Two notes on Argyrion," 271.
9. Ehling, "Two notes on Argyrion," 272.
10. Ehling, "Two notes on Argyrion," 273.
11. Tomlin, "Girl in Question," 49.
12. *CIL* 6.10234.
13. Cic. *Att.* 3.196.3; *Rosc. Amer.* 133. See Temin, *Roman Market Economy*, 201.
14. Plut. *Brut.* 25.

attention and provoked questions within the gossip network, which disseminated news of important activities throughout the community. These actions defied the "ethos" of Ephesus as "To be called an Ephesian was synonymous with magician, and magical books were called Ephesian scriptures."[15]

The book burning was not only a protest against magic and the dark forces empowering the practice, but also against economic control and manipulation over society. As noted, the most likely coin in Ephesus during this time was the denarius, about which Jesus gives commentary, inquiring of Caesar's image on the coin before declaring, "Give unto Caesar the things that are Caesar's and unto God the things that are God's" (Luke 20:24–25 NET). This passage likely alludes to 1 Macc 2:68, describing it as an "unambiguously revolutionary" remark of anti-pagan rhetoric.[16] Clearly, just as Jesus indirectly critiques the idolatrous nature of these coins, they served not as mere currency but as instruments of political propaganda. The denarii commonly displayed the reigning emperor on one side and a deity (such as Roma) on the reverse, symbolizing imperial theology.

Luke's readers would not have expected a liquidation of magical literature to be brought as an offering to the church. However, burning these assets—highlighted by their monetary value—suggests a protest, at least indirectly, against the imperial faces on the coins and the empire that minted them. This is thematically consistent with Peter's declaration that Simon's money should be destroyed (Acts 8:20) and Paul's disruption of revenue in Philippi (Acts 16:16–19).

With zero-sum qualities, this public demonstration multiplies the word of God, which grows in authority (ἴσχυεν, Acts 19:20), contrasting the evil forces that had exerted authority (ἴσχυσεν, Acts 19:16) over the false exorcists. After describing the worth of the magic books, Luke further qualifies the significant potency (κράτος, Acts 19:20) of the word of God, echoing Zechariah's statement: "He has displayed κράτος with his arm; he has scattered those who are proud in the thoughts of their hearts" (Luke 1:51 NET). With the success in Ephesus, "or after these happenings" (δέ ὡς οὗτος πληρόω, Acts 19:21), Paul determines (τίθημι, Acts 19:21) to go to Jerusalem. Luke then shifts from narration to quotation: "μετά ὁ ἐγώ γίνομαι ἐγώ δεῖ καί 'Ρώμη,'" with Paul's voice affirming, "After I go there, I must go to Rome." The word δεῖ indicates a sense of urgency, necessity,

---

15. Walaskay, *Acts*, 179.
16. Wright, *Jesus Victory of God*, 634.

destiny, and divine imperative, authoritatively used by Jesus (Luke 2:49; 4:43; 9:22; 12:12; 13:14, 16, 33; 15:32; 17:26; 18:1; 22:37; 24:7, 26, 44), then by Peter (Acts 1:21, 3:21, 4:12), and concerning Paul's destiny (Acts 9:15).

The Ephesian repentance motivates Paul to make his own gospel proclamation in Jerusalem, distinguishable from Peter's earlier record, and then expand his message to Rome. Inspired by the fantastic Pentecost at Ephesus, Paul acknowledges the greater effects of the Holy Spirit empowerment, hopeful that both key locations (Jerusalem and Rome) would react as Ephesus had, further crippling the dark powers. Paul sends his helpers Timothy and Erastus back to Macedonia, likely hoping for similar experiences in those locations while he remains in Asia, presumably to nurture the incredible emerging movement. If napkins and clothes could transmit Paul's type of empowerment, how much more so should his dispatched associates?

At each point in this study, opposition presents itself, attempting to hijack the gospel momentum in the form of greed. Luke's narration continues with the transition phrase "at the same time" (Κατά ἐκεῖνος καιρός, Acts 19:23). The reader is unsurprised that a notable contention arises with Demetrius, a silversmith, as the culprit who exemplifies the connection of greed and idolatry from Eph 5:5. While artisans were generally not in the elitist class,[17] the "basis for their social identity" was their trade and its potential wealth.[18] These craftsmen were of greater importance in a location like Ephesus, and were likely considered more socially significant given their support of Artemis's temple.[19]

This cult had been deeply embedded in Ephesian life for over a millennium.[20] The city claimed to be the birthplace of Artemis,[21] daughter of Zeus and sister of Apollo, having constructed three temples in her honor over many centuries.[22] The temple of Paul's day was elaborately known as one of the seven great wonders of antiquity.[23] It was the "most commit-

---

17. Seal, "Ephesus," *LBD*; see also Pericles 2.1–2.
18. Witherington, *Acts of the Apostles*, 593. See also Seal, "Ephesus," *LBD*.
19. Keener, *NT*, 384.
20. See Strabo, *Geogr.* 14.1.22–23; Hdt. *Hist.* 1.26; Ach. Tat. *Leuc. Clit.* 7.13—8.14; Xen. *Eph.* 1.2, 5.
21. Tac. *Ann.* 3.60–63; cf. Strabo, *Geogr.* 14.1.20; Aune, "Ephesus," 414.
22. Aune, "Ephesus," 414.
23. Paus. *Descr.* 4.31.8; 7.5.4.

ted cult in Asia," adored even more than Athena in Athens.[24] Pausanias, in the second century, notes Artemis as the most esteemed of the Ephesian deities,[25] substantiated by epigraphic findings recording 378 references to Artemis compared to seven total for other gods, including Dionysus, Zeus, Apollo, and Athena.[26]

Sandra Glahn remarks on the patron qualities of Artemis, noting the following regarding the goddess in Ephesus: "[Artemis] is frequently listed as the honoree of a building or statue dedication in monuments erected by couples or families, individuals. . . . Her priestesses are also honored with monuments. Artemis is associated with the city's festivals, parades, athletics, and public honors."[27] The Artemis temple cult owned significant amounts of farmland and had investments in many other industries to the extent that it was ingrained in every aspect of Ephesus's infrastructure, financing many public projects.[28] The populace knew the goddess as "savior,"[29] and many who threatened the cult faced execution.[30]

Demetrius's complaint was economic, as he secured a large volume of profit or business (ἐργασία, Acts 19:24) from the institution—a term also used in Philippi (Acts 16:16, 19). The Artemis cult generated a "lucrative tourist business from pilgrims travelling to the temple,"[31] which bolstered the silversmith's sales. Consistent with its ancient counterparts, this temple functioned as the core of banking operations, serving as a creditor and ideally providing safe storage, given its sacred space.[32] Demetrius appears to be influential both economically and socially, acting in a brokerage or even patronage position for other temple craftsmen, whom he gathers to remind them of the wealth (εὐπορία, Acts 19:25) associated with their businesses (ἐργασία, Acts 19:25).

This silversmith assumes in his statement that all the artisans are aware of the Holy Spirit's superior power, observed across all Asia (including Ephesus), which threatens to bankrupt them with widespread regional

---

24. Keener, *Acts: Exegetical Commentary*, 3:2872.
25. Paus. *Descr.* 4.31.8.
26. Glahn, *Nobody's Mother*, 83–84.
27. Glahn, *Nobody's Mother*, 85.
28. Keener, *Acts: Exegetical Commentary*, 3:2888.
29. IEph. 13.1255, 1265.
30. IEph. 9.1a.2.
31. Seal, "Ephesus," *LBD*.
32. Seal, "Ephesus," *LBD*. See also Dio Chrys. *Rhod.* 31.54.

effects from the cult's dissolution. Paul is accused of persuading the masses of the illegitimacy of idols while undermining the gods associated with them, thereby confronting the foundation of Ephesus's economic system.

Accordingly, Paul's assertions also threaten the broader pagan worldview. Generations later, Lucian of Samosata and Tertullian remark on the threat posed to temples by the Christian movement.[33] This threat extended to the imperial cult, which had hosted a temple in Ephesus to Roma and Divus Julius since the time of Augustus.[34] Moreover, in the later first century CE, near the time of Luke's writing, the city was emerging with four neocorate temples constructed there for Caesar worship, receiving high honor from Rome for doing so[35] and containing inscriptions of emperor deification.[36] The result was the intermingling in Ephesus of both the imperial and Artemis cults.[37]

With the dark powers interrupted, weakening, and nearly insolvent, a substantial threat loomed that Ephesus might be lost as a strategic location for evil. This is reflected in Demetrius's motivations when he warns of the danger associated with Paul's success, claiming that their businesses would fail if Paul abolished idolatry entirely from Asia. The complaint charges explicitly that Paul's success would render the temple of the great (μέγας, Acts 19:27) goddess Artemis worthless or without honor, thereby eradicating her greatness (μεγαλειότης, Acts 19:27). In Thessalonica, the Pauline mission was accused of turning the "world upside down" (οἰκουμένη ἀναστατόω, Acts 17:6). Ephesus later fears that Paul would destroy (καθαιρέω, Acts 19:27) the one who was "worshipped in all Asia and the entire world" (Acts 19:27).

Ephesus marks another occasion where Paul threatens "local patriotism,"[38] and Demetrius's plea hinges on successfully rousing the tradesmen. These men become passionately inspired by greed, generating an emotionally charged mob response similar to that in Philippi. They begin to shout (κράζω, Acts 19:28)—a response comparable to that of the evil spirits (Luke 9:39)—"Great (μέγας) is Artemis of the Ephesians" (Acts 19:28).[39] In a limited-good world, the fear was that once the cult (and its

33. Lucian, *Peregr.* 11–13; Tert. *Apol.* 37.
34. Cassius Dio, *Hist.* 51.20.6–7; see also Aune, "Ephesus," 414.
35. Oster, "Ephesus (Place)," 2:544.
36. Burnett, *Paul and Imperial Honors*, 72.
37. Brennan, "Artemis and Ephesian Haustafeln," 106–10.
38. Schreiner, *Acts*, 591.
39. Comparable to Anthia's cry in Xen. *Eph.* 1.11.5.

profit) began declining, it would likely continue on that trajectory toward obsolescence. Thus, they feel compelled to aggressively protect their indispensability and affirm their dark loyalty.

The mob reaction fills the premises with confusion (σύγχυσις, Acts 19:29)[40] as they rush (ὁρμάω, Acts 19:29) to the theatre, dragging Paul's companions.[41] This wording is akin to the description of Legion protecting their autonomy as the pigs "rushed" down the steep slope (Luke 8:33), and the crowd that "rushed" to stone Stephen (Acts 7:57). In an odd parallel to Pentecost, this inflamed group acts in one accord (ὁμοθυμαδόν, Acts 2:1; 19:29) as they seize Gaius and Aristarchus and drag them to the theatre.

Paul desires to intervene but is prevented by local disciples, including some Asiarchs, possibly protecting him from the aims of darkness attempting to disrupt his destiny in Jerusalem and Rome. Those Asiarchs, "leading citizens of Ephesus," came from the same class that selected priests for the imperial cult. This may indicate the extent of Paul's influence in Ephesus, where he had the support and protection of local officials.[42] However, if the Holy Spirit could transmit power through fabric, so also could God work among the apprehended disciples, Gaius and Aristarchus.

The confused crowd shouts unclear words (ἄλλος τις, Acts 19:32), their ongoing confusion (συγχέω, Acts 19:32) evident as many participants are ignorant of the gathering's purpose (πολύς οὐ οἶδα τίς, Acts 19:32). This indicates mob-like motivations rather than genuine conviction. They chanted, "Great is Artemis of the Ephesians," for two hours, akin to rhythmic acclamations at public events, accompanied by whistles and shouting.[43] The repetition, however, highlights the crowd's confusion and the emptiness of their protest.

The recurrence of μέγας (or its derivatives) represents a pattern in this study. Simon Magus was called μέγας (Acts 8:9-10, 13), Agrippa

---

40. Σύγχυσις, only used here in the NT, is employed in Gen 11:9 (LXX) for "Babel," the event that Luke uses to contrast to Pentecost. So also, this Ephesian greedy and cultic response demonstrates the anti-Pentecost event, compared to the earlier positive correlations. See Hamm, *Acts of the Apostles*, 79.

41. This confusion also has some parallel to Pentecost, but more evidently in contrast as this event appears more closely related to Babel (Gen 11:1-9).

42. Bruce, *Book of the Acts*, 376.

43. See Schnabel, *Acts*, 1422. See also Gaventa, *Acts*, 273, who finds some comparison in Heliodorus; see Arist. *Eth. nic.* 4.19; 7.8-9; 8.9; 10.8, 17; Chariton, *Chaer.* 1.5; 3.4; Ach. Tat. *Leuc. Clit.* 7.9.

I self-ascribed his greatness,[44] and at Philippi, idolatry was tied to μέγας profit (Acts 16:16). In Ephesus, the goddess of the cult is described with a form of μέγας, signifying her greatness (Acts 19:27–28, 34). However, in all this supposed greatness, ultimately "the only thing heathenism can do against Paul is to shout itself hoarse."[45] Eventually, the town clerk subdues the crowd, affirming their local myth of Artemis, who fell from "heaven" (διοπετής, Acts 19:35).[46] Artemis's fall from Zeus symbolizes being sent by the gods; similarly, Romulus's descent declared Rome's divine mandate to rule the world.[47] There is a possible connection to Luke 10:18, where Jesus observes Satan's fall,[48] as Paul's polemic undermines all cults by declaring that gods made by human hands are illegitimate.[49]

The clerk urges order, instructing the people not to engage in "extreme responses" (πράσσω μηδείς προπετής, Acts 19:36), incorporating πράσσω, which is used in their confession of extreme magical practices (Acts 19:19). He emphasizes that legal due process rests with the proconsuls, and accusations against Paul should be brought there, not addressed through mob action that undermines legal integrity.

While socioeconomic similarities between Ephesus and Philippi are notable—both faced threats to their social, political, and financial infrastructure—the contrast lies in the Ephesian leadership's appropriate public response. The clerk quickly assesses the situation, concluding that Paul and his companions have neither blasphemed the goddess nor desecrated her temple. Moreover, the clerk observes that the most urgent danger is that the greedily motivated pagan businessmen might incite a riot (στάσις, Acts 19:40), disturbing the Roman peace. Recognizing that the unruly influencers would have no power (δύναμαι, Acts 19:40) to defend against such a charge, he then dismisses the assembly.

---

44. Chilton, *Herods*, 192.

45. Haenchen, *Acts of the Apostles*, 578.

46. This is the current epicenter in the cosmic duel; Artemis is affirmed as falling from heaven; Jesus, when intensifying this feud with darkness, noted Satan's fall like lightning (Luke 10:18); and then Demetrius fears the absolution of the cult.

47. Livy, *Hist.* 1.16.6–7.

48. Schreiner, *Acts*, 595.

49. There could be a subtle counter-Pentecost parallel whereas the Holy Spirit fell upon gentiles (Acts 10:44–48; 11:15), in Ephesus, Artemis had fallen from heaven. However, at that location, Luke highlights the Spirit's superiority upon falling to earth.

Synthesis

Before Jesus entered Jerusalem, he encountered Zacchaeus, a symbol of dark occupation, whose demonstrated repentance was unparalleled in the Gospel (Luke 19:1–10). Likewise, the unparalleled repentance in Acts occurs at Ephesus just before the narrative shifts to Rome by way of Jerusalem—another location where "politics and religion were as heavily intertwined as religion and economics, and local civic pride was inseparable from the worship of the Ephesian Artemis."[50]

The greedy components are well evident in this section, with the double narrative providing two instances of such activity. First, Luke presents the invalid exorcists who, as charlatans comparable to Simon Magus and Elymas, were willing to summon any method (or name) to meet their aims. Interestingly, the Jewish magician in Cyprus was Bar-Jesus while the Jewish exorcists used the name of Jesus. More prominently observed were the greedy aspects of Demetrius and his fellow artisans. When their trade was threatened, they sought to stimulate their personal economy by causing a public uproar. This is comparable to the disappointed profiteers in Philippi who incited a mob reaction due to their loss of financial services. In contrast, many who brought forth their magic literature to be burned evidenced surrender—a vital weapon in the war against darkness—and demonstrated the strongest measure of repentance anywhere depicted in Acts.

The activity of the dark powers is also clearly depicted within the Ephesian double narrative. First, the evil spirit is presented as possessing a man who physically attacked the would-be exorcists. Secondly, the evil forces are noted to have long influenced a substantial portion of the populace, evidenced by the widespread burning of paraphernalia associated with sorcery. Thirdly, Demetrius textually functions as a keeper of the Artemis cult and, more precisely, the craftsman of wicked idolatry. The citizens of Ephesus proclaim the deific greatness of Artemis, comparable to Simon and Agrippa I, each known as great, while the Python spirit in Philippi generated great profit.

Moreover, the dark connection is evident between Bar-Jesus, described as a Jewish magician, and the failed Jewish exorcists. However, the ascribed "great" suffer the rebalancing of Luke's great reversal, evidenced by the Artemis cult being threatened with extinction and the businesses sustaining idolatry placed in jeopardy. An intriguing contrast in this story

---

50. Keener, *NT*, 384.

is Paul's assertion of illegitimacy of idols made with human hands, yet the affirmation of fabric (also made of human hands) displaying the Spirit's greater force.

Chapter 9: The Cosmic Duel from Jerusalem to Rome: The Culmination of the Battle (Acts 20–28)

Yes, and the Caesars too would have believed on Christ, if either the Caesars had not been necessary for the world, or if Christians could have been Caesars.[1]

—Tertullian

Introduction

Through the narrative analysis of key passages, this study has examined the cosmic victory over darkness in both literary components and narrative progression. In each instance, evil's attempts were thwarted, frustrated, or disappointed. Ultimately, these setbacks were not merely incidental but demonstrated that God's plans and purposes prevailed over the opposition, reinforcing the theological framework of divine sovereignty throughout Acts.

Applying the findings from Acts 1–19 to the final chapters of the book demonstrates that Luke is not simply narrating historical events but constructing a theological and political argument regarding the ultimate triumph of God's kingdom. Continuing the study with regard to Acts 20–28 thus serves as a crucial test case for the broader conclusions drawn from the earlier pericopes. This confirms the overarching trajectory of Luke's narrative and reinforces the implications of the church's role within the Roman world.

---

1. Tert. *Apol.* 1.

The Cosmic Duel in Acts 1–19

Prior to continuing the discussion of greed and the dark powers in Acts 20–28, this section briefly reiterates the developments discussed in Acts 1–19, beginning with events before Paul's emergence and continuing with the decreasing potency of the dark powers during Paul's mission.

Pre-Pauline Developments

Early opposition (Acts 1–5)

- Judas fails; Jesus's resurrection and the betrayer's demise reveal satanic defeat.
- Disciple group expands from 12 to 120, then by 3,000 at Pentecost.
- Temple-led persecution (Acts 3–4) proves futile; 5,000 disciples are noted.
- Ananias and Sapphira's treachery quickly ends, with no lasting harm beyond cautioning believers.
- After this, Satan is no longer actively mentioned; the church continues to grow (Acts 5:1–42).

Stephen's episode (Acts 6–7)

- Controversy over benevolent funds arises but is resolved without betrayal or death.
- After this successful outcome greed no longer threatens the church.
- Stephen's martyrdom introduces Saul, spurring the church's expansion beyond Judea.

Samaria (Acts 8:4–24)

- Spirit operates effectively without apostolic presence.
- Dark spirits are expelled, leaving Simon Magus powerless.
- Simon's bribery attempt fails, further diminishing his influence.

Caesarea (Acts 12:1–24)

- Peter's miraculous deliverance reaffirms divine victory.
- Agrippa I's sudden death demonstrates God's authority over oppression.
- The word of God multiplies anew (Acts 12:24).

Mirroring tactics

- Evil deploys traitors; God converts key antithetical leaders (Saul: 9:1-31, Cornelius: 10:1—11:18, Sergius Paulus: 13:4–11).
- Elymas (devil's "son," 13:9-10) is blinded rather than killed, signaling reduced threat by opponents.

Dark Powers Retreat

From this juncture, dark forces shift from offensive aggression to defensive retreat, as demonstrated by the narratives in Philippi and Ephesus.

Philippi (Acts 16:11–40)

- *Exorcism of divination spirit*: Challenges imperial greed and idolatry; a Balaam-like Python spirit ironically promotes Paul's message.
- *Mob-induced punishment*: Paul and Silas are stripped, beaten, and jailed but do not require a miraculous escape (unlike Peter in Acts 12).
- *Jailer's conversion*: Despite endangering himself, he survives, converting to the faith—no fatal consequence befalls the antagonists (unlike jailers in Acts 12).
- *Economic loss*: Slaveowners suffer profit damage; Lydia and the jailer (both generous) join the church, surpassing earlier single recorded conversion (Acts 13).
- *Judicial success*: Court officials release Paul, allowing him to rebuke Philippian leaders. While Paul expels a powerful spirit, dark forces cannot dislodge him.

Ephesus (Acts 19:11–41)

- *Miracle cloths*: Fabric touched by Paul proves more potent than evil spirits or charlatan exorcists.
- *Repentance from sorcery*: Many forsake magic, becoming traitors to the forces of darkness.
- *Surpassing idols*: Even cloth imbued by the Spirit outshines idols shaped by human hands.
- *Threat to Artemis*: The cult faces decline, yet Demetrius's opposition merely generates confusion rather than any true danger.
- *Effortless victory*: The Spirit's power triumphs with minimal resistance, cementing Ephesus as a milestone in the church's advance.

Increasing Potency of God's Kingdom

As dark forces shift to a defensive retreat, God's kingdom expands its influence and effectiveness:

- *Ephesus vs. Philippi*: Paul avoids beatings or arrest; charlatan exorcists suffer instead. The town clerk, not Paul, disperses the mob. Similarly, unlike the Jews in Corinth (Acts 18), the Ephesians lodge no complaint with their proconsul, and no miraculous intervention (e.g., prison deliverance or earthquake) is required.
- *Diminishing severity*: Early in Acts, Judas, Ananias and Sapphira, and Agrippa I meet violent ends. Later adversaries face milder outcomes:
    a. Simon (Acts 8:20–24): Threatened but left powerless, losing only his money.
    b. Elymas (Acts 13:11): Blinded instead of killed.
    c. Philippian slave owners (Acts 16:19–20): Suffered only financial loss.
- *Implication*: As the church's success grows, evil's potency wanes, requiring less severe rebuke.

Judicial Scenes

When viewed within the narrative arc, the trial scenes in Acts do not indicate legal apathy toward the church or an attempt to legitimize it to Rome. Rather, various imperial and pagan establishments feel threatened, including those in Philippi, Thessalonica (Acts 17:1–9), Athens (Acts 17:16–34), Corinth (Acts 18:1–17), and Ephesus. Paul appears fortunate to exit Philippi with boldness, yet he furtively leaves Thessalonica when charged with anti-imperial activity. At Corinth, Gallio the proconsul, like the town clerk at Ephesus, declines involvement.

Within the framework of the cosmic duel, the Spirit's emergence—not the integrity of the legal system—empowers Paul toward successful outcomes. The divine voice directs him to move deeper into Roman territory (Acts 16:10), assures him of fearlessness (Acts 18:9), and declares his destiny in Rome (Acts 23:11). The Spirit clears a path for Paul, despite potential legal opposition. Rather than conveying the harmlessness of the Christian movement, these episodes portray the kingdom's progression and its agent's maneuvering toward Rome. Even when imperial jurisprudence wavers, the mission's advance to the capital remains undeterred. Gamaliel's remark (Acts 5:39)—that if the movement is from God, it cannot be stopped—best situates the judicial outcomes in Luke's second volume.

Ultimately, Acts depicts the Spirit's steady advance over dark forces, toppling each greedy antagonist as the narrative builds toward Paul's Spirit-empowered arrival in Rome. The narrative structure anticipates a cosmic clash with Rome itself, epitomizing imperial greed and idolatry as the final bastion of darkness. This victory is both theological and socioeconomic, signaling the complete reordering of systems upheld by dark forces. Through these elements, Luke-Acts affirms the triumph of God's kingdom over imperial powers, framing the narrative as a declaration of war against darkness rather than a mere apologetic for the church's existence.

The Cosmic Duel in Acts 20–28

In Acts 1–19, seven distinct passages of Luke-Acts have demonstrated the author's repeated intersection of greed with the efforts of the dark forces. The expectation is that the remainder of Luke's text in Acts 20–28 will continue to emphasize socioeconomic ethics and the impending outcome of the cosmic duel, anticipating ultimate triumph over the dark powers.

Luke's expression of a cosmic battle in his writings has precedence. Second Temple Jewish writings, such as the War Scroll (1QM) from Qumran, often frame the battle between light and darkness as a confrontation with empires, particularly Rome, identifying Satan (or Kittim) as the angelic force over earthly kingdoms. Luke, familiar with Jewish textual traditions, likely would have considered these perspectives when narrating the church's engagement with empire.[2]

The "We" Passages and "The Way"

After departing Ephesus, Paul retraces his steps through previously visited locations (Acts 20:1–6), and then the narrator shifts to the first-person plural, a critical rhetorical device signaling escalating urgency. Bonz observes:

> The "we" passages do not represent historical, eyewitness accounts. But while they are, therefore, rhetorical, they were not created to add verisimilitude to Luke's historical narrative. Nor was Luke merely attempting to follow a literary convention for certain types of adventurous voyages. Rather, the "we" references serve as rhetorical shorthand for the Pauline Christians—those who are vicariously privy to Paul's example and who, as heirs to his legacy, have been called by him to continue his unfinished mission. They are Luke's intended audience, whose participation in the ongoing drama of God's salvation plan is signaled by the words of the Lukan prologue: "concerning the events that have been fulfilled."[3]

Accordingly, the "we" passages link Luke's audience to Paul's mission, inviting them to participate vicariously in the unfolding drama of salvation. This stylistic shift mirrors earlier usage during the journey to Philippi and culminates in the progression toward Rome. Likewise, "the Way" (ὁδός) functions as a similar signpost, first distinctly utilized when Elymas attempts to prohibit "the Way" (Acts 13:10) that is then alluded to by the Python spirit (Acts 16:17) and appears at Ephesus (Acts 19:9, 23) alongside the trajectory toward Rome.

---

2. Sanders, "Ethic of Election," 106.
3. Bonz, *Past as Legacy*, locs. 2036–39 of 3386.

Journey to Rome by Way of Jerusalem

Upon departing Ephesus and travelling through Troas, Paul restores Eutychus to life after his fatal fall from an upper window (Acts 20:7–12). This "otherwise unlikely scene"[4] underscores the Spirit's growing empowerment, reminiscent of how Jesus's own resurrection foreshadowed the impending triumph over darkness. In parallel fashion, Paul's miracle here foreshadows an intensification of spiritual power essential for future confrontations.[5]

Paul is eager to reach Jerusalem by Pentecost (Acts 20:16), seemingly hoping for a momentous spiritual renewal akin to the original Pentecost in Acts 2. While this may appear speculative, it aligns with Paul's larger pattern of seeking divine intervention at key festivals, and it resonates with the dramatic "Ephesian Pentecost" (Acts 19). Yet Luke, aware of Jerusalem's waning receptivity, signals that this city no longer yields fruitful ground for the Christian mission. As Bonz observes, "The Spirit does direct Paul to Jerusalem one last time, but only to emphasize that this city no longer bears any fruit for the Christian mission."[6] Consequently, Luke's narrative begins pivoting toward Rome, where the author envisions a decisive engagement with evil powers.

Paul's address to the Ephesian elders (Acts 20:17–38) further supports this pivot. While warning them of a spiritual duel and impending danger (Acts 20:28–31), Paul declares, "I have desired no one's silver or gold or clothing" (Acts 20:33 NET). This statement illustrates his eschewal of greed, aligning with Luke's recurrent theme of opposing wealth-driven exploitation. The community senses the rising conflict with evil; believers in Tyre plead with Paul not to proceed to Jerusalem (Acts 21:4), and Agabus prophetically warns him of ensuing bonds (Acts 21:11–12). Nevertheless, Paul presses on, convinced of his destiny, even though Luke's portrayal foreshadows Jerusalem's ultimate failure to replicate the Acts 2 experience. Instead, it is Rome to which Luke directs the reader's anticipation of God's unfolding plan.

---

4. Wright, *Paul: A Biography*, 344.

5. Thiessen, *Jesus and the Forces*, 183, suggests that overcoming death is in the same cosmic category as overcoming the evil forces.

6. Bonz, *Past as Legacy*, locs. 2049–50 of 3386.

Arrival in Jerusalem

When Paul and his companions reach Jerusalem, rumors of his presence fuel opposition (Acts 21:20–22). He agrees to fund the expenses for a group observing a ritual of piety (21:23–24). Meanwhile, the stance against idolatry is reaffirmed (21:25). Upon entering the temple, immediate conflict erupts as the dark powers threaten his journey to Rome by endangering his life. These tensions arise from allegations that Paul brought an Ephesian gentile into the temple (21:27–29). This recollection of the Ephesian Pentecost possibly reflects Paul's initial hope for a comparable event in Jerusalem. Roman soldiers then shield him from the mob (21:27–36). Yet they interrogate and misidentify him with a prior revolt, implying a dangerous reputation (21:38).

Paul's testimony, as a former persecutor turned advocate of the Jesus movement (symbolizing victory over darkness), intensifies the outrage (22:1–22). Roman soldiers prepare to flog him for further information, but Paul invokes his legitimately acquired Roman citizenship, thereby avoiding torture (22:28–30). His legal standing was legitimately acquired, in contrast to the bribery-secured citizenship by the Roman agent (22:28). Although Rapske contends Paul was unlawfully treated by the Romans,[7] Schreiner more accurately describes the narrative momentum, suggesting that imperial agents in Jerusalem show greater integrity than those in Philippi.[8] Their self-restraint contrasts with the "excessive disorder" and "lynch behavior" of the Jews.[9] Consequently, Paul's clash with darkness reveals that Roman officials offer him superior legal safeguards compared with both the Jewish leaders and certain other Roman authorities. They also "improve considerably" his conditions in custody, acting as lifesaving agents.[10]

This sequence parallels and diverges from Jesus's trial and death under Roman jurisdiction. Like Jesus, Paul stands before the Sanhedrin, testifying to Jesus's resurrection before the very council that conspired against him (Acts 23:1–11). There, a vision of the Lord assures him: "Have courage, for just as you have testified about me in Jerusalem, so you must also testify in Rome" (23:11 NET). The narrative reveals Paul's steady engagement with Rome through each encounter. Although his opponents strive more

---

7. Rapske, *Paul in Roman Custody*, 140.
8. Schreiner, *Acts*, 736.
9. Rapske, *Paul in Roman Custody*, 139.
10. Rapske, *Paul in Roman Custody*, 135.

fervently than they did to kill Jesus, they prove less effective. Even amid tension between Jews and Romans, Paul stays relatively passive yet prevails in the cosmic war.

The dark conflict intensifies in Jerusalem, shown by more desperate resistance than that faced by Jesus (Luke 19–21). The adversaries conspire to assassinate Paul without legal proceedings (Acts 23:12–22). Their plan fails when Roman soldiers, unknowingly permitting Paul's nephew to visit, learn of the plot. Initially, this might appear subversive,[11] but it confirms victory when imperial agents become ethical exemplars, overshadowing both Jerusalem's leaders and populace. As Walton argues, "The agents of the Roman Empire are shown to be far from perfect—although not as corrupt as they might be."[12] Seventy horsemen and two hundred infantrymen then escort Paul, supplying formidable military protection (23:23–35). This contrasts sharply with conditions in Philippi and heightens the reader's sense that Rome stands ready to receive him. This is another formidable twist in the cosmic war.

Caesarea

When Paul arrives in Caesarea, opposition persists (Acts 24:1–9). In his defense, he reaffirms the resurrection and references the funds he has collected for the Judean churches (24:10–21). Felix, intent on preserving Paul's safety, grants him a hearing to expound upon judgment and self-restraint (24:22–27). The greedy Felix had effectively procured his wife from another man, echoing the circumstances that led to John the Baptist's imprisonment (Luke 3:19–20). Paul's forthrightness, reminiscent of that earlier prophet, unsettles this imperial official and hints that Caesar might be, likewise, unsettled, perhaps toward repentance. Paul, however, remains in Caesarea for two years, likely due to Felix's avarice for a bribe.[13]

Festus succeeds Felix, and the Jews again plot to kill Paul. Recognizing this intensifying clash with darkness, Paul appeals to Caesar (Acts 25:1–12). As evil weakens, Paul's "Spirit-empowered prophetic speech" resonates.[14] He addresses Agrippa II, Bernice, and Festus, nearly persuading Agrippa

11. Rapske, *Paul in Roman Custody*, 149.
12. Walton, "Trying Paul or Rome," 140.
13. Rapske, *Paul in Roman Custody*, 313.
14. Wenkel, "Weaponry of Kingship," 95–108, continues the argument that Jesus provided an example of kingship for the Twelve to follow.

both to release him and to embrace the faith (Acts 25:13-32). This moment underscores Paul's influence over political officials, fulfilling his charge "to open their eyes so that they turn from darkness to light and from the power of Satan to God" (Acts 26:18 NET).

Mediterranean Voyage (Acts 27:1—28:10)

The final confrontation against the dark powers unfolds amid Paul's voyage across the Mediterranean. This setting recalls exodus and Passover imagery, woven throughout this study.[15] In biblical narratives, the sea often symbolizes evil forces. Luke may expect his reader to note that Zeus/Jupiter—the storm god and Roman patron—targets Paul to eliminate his threat. Yet the story mocks these deities, revealing that God's servant surpasses imperial and economic powers.

Paul sails in the perilous storm season, when most ships cease operations. Likely recognizing the sea's role in a cosmic duel, he anticipates battle on the waters (Acts 27:1-12).[16] Despite strong warnings, the vessel faces a fierce gale. Luke reports, "We then went for many days without seeing the sun or stars, with a major storm raging. All hope of safety was finally abandoned" (Acts 27:20 NET). Since human adversaries failed to kill Paul, the sea's darkness unleashes a grand offensive to bar him from Rome.[17]

In this crisis, the same divine voice that redirected Paul to Philippi (Acts 16:10), reassured him at Corinth (Acts 18:9), and guided him in Jerusalem (Acts 23:11) promises his safe arrival in the imperial capital. Paul's voice becomes dominant on the ship, overshadowing the commercial, political, and military figures who first ignored him. Salvation permeates this account, culminating when Paul urges everyone to break their lengthy fast and share a meal with sacramental overtones (Acts 27:13-32).[18]

This study began near Jesus's consecrated table—situated between Judas's conspiracy and betrayal. Eucharistic language reappeared at Eutychus's revival (Acts 21:7-11) and surfaces again here at sea, as darkness relinquishes its hold. Paul's pivotal role in preserving and encouraging the

---

15. Wright, *Paul: A Biography*, 375.
16. Schreiner, *Acts*, 719-20.
17. Bauer, *Acts as Story*, 241.
18. Curiously, this all occurs just following the Day of Atonement. See Wright, *Paul: A Biography*, 377.

ship's company (Acts 27:33–44) evokes divine care and rescue. To this, Wright notes:

> Luke has constructed Acts in such a way that chapter 27, the great voyage and shipwreck, functions as a kind of parallel to the climax of his Gospel, which is obviously the trial and crucifixion of Jesus [and Judas's betrayal]. That had been the moment when "the power of darkness" did its worst. This, now, is the moment when Paul has to face the worst that the powers can throw at him before he can arrive in Rome to announce Jesus as Lord.[19]

Indeed, it is as if Rome were symbolically present at Jesus's table—an event identified both as a "baptismal image" and a "Passover moment."[20]

Crew members discard grain (Acts 27:38), intensifying greed's role in the risky decisions to sail the vessel. Emperor Claudius had incentivized shipping grain to Rome in winter, likely commandeered from exploited regions. Because of these profits, the ship's operators risked their vessel.[21] As in Ephesus, however, evil turns against itself. The same storm meant to kill Paul destroys commercial assets, leaving Paul's prudence and leadership triumphant. He supersedes both captain and centurion, with Roman agents striving to protect him (Acts 27:21–44).[22]

Shipwrecked on Malta, near Rome at last, Paul encounters generous islanders. Yet darkness attempts one final strike, as a venomous snake bites him, evoking "the war between Satan and God."[23] Paul prevails and must again repel misguided adoration, refusing to be worshipped as a god (Acts 28:1–10).

Imperial Escort to Rome

Paul's concluding journey to Rome takes place on a ship whose figurehead features the "Heavenly Twins" (Acts 28:11). These gods supposedly ensure safe passage.[24] This imagery carries ironic force, suggesting that the very

---

19. Wright, *Paul: A Biography*, 376.

20. The shipwreck is akin to the crossing of the Red Sea—a Passover moment, a baptismal image. Wright, *Paul: A Biography*, 376.

21. Wright, *Paul: A Biography*, 377; and Suet. *Claud.* 18.1–2.

22. McKnight, *Acts: Participating Together*, 291.

23. Schreiner, *Acts*, 737.

24. Horace, *Od.* 1.3.2–5, 4.8.31–32; Vergil, *Aen.* 10.225–26; Cic. *Nat. d.* 2.6.15; Apuleius, *Metam.* 11.7; Paus. *Descr.* 2.17.6.

idols Paul opposed ultimately convey him safely, just as the Roman army and these deities together form the means of transit from Jerusalem to Caesarea and onward to Rome (Acts 28:11–31). The book of Acts concludes with Paul in Rome:

> Paul lived there two whole years at his own expense and welcomed everyone who came to see him. He announced the kingdom of God and taught the things about the Lord Jesus the Messiah with all boldness, and with no one stopping him. (Acts 28:30–31)

Luke depicts the imperial capital as more receptive than any city in Paul's missionary travels, with no sign of active resistance. Bauer remarks:

> [T]he book ends with the portrait of the gospel unconstrained by any force... proclaimed in the midst of the great and mighty power structures of the world. Finally, at Rome, even Paul's imprisonment, which is itself an expression of the power of imperial Rome, no longer provides any ultimate, or even serious, impediment.[25]

Luke thereby instructs his readers to expect that evil must be confronted and disturbed in Rome, targeting both avarice and idolatry—including the imperial cult. As Paul contested officials in Philippi and rattled Festus, so, too, he would confront Caesar. The text also implies that socioeconomic and military exploitation demand scrutiny, and that even Caesar himself may hear God's proclaimed word.

Synthesis

In Acts 20–28, themes of greed and generosity continue. Paul's avoidance of covetous behavior (Acts 20:33), his funding of the disciples' purity rites (Acts 21:23–26), and his offering for Jerusalem (Acts 24:17) all exemplify generosity. Meanwhile, greed appears in the bribery articulated by the Roman commanding officer (Acts 22:28) and by Felix (Acts 24:26), who endeavors to profit from and manipulate Paul's situation. Greed also motivates the centurion, shipowner, and captain (Acts 27:11, 38), who persist in a perilous voyage for economic gain, nearly costing lives. Yet generosity triumphs at Malta, serving as a sign of evil's defeat (Acts 28:2).

Acts 20–28 likewise reveals the dark forces. Paul explicitly refers to spiritual darkness in Acts 26:17–18, while dark powers remain implicit throughout his journey to Rome. Attempts on Paul's life by Jewish leaders

---

25. Bauer, *Acts as Story*, 247.

(Acts 21:31, 22:22, 23:12, 25:3), and the self-serving responses of Felix and Festus (Acts 24:24–26; 26:24–31) represent malevolent efforts to stop him from reaching Rome. The profit-driven decision to sail in hazardous conditions (Acts 27:11, 38), the storm, and the viper (Acts 28:3–6) also embody dark forces seeking to thwart Paul's mission.

Paul's sea voyage evokes parallels to Jonah's mission. Jonah journeyed by sea to a foreign seat of imperial darkness, Nineveh. In spite of his reluctance, astonishing repentance ensued. However, through the parallel of trials of the sea voyage to Rome, another seat of empire, Luke's readers realize that Paul, as an empowered and willing representative of Jesus, is even greater than Jonah (Luke 11:32).[26] Evoking a connection to Jonah further underscores the expectation of a remarkable act of repentance in Rome. As Wright observes, "The dark powers have done their worst. Once again Paul . . . has put his faith in the God who raises the dead, the God who wins the victory over the forces of evil."[27]

---

26. Wright, *Paul: A Biography*, 379.
27. Wright, *Paul: A Biography*, 382.

Chapter 10: Subverting Empire— Limited Good, Symbolic Challenges, and Social Upheaval in Acts

The Christians are the occasion of all the mischief in the world. If the Tiber overflows, and Nile does not; if heaven stands still and withholds its rain, and the earth quakes; if famine or pestilence take their marches through the country, the word is, Away with these Christians to the lion.[1]

—Tertullian

Chapter 10 interprets the cosmic duel through the lens of several theories that demonstrate the potential threat to imperial domination. First, the Spirit is considered according to the concept of limited good, integrating this socioeconomic framework with Luke's depiction of spiritual opposition. It then situates the church's interactions with Roman power, economic systems, and religious structures within the broader sociopolitical landscape, drawing on insights from Horsley and MacMullen.

Spirit and Limited Good in Defeat of Evil

The concept of limited good, as proposed by George Foster, contends that all desirable resources—material, social, or symbolic—exist in finite quantities within a given community.[2] This perspective, derived from Foster's

---

1. Tert. *Apol.* 40.1.
2. Foster, "Peasant Society," 293–315; "Second Look," 57–64.

analysis of peasant societies where scarcity defines daily life, frames existence as a zero-sum game: any gain by one individual or group corresponds to a loss for another.³ It is not merely a response to material paucity but a deeply embedded cultural viewpoint shaping behaviors, relationships, and social structures. In such contexts, resources like land, food, and water are perceived as non-expandable; acquiring more typically means dispossessing a neighbor, and an increase in one family's harvest signifies a reduction in another's.⁴ This outlook extends to intangible goods like honor, power, and reputation, viewed as part of a closed system in which any increase in one realm necessitates a decrease elsewhere.

A defining feature of the limited good perspective is its inherent sense of depletion, wherein all good things—tangible or intangible—are believed to diminish over time.⁵ This belief fosters anxiety about acquisition and a communal vigilance against perceived imbalances, for when one household gains wealth or social standing, it is seen as destabilizing the community's equilibrium.⁶ Consequently, conspicuous consumption and accumulation are discouraged, and those who amass excess resources or status are viewed with suspicion. The same zero-sum logic applies to symbolic and relational dimensions: honor is treated as finite, and strengthening certain social bonds may weaken others. This perception of ever-diminishing opportunities fuels envy and rivalry, underscoring the conviction that every gain must come at another's expense.⁷

Although most observable in agrarian societies, the concept of limited good also manifests in urban and metropolitan settings, where competition for resources, power, and influence intensifies.⁸ Urban centers, with their dense populations and concentrations of wealth and power, amplify the finite nature of commodities such as housing, employment opportunities, and social capital.⁹ For instance, the availability of prime real estate is

---

3. Foster, "Peasant Society," 293–315.
4. Foster, "Peasant Society," 293–315.
5. Foster, "Peasant Society," 293–315.
6. Foster, "Peasant Society," 293–315.
7. Foster, "Peasant Society," 293–315.

8. See Harvey, *Rebel Cities*; *Urban Experience*; Massey and Denton, *American Apartheid*; Glaeser, *Triumph of the City*; Logan and Molotch, *Urban Fortunes*; Low, *On the Plaza*; Simone, *For the City*; Putnam, *Bowling Alone*; Bourdieu, *Distinction*; Sassen, *Global City*; and Zukin, *Loft Living*.

9. To consider such contexts in the ancient setting, see Horsley, *Paul and Empire*; Malina, *NT World*; Friesen, *Imperial Cults*; "Poverty in Pauline Studies," 323–61; Garnsey

limited, and rising demand drives prices higher, making access increasingly exclusive.[10] The acquisition of a desirable property by one party can feel like a direct loss to others who are priced out. Success in these arenas reinforces perceptions of scarcity, as achievements are seen to draw from a restricted pool of opportunities.[11]

In both rural and urban contexts, the belief that good things are finite shapes individual behaviors and societal norms.[12] Fear of depletion and the desire to maintain balance influence cultural values, economic practices, and political systems.[13] In traditional societies, this often results in an emphasis on redistribution and communal sharing, discouraging the hoarding of resources or power by a few.[14] Yet in metropolitan settings, these dynamics are complicated by cultural, ethnic, and economic diversity, heightening tensions as communities vie for access to resources, opportunities, and recognition.[15] Such tensions become particularly acute where inequality is stark and resource distribution appears inequitable, sometimes manifesting as social movements, political unrest, or systemic discrimination. Thus, the limited good worldview persists across diverse societal landscapes.

Several scholars have applied the limited-good theory to New Testament studies.[16] However, most agree that Luke wrote to an (Hellenistic) educated reader—perhaps even a member of the aristocracy. If true, then a limited-good worldview might have been less intrinsic to an elitist audience in an urban setting. Nevertheless, the epic qualities of Luke-Acts, which function as a bridge between high and popular literature,[17] made such historiography accessible to more common readers. In this context, Theophilus, as noted throughout this project, may represent the status of the recipient Luke intends the reader to imagine. A more common

---

and Saller, *Roman Empire*; Fitzgerald, *Greco-Roman Perspectives*; Ste. Croix, *Class Struggle*; Meeks, *First Urban Christians*; and Hanson, *Cities of God*.

10. Zukin, *Loft Living*, x; Logan and Molotch, *Urban Fortunes*, 18; Low, *On the Plaza*, 86–87.

11. Low, *On the Plaza*, 18–19; Logan and Molotch, *Urban Fortunes*, 34.

12. Low, *On the Plaza*, 20–21; Harvey, *Rebel Cities*, 80.

13. Low, *On the Plaza*, 64–65.

14. Low, *On the Plaza*, 56–57; Harvey, *Rebel Cities*, 70–71.

15. Harvey, *Rebel Cities*, xi; Logan and Molotch, *Urban Fortunes*, 34.

16. See Malina, *NT World*, 87–110; Rohrbaugh, *Social Sciences*, 17–42; Neyrey, *Honor and Shame*, 8–25; DeSilva, *Honor, Patronage, Kinship, Purity*, 31–59; and Esler, *Community and Gospel*, 50–75.

17. Bonz, *Past as Legacy*, loc. 2235 of 3386.

populace—those benefiting from the great reversal—would have been far more inclined toward a limited-good worldview and its zero-sum implications, nurtured by Rome's socioeconomic policies.

Luke uses limited-good conceptuality in his writings as directly noted in narrative events. For example, Simon Magus loses power upon Philip's arrival in Samaria (Acts 8:4–24) and the threat to Bar-Jesus/Elymas upon Paul and Barnabas's audience with Sergius Paulus (Acts 13:4–11). Moreover, the depletion of profit in both Philippi (Acts 16:11–40) and Ephesus (Acts 19:8–41) illustrates this phenomenon. Other portions of Luke's texts demonstrate this factor. Examples include Mary's remarks on the elevation of the lowly and hungry, contrasted with the downfall of the wealthy and rulers (Luke 1:52–53). Simeon also expresses that Jesus will cause the "rising and falling of many" (Luke 2:34). In the Sermon on the Plain, Jesus offers blessings and woes in a way that reflects zero-sum qualities (Luke 6:20–26). Additional examples include character juxtapositions of the Pharisee and the sinful woman (Luke 7:36–50), the wealthy man and Lazarus (Luke 16:19–31), and the Pharisee and tax collector (Luke 18:9–14).

Undoubtedly, Luke's writings (and their oral retelling) circulated among people of diverse social strata and across multiple regions, many of whom would have held a limited-good worldview. These recipients were also likely familiar with Second Temple Jewish eschatological texts that envisioned a final battle between light and darkness, resulting in the restoration of God's kingdom and the exile of its imperial foes.[18] Throughout Luke-Acts, a progressive reallocation of power unfolds: the Gospel's opening sections establish its eschatological implications (highlighted in chapter 3 of this study). The examined pericopes of this project detail socioeconomic rebalancing wherein societal mechanisms of control are challenged, along with the evil powers supporting them. Likewise, literary features in chapter 7 portray God's kingdom gaining strength as it advances toward Rome. The dark powers are increasingly subdued, culminating in what appears to be a final effort to hinder Paul's arrival in the imperial capital. Upon reaching Rome, Paul preaches with boldness and without hindrance, signaling the ultimate defeat of evil. The text repeatedly emphasizes judgments upon dark powers and their agents—from Satan's fall to Agrippa I's death. From a limited good perspective, with its zero-sum dynamic, the

---

18. 1QM (War Scroll) 1.10; 1 En. 37–71; Pss. Sol. 17.26–27; Jub. 1.28–29; 4 Ezra 7.28–30; T. Mos. 10.1; 2 Bar. 40.1; Sib. Or. 3.702–4; Wis. 4.20.

ascendance of God's power entails the corresponding diminishment—indeed, the depletion—of malevolent forces.

Ephesus furnishes a compelling illustration of this dynamic: widespread repentance leads to the abandonment of magical practices and temple cultic rituals, rendering both nearly obsolete. Concurrently, the Holy Spirit's efficacy grows through tangible acts, such as cloths imbued with divine power, thereby amplifying God's word. A limited-good worldview might interpret Paul's determination to reach the imperial center—fueled by events in Ephesus—as both a culmination and a further test of the zero-sum trajectory outlined in Acts 1–19.

Building on earlier findings about socioeconomic subversion and the erosion of dark powers, Luke's audience would interpret Paul's relative safety in Rome as evidence of God's Spirit expelling evil and exposing avarice. It would also be seen as the Spirit overturning idolatry at the core of imperial authority. This view accords with the Lukan corpus, where satanic and demonic influence recedes steadily, leaving only human rulers entrenched in darkness. Thus, the final conflict in Rome functions as the "endgame," confirming the cosmic duel motif centered on the downfall of greed. It demonstrates that as God's power increases, evil forces reach exhaustion, fulfilling the trajectory established in the previous chapters and culminating in an eschatological finale.

Horsley's Legion Hypothesis

Exorcisms fulfill a critical role in the cosmic duel with limited-good implications. In the collectivist culture of the first-century Mediterranean setting, illness was not primarily regarded as a personal dilemma but as an indication of community issues, with afflicted members symbolizing disorder in corporate life. Consequently, disease served as a "sign or emblem that marked what a group values, devalues, and preoccupies itself with."[19] Many of Jesus's actions constituted "political acts," demonstrating a sense of "treason" through his superior power in reorganizing his social world.[20] Jesus's exorcisms represented a social reordering that restored appropriate physical and social balance.[21]

---

19. Pilch, *Healing in NT*, locs. 1254–55 of 2182.
20. Pilch, "Jesus's Healing Activity," 154.
21. Pilch, *Healing in NT*, locs. 1251–53 of 2182.

Horsley further draws on a cultural anthropological perspective, describing exorcism as being interrelated with "political and economic forces," functioning as an alternative (and even competing) power.[22] Jesus's works provided an alternative to the powers that had led to social disintegration. Horsley applies these insights to Second Temple Judaism, referencing the War Scroll (1QM) found at Qumran. In it, the sons of light battle the sons of darkness, who are described as being "in close collaboration with the invading Romans" in a culminating cosmic duel.[23]

Horsley's assessment frames spiritual possession as a depiction of colonialism. Just as Douglas associates physical orifices with social openings,[24] Horsley views possession as the invasion of foreign and unclean spirits. This symbolizes corporate possession and occupation by external powers, particularly Rome, who have entered the social gateways through a series of imperial impositions.

Horsley applies his model to Mark 5:1–20 (corresponding to Luke 8:26–39), contending that the designation "Legion" represents Roman military presence. He argues that the narrative sequence involving a "herd" of swine uses terminology associated with soldiers, with their being "dismissed" by Jesus reflecting a military command. Their subsequent "charge" into the sea mirrors military action and evokes the Mediterranean, symbolizing the empire's origin.[25] Moreover, their drowning signifies not only their expulsion but also, through exodus imagery, an imperial defeat (Exod 15:1–10).[26]

This interpretation is broadly shared by others who note that the tenth legion, stationed in the region and active in suppressing the Jewish Revolt, ironically used the boar (swine) as its symbol.[27] Significantly, to many Jews, the boar imagery was particularly offensive, representing an unclean animal.[28] Moreover, the swine located on a hill correlate to Rome as the proverbial "city on a hill." According to Perrin, "Luke's readers may well have read between the lines to learn that the powerful forces of pagan Rome would

---

22. Singer, "Reinventing Medical Anthropology," 181.
23. Horsley, *Jesus and the Powers*, 118; see also 1QM 1:3–4, 13–14; 17:5–8; 18:4–5.
24. See Douglas, *Purity and Danger*, 122–29, regarding orifices.
25. Horsley, *Jesus and the Powers*, 112, 127.
26. Horsley, *Jesus and the Powers*, 112, 127.
27. Wallis, *Galilean Wonderworker*, 119.
28. Witmer, *Jesus, Galilean Exorcist*, 172.

one day succumb to Jesus's power."[29] The text includes additional associations with uncleanness, including references to gentiles and tombs, offering a broader indication of impure idolatry tied to the imperial presence.[30]

Jesus's exorcisms, like his healings, restored appropriate social order (Luke 4:33–35; 6:18–19; 7:21; 8:2, 35; 9:1, 37–42; 11:14; 13:11–12, 32). While demons are not mentioned after Luke 13:32, unclean spirits—absent from the Gospel after 13:11–12—are referenced four times in Acts (5:16, 8:7, 16:18, 19:12). Each instance illustrates the restoration of proper social balance. Additionally, the devil appears twice in Acts, although passively: first, in Peter's proclamation of Jesus's victory (Acts 10:38), and second, in Paul's rebuke of Elymas (Acts 13:10–11). Overcoming evil—and blinding the magician—leads to Sergius Paulus's reception of Paul's message. While the magician moves from light (seeing the sun) to darkness, this imperial agent's movement from darkness to light symbolizes his alignment with Luke's appropriate social, theological, and spiritual framework.

Satan's chaotic reign had also been a threat when Jesus sent out his disciples (Luke 10:18; 13:16). However, though Satan had sown disorder among them (Luke 22:3, 31; Acts 5:3), the Acts narrative demonstrates the Spirit's ultimate triumph over these disruptions (Acts 20–28). An intrinsic quality of evil spirits was their ability to weave an unnatural tapestry within the possessed, rendering the individual polluted due to that spirit's occupation (hence their designation as impure). This blending of incompatible substances was a hallmark of uncleanness according to Old Testament purity codes. Jesus's exorcisms thematically connect to Zech 13:2, which speaks of purification from idolatry, which is particularly significant in Acts where the Mediterranean region's prevalent paganism was evident. In contrast with the evil spirits' pollution, the power of the Spirit progressively generates order and purity.

In Samaria, unclean spirits are both explicitly mentioned (Acts 8:7) and implicitly present in Simon Magus's empowerment. Similar themes of pagan worship emerge in other accounts, including the divine attribution of Agrippa I, Paul's encounter with Elymas in Cyprus, and the spirit of divination in Philippi. Additionally, the expulsion of occupying forces occurs by garments Paul had touched in Ephesus. These episodes are intertwined with idolatrous practices in society, from the Artemis cult to Caesar

---

29. Perrin, *Luke*, 159.

30. Perrin, *Luke*, 157–59; see also *Jesus the Temple*, 160.

worship. Yet, in every case, idolatry and the associated dark spirits are confronted and decisively defeated.

Horsley's reading underscores a dark conflict in Luke-Acts, revealing the Holy Spirit's superior power over evil, with Jesus's expulsion of demons (and possibly healings) as micro-level responses to the macro-level reality of imperial occupation. Applied to Acts, this theory suggests that as the disciples expand "to the ends of the earth" (Rome), dark forces are expelled by the Spirit's dominant power. This is evidenced by events in Samaria, Cyprus, Philippi, and Ephesus. This trajectory positions the book's conclusion as a climactic escalation of the Spirit's war against evil, culminating in Rome.

Rome was the logical endpoint of this cosmic trajectory, functioning as the most tangible symbol of institutional evil and unholy possession on earth. The Roman imperial system aggressively occupied and extracted resources from various lands, maintaining its self-serving order through violence and oppression. Such an arrangement constituted an unclean relationship wherein an alien force violated purity, caused socioeconomic disruption, and perpetuated idolatry.

The literary focus on Paul's journey to Rome applies and tests the interpretive framework developed earlier. It demonstrates that the exorcistic dynamic at work in Samaria, Caesarea, Philippi, and Ephesus continues consistently as it moves toward the empire's center. If dark powers are disrupted in smaller contexts, their final confrontation in Rome represents a far-reaching cosmic exorcism, releasing creation from imperial captivity and signaling a socioeconomic rebalancing akin to that already demonstrated. In this view, Acts becomes more than apologetic: it proclaims a resolute conflict with imperial interests.

Ephesus, where dark spirits yielded even to Spirit-empowered cloth and cultic temples emptied out, foreshadows Paul's (and Luke's) vision for Rome (Acts 19:21). In this respect, Horsley's theory—integrated with the findings of this study—highlights the political implications of an exorcism movement initiated by Jesus in Galilee and progressively entrusted to his disciples across the Mediterranean. Positioning Rome as the final arena of this escalating duel tests the same forces and motifs documented earlier. It allows readers to anticipate similarly disruptive—yet ultimately triumphant—encounters at the empire's core, confirming the study's broader conclusions about the diminishing power of darkness in Luke's account.

MacMullen's Enemies of the Roman Order

Ramsay MacMullen's framework for imperial subversion helps test this study's findings on the cosmic duel in Luke-Acts. That narrative depicts the early church as a disruptive force challenging idolatry and imperial ideology. These overlaps between Roman perceptions of subversion and Luke's portrayal of Christianity invite closer engagement with MacMullen's categories, especially prophecy, philosophy, magic, and urban unrest. MacMullen's work, including *Enemies of the Roman Order: Treason, Unrest, and Alienation in the Empire*, integrates historical, political, social, religious, and economic factors. It shows how Rome responded to perceived threats comparable to Christianity. He categorizes disruptive factors beginning with Cato and Brutus, then philosophers, magicians, diviners, prophets, astrologers, urban unrest, outsiders, and an appendix on famines and brigandage. This study reorganizes those categories to show how Acts aligns with what Rome deemed subversive, clarifying whether Luke presents Christianity as anti-imperial or merely religious.

Metaphysical Dangers—Philosophy, Prophecy, Magic, Divination, and Astrology

Introduction

Philosophy, prophecy, magic, divination, and astrology each represented distinct yet overlapping sources of power in ancient Rome, often challenging imperial structure. Philosophy, emphasizing knowledge, critiqued tyrannical governance and socioeconomic ethics, including wealth-driven ambition and exploitation of lower classes.[31] Prophecy offered divine revelation that could conflict with Rome's political narrative.[32] Magic sought to influence visible and invisible realms, empowering marginal groups and provoking deities' suspicion. Divination and astrology likewise interpreted future events, sometimes undermining Roman methods and disturbing the social order. These practices lay beyond state regulation,[33] so emperors passed laws banning them, punishing practitioners with expulsion or execution while confiscating or burning associated materials.[34]

---

31. MacMullen, *Enemies of Roman Order*, 46–48, 51–55.
32. MacMullen, *Enemies of Roman Order*, 134, 137–40.
33. Gupta, *Strange Religion*, 13–14.
34. MacMullen, *Enemies of Roman Order*, 97–98, 128–32, 134–36.

Philosophy and Prophecy

Applying MacMullen's imaginative reading not only affirms but also expands Walz's assessment regarding Theophilus's likely perspective of the alternate magic practiced by the church.[35] For example, the church's authoritative and prophetic speech mirrored certain philosophical critiques, including socioeconomic ethics and authoritative demonstrations of governance. Skinner observes, "What they teach about Jesus Christ asks people to embrace new religious, social, political, and economic values. This sometimes puts proclaimers and audiences at odds with the established social order."[36] Moreover, Paul's discussions in the hall of Tyrannus (Acts 19:9), debates at the Areopagus (Acts 17:18–20), and discourse with Felix (Acts 24:25) each appear philosophical.

Likewise, prophecy plays a central role in Luke-Acts. It shapes moments such as Pentecost (Acts 2:17–18), Agabus's famine prediction (Acts 11:27–30), and warnings of Paul's arrest (Acts 21:10–14). In MacMullen's framework, prophecy primarily refers to foretelling, which heightened Roman suspicion toward groups claiming divine insight into future events (which might conflict with the imperial narratives). MacMullen discusses the role of παρρησία among ancient philosophers, a term revisited multiple times in this study. It appears in the final passage of Acts (28:30–31), identifying bold public speech as a chief means of resisting tyranny. This study shows how παρρησία challenges greed and economic exploitation within imperial structures. The prophetic voice in Acts confronts spiritual and material corruption, especially the economic greed that props up oppressive systems. MacMullen's insights confirm that prophecy was dangerous not just for its predictions but also for its capacity to unsettle power structures.[37]

Magic

What many consider miracles, an ancient audience perceived as magic.[38] Yet, there was "no period in the history of the empire in which the magician

---

35. Walz, "Cursing Paul: Magical Contests," 168.

36. Skinner, *Intrusive God, Disruptive Gospel*, 137.

37. MacMullen, *Enemies of Roman Order*, 64–66. Examples include: Musonius Rufus, *Exile*; Epictetus, *Disc.* 1; Pliny, *Pan.* 1; Eur. *Phoen.* 388–89; Seneca, *Ben.* 7; Plut. *Mor.*; Dio Chrys. *Or.* 13–14; Cassius Dio, *Hist.* 67; Favorinus in Philostr. *Vit. Soph.* 489.

38. Crossan, *Historical Jesus*, 307.

was not considered an enemy of society."[39] Acts depicts magical contests in confrontations with Simon Magus (Acts 8:9–24) and Elymas (Acts 13:8–12), who pursued supernatural power for personal gain. Rome saw magic as illicit, private power threatening the imperial order, which placed the emperor at the pinnacle of religious authority. Hence, the early church's miracles and exorcisms fell under suspicion as unauthorized supernatural practices, especially when they undermined economic structures. Similarly, events like the deaths of Judas (Acts 1:15–20), Ananias and Sapphira (Acts 5:1–11), and Agrippa I (Acts 12:21–23) display divine judgment resembling magical intervention. They heighten perceptions of supernatural activity.

Divination

The book of Acts depicts divination-like practices, including the casting of lots to replace Judas (Acts 1:26), mirroring Roman diviners who interpreted entrails (Acts 1:15–20). Paul's vision of safe passage to Rome (Acts 23:11) and other visions also recall forms of divination. The empire might have read events like the earthquake in Philippi (Acts 16:25–26) or Peter's Pentecost signs (Acts 2:16–21) as astrological omens. While the church in Acts defies neat categorization, it intersects strongly with philosophy and prophecy. Ancient audiences likely saw magic, divination, and astrology as intertwined. Overlapping features among these variables suggest that by the time Paul reached Rome, the disciple movement was deemed subversive.

Subversive Forces—Brigandage, Famines, Insiders, and Outsiders

Introduction

MacMullen identifies four additional categories relevant to Acts, each with overlapping features. Brigands, synonymous with bandits, often operated on Rome's margins. Economic crises, including famines, exacerbated this threat, highlighting Rome's wealth and power disparities. Additionally, Roman politicians were vulnerable to subversive behavior.

Several variables align with "social banditry," offering a framework for understanding Luke-Acts, though with modifications. In the first century, social banditry arose in vulnerable peasant communities oppressed by

---

39. MacMullen, *Enemies of Roman Order*, 125–26.

Rome.[40] Heavy taxation, debt, land seizures, and foreign control spurred bandit movements seeking justice and reparation from policymakers.[41]

In Horsley's model, social banditry functioned as a revolutionary resistance to injustice, often preceding revolt.[42] These movements addressed immediate injustices, not broader systemic transformation. Wright identifies three key traits: concern for the marginalized, nonviolent factions, and ambiguous peasant-government interactions.[43] Because of stark wealth disparities, social banditry rose in first-century Palestine, contributing to the First Jewish Revolt, soon after Paul's arrival in Rome (Acts). Simultaneously, Christianity emerged in Luke's narrative to confront Roman injustice.

While social banditry usually involved peasants, the church in Acts reflects Wright's banditry markers—socioeconomic concerns, nonviolence, and cross-class engagement—adapted to urban contexts. A strength of the early church was the effectiveness in developing community ties among the marginalized.[44] However, when the state disapproved, it labelled such movements as terrorism.[45] This study's evidence suggests the church in Acts faced a similar perception.

The Threat of Banditry

Paul's arrest in Jerusalem, stemming from a modest disruption, leads to his Roman trial. A centurion labels him σικάριος (Acts 21:38). This charge implies Roman suspicion of Paul's link to the Sicarii, a group "associated with revolt, robbery, and assassination."[46] Though banditry was often rural, Josephus highlights the Sicarii's bold urban operations, especially during festivals like Pentecost.[47] Their emergence stemmed from "the alienation of the people

---

40. Murphy, *Early Judaism*, 286.
41. Murphy, *Early Judaism*, 286.
42. Horsley, *Jesus Spiral of Violence*, 25, 37–39.
43. Wright, *Jesus Victory of God*, 215.
44. See Stark, *Cities of God*.
45. Horsley, *Jesus Spiral of Violence*, 20–21. See also Murphy, *Early Judaism*, 289.
46. Wenkel, "Sicarii," *LBD*, states, "In the Roman Empire, although it is difficult to separate 'Sicarii' from 'robbers,' the use of σικάριος (sikarios) in Acts 21:38 indicates a political agenda, not simply the theft of money and goods."
47. Josephus, *J.W.* 2.254–57 and *Ant.* 20.162–63; 185–87.

of the countryside, due to the hardships of direct Roman rule."[48] This hybrid movement incorporated both "urban poor and the rural peasants."[49]

Comparing the church to banditry, including the Sicarii, requires some creativity, yet distinctions remain. Still, Acts shows justice served on greedy traitors exemplifying systemic wealth imbalance (e.g., Judas, Ananias, Sapphira). Agrippa's actions (Acts 12:1–24) depict apostolic leaders as criminals or terrorists, a Roman strategy to suppress perceived threats. The narrative records Herod Agrippa I's divine execution, Elymas's blinding, and Simon Magus's earlier disempowerment. A Roman reader like Theophilus might see this epic or novelistic progression in two ways. Whether read as history or prophetic imagination, Acts shows the Jesus movement confronting socioeconomic exploitation with harsh methods. This outcome unsettles the Roman order in ways matching Wright's banditry: too minor for military suppression yet sufficiently disruptive.[50]

Social banditry had a "fluid" association with other popular movements opposed to Rome,[51] arguably including the church in Acts, which expanded from the peasant areas of Galilee ultimately into Roman urban centers. Societal unrest appeared in Philippi, Thessalonica, Corinth, Ephesus, and Jerusalem. Although banditry was mainly rural, Acts depicts a mobilized metropolitan counter-movement. Social bandits often "abandoned their land and lived outside the law."[52] Jesus and his apostles display detachment from property—first in Galilee (Luke 5:11, 18:29) and then in Jerusalem where they sell land and face judicial trouble while associating with cryptic deaths of would-be elitists (Judas, Ananias and Sapphira). Luke implies Agrippa I targeted the apostles for such activities. A perceptive reader might see Barnabas, who sold land, and Paul as agents of sociopolitical reform. Paul's travels left public controversy and challenged Roman order.

Before Jesus intervened, Paul displayed aggression toward Christians, revealing a militant personality as he was "breathing out murderous threats" (Acts 9:1 NIV). This aggressiveness emerges at Philippi, where he defied Roman ethos, disrupted profit, and aided the exploited, hallmarks of social banditry. Like bandit Bulla Felix freeing Roman prisoners,[53] Acts narrates similar

48. Freyne, "Galilee: Hellenistic/Roman," 2:897–98.
49. Levine, "Jewish War," 3:840.
50. Wright, *Jesus Victory of God*, 214.
51. Wright, *Jesus Victory of God*, 218.
52. Murphy, *Early Judaism*, 286.
53. Cassius Dio, *Hist.* 77.10.1.

releases: Peter (Acts 12) and Paul (Acts 16). In Thessalonica, Paul leaves under suspicion of undermining Roman ethos, much like a stealthy criminal.

Rome's robust roads and military force aimed to deter bandits,[54] yet Paul exploited those same routes for political rebellion in urban centers. Social banditry thrived through a "favorable relationship with the peasants," the inferior class.[55] By the second century, Celcus notes the church's appeal among the marginalized,[56] affirming Luke's focus on the poor benefiting from reversal.

Bandits sometimes gained power and wealth.[57] Similarly, the Jerusalem church benefited when funds were laid at the apostles' feet, introducing greed (e.g., Judas, Ananias, Sapphira, Simon Magus). Acts of the Apostles shows the church countering this threat through redistribution. Bandit groups often gathered around charismatic leaders,[58] as seen in John the Baptist, who left home while advancing a political message. Such leadership likewise appears in Jesus's ministry, the Jerusalem church, and Paul's broader mission.

Bandit leaders were often romanticized by supporters, including in literature, yet criticized by opponents, as seen in Luke's account.[59] Paul's reputation is shaped by gossip (Acts 14:19; 17:13; 18:12–13; 21:27–28; 24:1–9) and Tacitus's state-biased writings.[60] Writing between 115 to 120 CE, Tacitus depicts the church as vile, criminal in origin, and antisocial. He claims this justified Nero's blame for Rome's great fire and the gruesome martyrdoms that followed. This exemplified the balance of romantic literature (like Acts) to that of detractors.

The Threat of Famines

Other "ecological factors" also contributed to rising banditry.[61] A key shift in Acts is the Antioch congregation's emergence, enabling Mediterranean

---

54. Meeks, *First Urban Christians*, 17.
55. Heard and Yamazaki-Ransom, "Revolutionary Movements," 790.
56. Origen, *Cels.* 3.59.
57. Crossan, *Historical Jesus*, 170.
58. Hanson, "Jesus and Social Bandits," 292.
59. MacMullen, *Enemies of Roman Order*, 192–93.
60. Tac. *Ann.* 15.44; Minucius Felix, *Oct.* Minicuis Felix also accused the church of cannibalism.
61. See Hanson, "Jesus and Social Bandits," 291, regarding ecological factors.

expansion. This coincides with Agabus's predicted famine (an ecological factor) and the church's aid to Judea. Agrippa I's mismanagement, tied to a trade war, aligns with his persecution of James and Peter. The famine likely spurred a movement resembling adapted social banditry, targeting the empire's injustices and disciplining economic elites.

Acts 4:31 shows the Jerusalem church praying for political boldness (παρρησία),[62] followed by "ecological factors," including structural shaking reminiscent of an earthquake. A similar quake occurs in Philippi when Paul confronts colonial power. The term reappears in Thessalonica (Acts 17:13) and in Rome (Acts 28:31), linking seismic and political disruption. Luke uses earthquakes as narrative signposts, while Tertullian notes Rome's blame of Christians for ecological disasters.[63] Nero, ruling during Paul's presumed arrival, accused Christians of igniting Rome's great fire. Luke's account of a noteworthy fire in Ephesus (Acts 19:18–20) echoes that suspicion and implies growing Christian impact on imperial centers.

Insider Threats

MacMullen notes how military deserters often fueled banditry, citing Maternus as an example.[64] Luke highlights Cornelius, a centurion who converts under Peter's influence. The Philippian jailer also demonstrates subversive change upon conversion. By Acts 27–28, the centurion guarding Paul yields to him, symbolizing Rome's subordination at the narrative's close.

Rome also feared prominent politicians who might threaten imperial authority. Figures like Cato, Brutus, Cassius, Cremutius Cordus, and Thrasea Paetus exemplify such betrayal. Stark posits that religious movements generally begin among the privileged, explaining Christianity's rise.[65] Both Cornelius, a centurion, and Sergius Paulus, a proconsul, illustrate the church's influence. They each depict an archetype of the church's effectiveness, influence, and disciple targets. However, a reader like Theophilus might question if these Roman officials violate Christian virtues (by promulgating Roman ethics) if they will meet the same fate of others who betray the apostolic ethos (Judas, Ananias, and Sapphira). Such a proposition generates a fundamental tension among these Roman characters. While

62. Alternate translation is "truth to power."
63. Tert. *Apol.* 40.1.
64. Herodian, *Hist.* 1.10.1–6.
65. Stark, *Triumph of Christianity*, 88. See also *Rise of Christianity*.

later events in Acts do not explicitly indicate the conversion of additional Roman or civic leaders—apart from the Asiarchs in Ephesus who generally were associated with the imperial cult. However, Luke shows the Holy Spirit favoring Paul by dissuading political influencers from interference (Acts 18:12–17; 19:28–41; 24:1–27; 25:1–12; 28:7–10).

Outsider Threats

MacMullen frames communities as "outsiders" as those existing within imperial confines who form an alternate society while describing Christians as the "supreme proof" of such movements.[66] Therefore, as the church integrated into all facets of Roman society, it posed a risk. Douglas's purity guidelines, applied to societal boundaries, suggest that as outsiders infiltrated the core of the Roman world—represented by Paul's arrival in Acts 28—they generated severe concerns about cultural and political purity at the imperial capital. Yet, the early church aimed to disciple both elites and the marginalized, leading Tertullian to note Christian presence at every social level by the second century, including the palace and Senate.[67] Clearly, allowing influence by "outsiders" posed a relevant risk to the imperial infrastructure.

Urban Unrest and the Threat to Idolatry

MacMullen contends that urban life posed a notable threat to Roman stability. He identifies urban unrest as a primary source of danger. Discontent and feuds often reached public venues like theatres and amphitheaters.[68] Luke-Acts describes various urban disruptions, starting with Jesus's measured actions in rural Galilee and culminating in his entry into Jerusalem (Luke 19–21). The same city later witnesses apostolic disruptions (Acts 1–7). These accounts hint at borderline or potential unrest. Moreover, Paul's social encounters sparked borderline or overt disruption (Acts 9:1–31; 13:13–52; 14:8–20; 17:1–15, 16–34). He also incited major unrest and rioting (Acts 14:1–7; 16:16–40; 17:1–9; 18:1–7; 19:23–41; 21:27–36).

Luke's narrative also highlights MacMullen's view that Rome's greatest internal threat came from upper-class Greeks defending their Hellenistic

---

66. MacMullen, *Enemies of Roman Order*, 217.
67. Tert. *Apol.* 37.4; *Scorp.* 4.1–4; 5.1–3.
68. Stark, *Cities of God*, highlights the urban effectiveness of early Christianity.

"purity."[69] Pagan idolatry served as the hallmark of Greek socioreligious identity. This practice also held key political and historical implications. Idolatry intersects with dark powers and socioeconomic exploitation, as discussed in chapter 10 in the context of Ephesus. The book of Acts records a robust polemic against idolatry, including temple criticism across the Mediterranean. Examples include Stephen's speech (Acts 7:47–50), Lystra (14:11–18), the Jerusalem Council (15:20–29), the Areopagus (17:16–34), Corinth (18:12–17), and Ephesus (19:23–41). Similar critiques surface in Paul's remarks to Ephesian elders (20:19–21), his Jerusalem arrest (21:27–36), Agrippa II hearing (26:18), and Malta encounter (28:3–6). Each instance challenges pagan worship and often sparks disruption.

Cicero emphasizes *cultus deorum*[70] as reverence for the gods rooted in social and "national obligation."[71] The gods governed human destiny through blessings or curses. Thus, *pax deorum* required obedience and ritual reciprocity.[72] Homer's *Iliad* depicts mortal vulnerability under divine power while Porphyry likewise explains the appeasements demanded by these deities.[73]

The Roman worldview formed a socioeconomic "pyramid," placing chief gods at the apex, then lower gods and Caesars, followed by elites, and finally slaves.[74] This hierarchy was inherently theological. Luke's "great reversal" upended that structure, challenging imperial theology. By bypassing that hierarchy, Luke-Acts presents a countercultural movement akin to heresy against imperial theology. Those embracing Christianity became apostates under Roman belief. Livy cites divine anger against foreign cults, causing widespread disaster.[75] The gods also targeted the Roman army, seen in Germanicus's death. Suetonius observes that his loss sparked a citizen revolt against the gods.[76]

A century after Luke, Tertullian notes how Christians were blamed and persecuted for natural, geological, and meteorological disasters.[77]

---

69. MacMullen, *Enemies of Roman Order*, 189, 125–26.
70. Cic. *Nat. d.* 2.8.
71. Gupta, *Strange Religion*, 17.
72. Gupta, *Strange Religion*, 15–16.
73. Homer, *Il.* 24.525–33; Porphyry, *Abst.* 2.16.
74. Gupta, *Strange Religion*, 20–21.
75. Livy, *Hist.* 4.30.9–11.
76. Suet. *Cal.* 5.2.
77. Tert. *Apol.* 40.1.

Viewed as a foreign cult, they were labelled atheists for rejecting idolatry.[78] Thus, the church endangered Rome's social and political stability by angering its gods. Should Caesar tolerate such a group, those gods might punish emperor and empire. Tertullian echoes this perspective.

If Hellenistic tradition-keepers posed Rome's greatest threat, the church's war on dark powers entangled both Rome and Greece. Unless the empire acted decisively, Greece might blame Rome for tolerating anti-idolatrous treason. A Roman official reading how Ephesus nearly lost the Artemis cult (Acts 19) would see little sign of harmlessness.

Luke's critique of Rome's imperial cult is indirect but present. Divine honors grew more common in the late first century. Bird observes that "Luke's critique of idolatry is not partitioned from his suspicions about Roman authority because the two were intertwined."[79] Threatening Ephesus's Artemis cult, even hypothetically, hints at the potential loss of Caesar worship. Meanwhile, Luke records Paul's plan to visit Rome (Acts 19:21), anticipating similar imperial disruption as Ephesus.

Rome labelled the church atheist for rejecting idols and imperial cult rituals.[80] Thrasea Paetus, a philosopher and insider, was executed by Nero for similar nonparticipation.[81] Christians as outsiders would face even greater suspicion and hostility. Pliny the Younger similarly highlighted Christianity's refusal to worship Roman gods and its distinct socioeconomic ethics. Writing around 112 CE (approximately contemporaneous with Luke's writing), he resolved to execute Christians who did not recant.[82] He noted the movement's growth in rural and urban areas, affecting industries linked to temples and idols.[83]

Summing up the Threats to Empire

The church intersects with all MacMullen's Roman threat categories, though with varied nuances. Philosophical and prophetic traits are most evident, while magic, divination, astrology, and urban idolatry remain plausible.

---

78. Josephus, *Ag. Ap.* 2.148; Cassius Dio, *Hist.* 67.14; Mart. Pol. 3.2; Euseb. *Hist. eccl.* 3.13; Lucian, *Peregr.* 13; Porphyry, *Christ.* 1.2.3; Josephus, *Ant.* 14.68–78; Tac. *Hist.* 5.9.

79. Bird, *Bird's-Eye View*, 256.

80. See Epistle to Diognetus 6.3–4; Justin Martyr, *1 Apol.*

81. Tac. *Ann.* 16.21.

82. Pliny, *Ep.* 10.96–97.

83. Pliny, *Ep.* 10.96–97.

Banditry and political defection appear more subjective and less convincing. Yet portions of Acts imply a compelling scenario of church-empire tension. From a pagan view, the church does not appear benign. Theophilus, likely an aristocratic reader, would see evidence of conflict. However, when considering the narrative of the early church in Acts that overlaps with these various Roman threats, the weight of evidence produces a compelling scenario. Rather than appearing nonthreatening to Roman order, the church, when viewed from the perspective of a pagan, would present Theophilus, a presumed reader within Roman aristocracy, with substantial evidence of various tensions between church and empire.

A more creative proposal argues that rather than appearing neutral, Acts can be read as flaunting the church's power as existing outside of Roman regulation and even surpassing imperial forms of authority. Cicero's method of "guilt by association" creates a scenario in which readers of Acts of the Apostles perceive the church as aligned with each of MacMullen's categorical threats. Moreover, the original audience would likely recognize that Rome had responded to individuals and movements for far less subversive actions than those Luke reports. Likewise, early in Acts (5:34–39), Gamaliel makes comparison of the apostolic group to political revolutionaries. Meanwhile this idea emerges in the latter division of Acts (21:38), also in Jerusalem. Both times the movement is connected to subversive activity as Luke himself generates a lingering literary question.

Applying MacMullen's model reveals escalating conflict between the church and imperial authority in Acts. Earlier texts showed how the gospel clashed with economic structures in Cyprus, Philippi, and Ephesus. The unrest in those locations reflects disturbances that Roman officials wanted to quell. Luke thus portrays the church as dismantling the imperial status quo, not merely existing passively. MacMullen's categories clarify whether the early church was countercultural or deeply subversive, affirming that Acts depicts a divine-imperial battle.

Synthesis

This chapter has systematically tested the findings from the detailed textual analysis of seven key pericopes in Acts by applying them to the final arc of the narrative (Acts 20–28). Throughout the dissertation, Luke's presentation of economic ethics, spiritual opposition, and imperial structures reveals a pattern of divine power confronting and ultimately overcoming the forces of greed and darkness. This concluding chapter has extended that analysis by demonstrating how the broader cosmic struggle in Acts reaches its climax in Rome, where Paul, empowered by the Holy Spirit, arrives at the very heart of imperial power. This progression affirms that Luke's portrayal of the church's expansion is not merely historical but profoundly theological, with economic and sociopolitical implications.

The limited-good framework has provided a lens through which Luke's theological vision can be tested. Earlier pericopes established how the gospel's movement diminishes existing economic and religious structures—for example, in Philippi (Acts 16), the Spirit's intervention displaces economic exploitation tied to divination, and in Ephesus (Acts 19), the proclamation of Christ threatens the city's economy by destabilizing Artemis worship. By applying this framework to Acts 20–28, this chapter has shown that the zero-sum implications of the Holy Spirit's work remain consistent: as the kingdom advances, opposition intensifies, confirming that Luke depicts the gospel as a direct challenge to Rome's socioeconomic and spiritual order.

Furthermore, this chapter has tested the Legion hypothesis (Horsley) against the narrative of Acts, particularly regarding how possession, exorcisms, and social concerns interact within Luke's theological framework. The earlier textual analyses demonstrated that Luke connects exorcisms with broader societal and economic structures, portraying them as acts of resistance against systems of power. This model was applied to Paul's encounters in Acts 20–28, where his imprisonments, trials, and interactions with Roman authorities reinforce the notion that spiritual opposition mirrors imperial resistance. The study found that Luke's portrayal of Rome aligns with his depiction of demonic forces elsewhere, further supporting the argument that Acts presents a dual confrontation—against both spiritual and imperial powers.

Similarly, the MacMullen framework of Roman threats was applied and tested within Acts 20–28. The earlier textual investigations demonstrated that Christianity's engagement with prophecy, public speech (παρρησία), and economic structures positioned it as a disruptive force in the Roman world. By extending these insights to Paul's final journey, this chapter has confirmed that Luke's presentation of the church aligns with categories Rome viewed as subversive—philosophical movements, prophetic sects, and urban agitators. The disturbances in Philippi and Ephesus earlier in Acts foreshadow the growing imperial opposition in Acts 20–28, culminating in Paul's trial and arrival in Rome. This progression reinforces the pattern identified in the earlier pericopes: wherever the gospel advances, it disrupts economic, religious, and imperial power structures, confirming that Luke portrays the church as a force of divine upheaval.

This chapter has confirmed that the themes of economic reversal, confrontation with dark powers, and resistance to empire—established in the earlier pericopes—persist and escalate in Acts 20–28. Luke does not present the gospel as a peaceful addition to the Roman world; rather, he portrays it as a force that dismantles, disrupts, and replaces existing power structures. The cumulative evidence suggests that Acts does not function as a political apology for Christianity within the empire, but rather as a theological manifesto of divine victory over imperial and spiritual domination.

This study, therefore, reinforces that Luke presents the early church as engaged in a cosmic battle—one in which the victory over greed, exploitation, and oppression is realized through the work of the Spirit. If Theophilus or any other Roman elite were to interpret Luke-Acts through this lens, it would have been difficult to see it as anything other than a subversive text, presenting a kingdom in direct opposition to Rome. This final chapter, by testing and applying the findings from the earlier pericopes, affirms that Luke's overarching message is not imperial accommodation but rather the inevitable triumph of God's kingdom over all forces of darkness, including those of Rome itself.

Conclusion—From Darkness to Light: Greed and Liberation in Luke-Acts

[T]he relationship between Acts and Empire clearly remains an unfinished and important discussion.[1]

—Jeremy Punt

Synthesis

THE INTRODUCTION OF THIS study lays the theological and literary foundation for understanding Luke-Acts as a unified narrative that depicts a cosmic conflict where greed and dark spiritual powers are closely linked. These two motifs, often treated separately in scholarship, function in tandem throughout the Lukan corpus, particularly within seven key pericopes in Acts. In these seven foundational passages, Luke presents greed not merely as an ethical issue but as a weapon of the dark powers. Current scholarship tends to isolate socioeconomic, spiritual, and political themes, especially in Acts 10–28. This study bridges those divides. Luke-Acts is perceived as prophetic historiography—a narrative shaped to reveal theological truth and confront imperial ideology.

The study begins with a brief overview of the interplay of spiritual evil and economic injustice in Luke's Gospel. Jesus's confrontation with these opposing forces sets the stage for Acts as a continuation of that struggle. The chosen pericopes in Acts continue to present greed as a spiritually

---

1. Punt, "Countervailing 'Missionary' Forces," 45.

charged force and the dark powers as enmeshed with sociopolitical structures—foreshadowing a final confrontation in Rome.

Cicero (106 to 43 BCE), the Roman lawyer, orator, and rhetorician, employed a persuasive tactic called "guilt by association" to undermine his various opponents.[2] In the Roman setting "a man's friends and associations reveal to the community who he was."[3] This study evokes Cicero's rhetorical strategy of "guilt by association" as a device employed by Luke, who utilizes a similar tactic by grouping together a series of suspicious variables to render an implicit judgment. By linking Judas, Ananias, Sapphira, Simon Magus, Agrippa I, Elymas, the sons of Sceva, the Philippian citizens, and Demetrius to greed, Satan, unclean spirits, idolatry, and sorcery, Luke constructs a narrative that links Rome to evil and greed through "guilt by association."[4]

First, Judas's avarice is apparent in his acceptance of a bribe in exchange for his betrayal (Luke 22:1–6). Moreover, the sizeable amount of this transaction is implied by Luke's record that Judas was able to use it to secure valuable real estate. In doing so, Luke associates Judas with various rapacious forces that enabled him to benefit from an economic policy that burdened the majority class. Luke identifies Judas in connection not only to the sociopolitical powers of greed and economics but also to the forces of darkness, specifying that he is directly engaged by Satan (Luke 22:1–6).

Ananias and Sapphira were also guilty by association. First, the initial evidence of this couple's guilt was that they enjoyed a superior economic standing compared to the majority populace, who lived at subsistence levels or in poverty. They held real estate assets in proximity to Jerusalem, indicative of wealth and power in that region. By association, they related to the wealthy class that exploited the poor. Additionally, their betrayal of theological ethics connected them to Judas. Luke aligns them as character foils to Barnabas, indicating that they were eager for an enhanced honor standing within the church comparable to the significant figure. Finally, Peter's declaration that Satan had entered their heart robustly described unequivocal dark collusion.

2. Aldrete, "Cicero."

3. Hammar, "Making Enemies," 207. Examples include Cic. *Cat.* 3.16, 25; 4.11–12; *Phil.* 2.61; *Rosc. Amer.* 68; *Agr.* 1.22.

4. Conversely, this same rhetorical mechanism could lead Theophilus—an assumed Roman elite—to view Peter and Paul, key representatives of the Palestinian and broader Mediterranean contexts, as guilty by association. This is because bandit-like behavior, magic, and anti-idolatry are each inherently anti-imperial.

Likewise, Simon the magician's guilt was evident on multiple levels. First, he was a blatant practitioner of dark forces, as Peter denoted him as being bound to wickedness. Additionally, his occupation involved achieving wealth through a presumed system of exploitation within the Samaritan community. This awarded him significant honor status and economic benefits. He welcomed the attribution of being called "the power of the god called great," associating him with the dark powers of idolatry that also motivated Judas, Ananias, and Sapphira. Furthermore, Simon evidently assumed that Peter's character was as venal as his own, attempting to insinuate himself into the apostolic group and accelerate his acquisition of power through bribery. In doing so, he was perhaps guilty not only of bribery but also of flaunting his conspicuous wealth to reassert his self-importance and social status. His acquisitive display reflected the habits of those accustomed to using excess wealth to manipulate others.

King Agrippa I also fits the category of guilt by association. Luke brackets Agrippa I with the dynasty proceeding from Herod the Great, linking the last king of the Jews to a system of economic oppression and numerous acts of murder, including Herod Antipas's execution of John the Baptist. Furthermore, Agrippa I personally incriminated himself through James's execution and his intention to kill Peter, decisions driven by his rapacious need for public approval. His usury was evident in his implied trade war with the vulnerable populace in Tyre and Sidon during a time of famine. Luke expected his readers to recognize these historical elements. They would grasp that Agrippa I's career was characterized by the systematic abuse of those who stood in his way, driven by his thirst for praise, power, and economic security. His infatuation with Rome, realized in his relationships with Caligula and Claudius, further indicted him as culpable by association with the oppressive empire. Luke makes his guilt abundantly clear by highlighting that Agrippa I allowed himself to be worshipped as a cultic figure, flagrantly crossing the threshold of idolatry and aligning himself with the forces of darkness.

Moreover, Luke associated all these negative characters together. In each of these challenges to the early church, these figures emerge as connected to the dark powers, and these instruments of greed and oppression are resisted and defeated. After securing a field with the proceeds of his malfeasance, Judas's profane death occurred on that same plot of land, making the location a symbol of exile. Ananias and Sapphira met immediate death, and their shameful demise was well attested. They were left unable to hoard their remaining wealth or acquire apostolic honor. Luke specifies that Satan entered these characters, each of whom was an insider to the church group (Luke 22:3; Acts 5:3). However, after these accounts, Luke never again refers to Satan as entering villainous characters, nor are insiders portrayed as opposing the church. This progression demonstrates that the threats were neutralized.

Luke's next two stories more subtly reveal associations with evil through powerful and well-known figures who were outsiders to the church. In Samaria, Simon's powers were nullified when Philip arrived and freed the populace from unclean spirits. The magician was rendered impotent, rejected from ecclesial leadership, and left only with the option of dramatic repentance. Herod Agrippa I, concluding the Palestinian section, marked an important transition in the narrative. He served as a type to show that the church's primary confrontation with dark powers would center on the forces of Rome and its cultic worship. Agrippa I's violent acts and economic extortion culminated in a dishonorable and polluted death.

In each case, the victory over darkness is not only depicted in the church's resistance to greed but also in the justice meted out to the villains and the growing vibrancy of the church. Following Judas's betrayal, the church's triumphant advance was signified by Jesus's resurrection and ascension, Peter's emergence as a leader, and the multiplication of disciples, leading to and emanating from Pentecost. The Jerusalem temple elites' increasingly ineffective persecution corresponded to the dark powers' futile attempts to corrupt the church from within.

Not only did the attempts to infiltrate the disciple group lessen following Judas, but the church's challenges galvanized its purity and growth. Peter's immediate response, articulating God's judgment against the conspiracy and embezzlement in Acts 5, instilled fear and awe, tightening social boundaries and deterring further treachery. The Jerusalem church continued to expand, even surpassing Pentecost's successes. In Acts 6, a potential crisis of fraud and greed was honorably resolved, avoiding incrimination and strengthening the church's unity.

When persecution intensified after Stephen's death, the church mobilized and expanded to Samaria, where Peter symbolized victory by rejecting Simon's bribe. The narrative continued with the Ethiopian eunuch's conversion, Saul of Tarsus's reversal from persecutor to disciple, and Cornelius's Spirit baptism and table fellowship in Caesarea. Christian unity was further evident in Acts 11, as the Antioch church dispatched financial assistance to Judea during a famine. Even when James was executed and Peter imprisoned, the latter's miraculous release affirmed the church's unstoppable growth, preparing for dramatic expansion toward Rome.

These narrative blocks construct an image of the Spirit's power disrupting the dark powers of greed, idolatry, and imperial oppression. The Spirit's arrival in Rome is anticipated as a continuation of these triumphs. Luke implicitly indicts Rome as bound in unrighteousness and in need of repentance, paralleling Peter's rebuke of Simon in Samaria.

The story of Acts then transitions into the gentile world, spreading across the Mediterranean region. The war with the dark powers becomes further evident through clashes with competing religious thought in diverse locations, including Rome itself. In Acts 12, "the language echoes Greco-Roman ruler cults and functions not only to close out the first half of Acts but to foreshadow chapters 13–28."[5] This observation substantiates the relationship between Agrippa I (at this chapter's conclusion) and the idolatrous, pagan, and imperial situation that the church must confront all the way to Rome.

Paul's mission in the broader Mediterranean setting of Acts illustrates escalating components of greed and spiritual forces in three key pericopes. First is the account at Cyprus involving Bar-Jesus, also known as Elymas, who serves as an advisor to Sergius Paulus, the proconsul. Elymas, being both a magician and a Jewish false prophet—a double faux pas in Luke's writing—is characterized by selfish behavior that exploits his clientele. His position with the proconsul offers him significant socioeconomic opportunities, whereby his greed motivates him to blockade gospel transmission, being aware that such reception would eliminate his job security.

Secondly, in Philippi, the institution of human slavery is linked with a dark possessive entity to generate remarkable profit margins. Each of these components is inherent of greed, further evidenced by the public's response when the commercial process is disrupted. This upheaval prompts an outrage that circumvents the proper legal process.

Thirdly, in Ephesus, the itinerant exorcists' greed is at least implicit. Meanwhile, the organization of silversmiths by Demetrius agitates the city, highlighting the greedy motivations of this union. With their profit margins reduced and the socioeconomic security of Ephesus threatened, the population responds with desperation (and greed).

---

5. Schreiner, *Acts*, 410.

Likewise, the presence of dark forces is clearly attested in these three sections. First, Elymas's sorcery and false oracles are associated with demonic evil in the Jewish worldview that Luke assumes. Moreover, Paul's description of Elymas as a "son of the devil" cements such a perspective. Secondly, the dark entity producing divination in Philippi is connected to idolatry and pagan practices—an antithetical source to the Holy Spirit—and is also connected to evil in Luke's writings. Meanwhile, the undercurrent of the imperial cult adds a more implicitly veiled presence of evil at Philippi. Thirdly, in Ephesus, Luke indicates the generic presence of evil spirits when fabrics that Paul has handled disrupt these forces. This is further conveyed in the specific episode of seven inauthentic exorcists confronting a possessed man. Moreover, the burning of dark literature and paraphernalia indicates the prevalence of magic in that location, and their dedication to the Artemis cult reinforces widespread pagan loyalties.

Victory over evil is witnessed when Elymas seeks to block gospel transmission. Not only is he rendered blind, but proconsul Sergius Paulus becomes a strategic convert. While Elymas's ongoing opportunities seem bleak, the reader expects optimism in Cyprus, which now has a disciple in a place of authority, giving hope for "the ends of the earth" (Acts 1:8). Unlike most of the villains from the Palestinian section, Elymas need not suffer death to be defeated, nor does he attempt to infiltrate the apostolic group as Simon Magus did. This highlights a clear progression in the feud against evil: the dark powers have now been maneuvered to a defensive, not offensive, stance.

Meanwhile, in Philippi, the Python spirit is expelled, and the girl is liberated from an occupying force, a signpost that exploitative socioeconomic practices have been placed on notice. Lydia and the jailer are ideal disciples in positions of influence, and they exhibit generosity within the region. The addition of these two influential converts exceeds the notable single conversion of Sergius Paulus in Cyprus. Victory is further observed when Paul speaks truth to the powers of the local colony. Imperial agents experience the fear of God, and Paul is able to walk away following a series of subversive acts, not the least of which is interrupting the Philippian economy.

Paul remains safe while incarcerated (unlike James, who had been killed), and the Roman representative (jailer) was afraid. The earthquake declares "God as sovereign over the Roman Empire and its colonies,"[6] so Paul remains in jail (unlike Peter) even though persons accused of treason

---

6. Schreiner, *Acts*, 511.

CONCLUSION

"were usually expected to flee into exile," resulting in a "loss of citizenship."[7] However, the reader later learns that Paul's retention of citizenship was the means toward Rome, a too-valuable asset to relinquish in Philippi by running away. Nevertheless, judicial due process ultimately prevails, permitting Paul's freedom. This allows him a key opportunity that an escapee would never have been afforded: the ability to publicly criticize the officials.

Unlike the story involving Agrippa I's death, the guard in Philippi does not die; instead, the imperial representative becomes a disciple, even with Paul's relative passivity (compared to his assertive actions blinding Elymas to enable Sergius Paulus's gospel reception). Furthermore, the initial witness to the jailer is evidently the possessive spirit, which, like Balaam, had attempted to disrupt the movement but instead became a temporary evangelist, resulting in "free publicity" for Paul.[8]

Elymas had been blinded, demonstrating that the Spirit would react with more subtle responses, yet in Philippi, the jailer (an imperial representative of order) turns the blade on himself but is then rescued by Paul. Finally, in Ephesus, the only injured persons in the narrative are the itinerant exorcists, having been attacked by the evil spirit, rather than suffering because of an act of God. Moreover, Elymas and the Philippian magistrates receive an apostolic rebuke. However, the only words of correction in Ephesus come from the town clerk, with no need for a divine earthquake or courageous words from the apostle. This is a sign that evil's effects are diminishing.

The sequence of successful interactions with political officials is also noticeable, including Cornelius, the jailer in Philippi, and Sergius Paulus. While Gallio in Corinth and the clerk at Ephesus are not disciples, their beneficial judgments demonstrate the progressive empowerment of the church, a factor noted in Philippi where the authorities suffer correction; and in Thessalonica, the political powers are less successful in apprehending suspects despite a serious anti-imperial accusation. This shift is significant as the narrative moves toward Paul's encounters with the dangers of Jerusalem and then Rome. There is greater hope for the transformation of the empire if rulers remain unconverted but ambivalent (or incompetent) in their judicial rulings. Moreover, rather than Paul being stripped of his clothes as in Philippi, it is the charlatans who are rendered unclothed at Ephesus. Likewise, Paul has expelled the spirit in Philippi; meanwhile,

7. Rapske, *Paul in Roman Custody*, 43.
8. Longenecker, "Acts," 967.

despite the officials attempting to exorcise him from the city, he leaves only after issuing a public rebuke to them and on his own terms.

The evil forces in the cosmic duel utilize traitors, beginning with Judas's successful treachery. However, the church in Acts is successful in turning operatives of darkness into agents of light, including Saul of Tarsus, Cornelius, Sergius Paulus, the Philippian jailer, and the dark forces which betray each other in Ephesus in the confrontation between the charlatans and evil spirits. Also, the effectiveness of the charlatans is so diminished that they attempt to use the names of their competitors (Paul and Jesus) to maintain their craft. Yet the dark powers are so confused that they turn on each other. Simply put, the charlatan and the possessive spirit become destabilized by the mere presence of Paul.

Meanwhile, the power of God is so enhanced that the fabric handled by Paul transmits his deeds, as the dark powers become subordinate even to materials associated with the Spirit. At Ephesus, the people react with a spontaneous sign of repentance, burning their magic books in an ideal expression of Lukan discipleship, relinquishing their power and its monetary potential for the kingdom of God. Meanwhile, pagan idolatry is so threatened that a patron cult of Ephesus is on the trajectory of extinction. An angry mob reacts, yet, unlike at Philippi, the local authorities administer justice, offering additional optimism for when Paul reached Rome.

A reader like Theophilus, presumably of Roman elite status, reading Acts as a pagan in the likeness of MacMullen's imaginative approach, would assess the stark imperial implications that, in Cyprus, a superior form of power to magic had captivated the leadership and had converted the proconsul while binding the sorcerer who was under Roman patronage. In Philippi, long-standing pagan divination connected to an ancient cultic setting is expelled; the Roman ethos is interrupted; and by inference, the divine honors of that city are put on notice along with its leadership. Following Cornelius, in Cyprus, the proconsul converts. In Philippi, a representative of the empire becomes a disciple engaging in subversive acts. Finally, in Ephesus, idolatry is agitated and nearly eradicated (as reported by Luke), while the silversmiths are nearly put out of business because another ancient cultic deity (and the imperial cult by implication) is threatened with extermination. Meanwhile, the people abandoned their magical powers, something they were uncompelled to do because of the existing imperial laws, yet were prompted to do by the Holy Spirit.

In each case—economic destruction, pagan obsolescence, and the transfer of loyalty from unapproved magic to the superior power of the church—Paul recognizes upon viewing the Ephesian response that he must go to Rome. Since he has been able to confront and threaten the Artemis cult, which is worshipped by the "entire world" (Acts 19:27), he seeks a comparable response at the imperial capital. There, encountering the leader of the whole world, Paul might not only threaten Caesar's cult but inspire a demonstration of repentance that drastically adjusts the empire's trajectory when darkness is defeated at its epicenter.

Reflection

This study affirms that themes and motifs in Acts should be read together in unison with the broader narrative.[9] Existing academic efforts related to this study offer an abundance of works related to socioeconomic ethics in Luke-Acts, alongside other publications dedicated to Luke's view of Rome and studies examining Lukan spiritual phenomena, including the dark powers. However, resources that engage in an intersection of all three dynamics simultaneously are largely nonexistent.[10] The objective of this project is to address these topics jointly, discovering the overlap in Luke's themes of socioeconomic ethics and spiritual phenomena and how these connections shape the reading of Acts.

In addition to identifying the socioeconomic factors within the seven pericopes, this study employs social, economic, and political history to argue the significance of the following:

- Judas's land transaction and his representation of both the Judean economic structure and the demise of the dark powers (Luke 22:1–5; Acts 1:15–20).

- The social stationing of Ananias and Sapphira within the Jerusalem economic paradigm, enhancing existing views of their greedy activity as a grasp for honor acquisition within the church, alongside their demise as indicative of the fate of evil forces (Acts 5:1–11).

- The exploitative regional patronage of Simon Magus in Samaria, which functioned in conjunction with idolatry. Simon's actions

---

9. Gaventa, "Toward Theology," 146–57.
10. For details, see appendix C.

mirrored the systemic operations of Rome throughout the empire, yet his impotence ultimately symbolized the fate of the dark powers and the organizations and systems they empower (Acts 8:4–24).

- Herod Agrippa I's economic liability during a famine, where he operated as a representative of Roman oppression and worship. His demise represented the ends of the imperial cult, general idolatry, and the powers of evil (Acts 11:27—12:24).

- Elymas's patronage relationship with Rome and his interests aligned with imperial priorities (Acts 13:4–12). His opposition functioned to demonstrate how the dark powers might attempt to hinder the gospel's transformative reach into imperial agents (and Rome itself), yet his defeat is indicative of the powers' ultimate destiny.

- Philippi's exemplification of Roman systems of exploitation with tangible and spiritual occupation (Acts 16:16–21), and Ephesus's depiction as a spiritual stronghold of magic and idolatry (Acts 19:11–41). However, each functioned as a test case for the Spirit's disruptive power over cultural and imperial power bases.

In both Philippi and Ephesus, the impact of the Holy Spirit is significant, offering an implicit indictment of Roman economic systems, the imperial cult, and general idolatry while disrupting the local (and broader) ethos.

The presence of the dark powers is also identified in many of these passages, yet with a more nuanced perspective. Satan's occupation of Judas, Ananias, and Sapphira is indicative of the evil forces' desire to possess persons, locations, and institutions (Luke 22:1–6; Acts 1:15–20; 5:1–11). Likewise, magic serves as a means of societal control and exploitation, empowered by dark spirits, often operating in unison with imperial economic forces (Acts 8:4–24; 13:4–12). Moreover, idolatry represents a systematic and natural intersection with Rome (Acts 11:27—12:24; 16:11–40; 19:8–41). Additionally, this study argues that spiritual possession of populations, with the intent to manipulate and control them, is part of the Roman ethos (Acts 16:11–40).

A cumulative consideration of these discoveries yields a perspective regarding how these variables impact the narrative conclusion of Acts of the Apostles. This study not only affirms socioeconomic ethics as a vital component of the cosmic-conflict perspective, but, more significantly, highlights greed and profit-generating endeavors as central vices of the dark powers. In short, this study argues that Acts portrays early Christianity's most prominent tangible mission as disrupting socioeconomic exploitation and its enabling powers. Meanwhile, the strongest resistance comes from those people, institutions, and spiritual powers seeking to preserve systems of socioeconomic influence and control.

A secondary consideration of this study was to determine how these seven Lukan passages connect socioeconomics and spiritual activity to enhance broader Lukan theology. Examining socioeconomic greed and evil spiritual forces in tandem reveals an ongoing conflict between God and dark powers in Luke-Acts, where socioeconomics serves as a weapon of warfare, closely linked to Rome and idolatry. Read in this light, the cosmic conflict (with human and institutional operatives) becomes more apparent, particularly in Acts 20–28. The reader anticipates that the battle with evil, along with the confrontation of idolatry, political exploitation, and socioeconomic greed, will logically culminate in Rome, continuing the sequence established in the study's pericopes.

This intersection with Rome is further compelling when considered in the light of other dynamics of this study, including the implementation of MacMullen's imaginative reading identifying enemies of the Roman empire. Theophilus—most plausibly assumed to be a Roman elite—would likely have perceived the Holy Spirit as a competitive and threatening power to the Roman imperial cult. Luke presents the Spirit in a way that can be understood as a superior form of "magic," commanding influence and control deemed illegal under Roman law. Leaning on MacMullen's assessment of Roman threats, various actions and characteristics of the church could be seen as imperially subversive. Paul's anti-idolatrous stance, for example, posed a threat in at least three ways:

a. subverting the empire by potentially disturbing the Greek aristocracy, whom MacMullen contends were the most substantial threat to Roman order;

b. contending with the tenets of the Roman imperial cult; and

c. upsetting the pagan gods, who, in response, might punish Rome for permitting the activity of a group abolishing idolatry.

Given these characteristics, Theophilus could have viewed the Jesus movement as a form of resistance, comparable to but more potent and sophisticated than social banditry. Like the Sicarii, the church's actions could be perceived as aggressive urban protests, eliminating or seeking revenge on key figures—amounting holistically to a form of terrorism that disturbed

Roman order and peace. Such a perspective would make it unsettling for Theophilus to support the church's emergence in Rome.

Additionally, Horsley and others argue that Jesus's exorcisms were political in nature, representing the expulsion of occupying forces. When applied to Acts, it is noteworthy that the exorcism of dark powers in locations such as Samaria, Cyprus, Philippi, and Ephesus emerged as a key ministry component, motivating Paul's activity in Rome. The trajectory established throughout Acts suggests that something controversial would occur upon reaching Rome, particularly considering Paul's eventual audience before Caesar. The aims of the Holy Spirit would be:

a. to speak boldly "truth to power," even to Nero himself;

b. to offer a rebuke against idolatry in a city renowned for its idols;

c. to expel dark spirits; and

d. to engineer a sign of the "great reversal" comparable to the Ephesian response or the liberation of the slave girl in Philippi.

Any of these individual actions would warrant a strong judicial response from Roman authorities. The combination of these markers challenges—and potentially eliminates—the dominant hypothesis that Luke wrote apologetically, suggesting an irreparable relationship between the church and Rome without reform from either entity.

Appendix A—The Cosmic Duel of Luke-Acts and African Traditional Religion(s): Implications for the Contemporary Prosperity Gospel

A COMPARISON OF THE cosmic duel in Luke-Acts and its corresponding elements in African Traditional Religion(s) (ATR), as applied to a specific theological issue within African Christianity, the "prosperity gospel," illustrates how liberation and postcolonial thought can inform and engage each other. For example, the history of colonialism in the African setting offers an opportunity to use the Lukan texts for the purpose of drawing on contemporary appeal, not as an interpretation of a text, but rather as an intimation.

Comparative Analysis of Luke's Cosmic Duel and African Traditional Religion(s)

The concept of the cosmic duel encapsulates the battle against dark spiritual forces that manifest in greed, idolatry, and systemic oppression. In Luke-Acts, this conflict is depicted in various scenes. These include Jesus's confrontations with demonic forces (Luke 4:31–37), various exorcisms (Acts 16:16–18), and narratives such as Ananias and Sapphira's deceit (Acts 5:1–11), where greed signals allegiance to dark powers. This dualism contrasts the kingdom of God with the activities of evil, illustrating how spiritual forces shape sociopolitical realities and challenge moral order.

Similarly, ATR conceptualizes the universe as a contested space where spiritual forces influence human life and society.[1] The Supreme Being,

---

1. Mbiti, *Introduction to African Religion*, 32.

divinities, ancestors, and spirits (both benevolent and malevolent) form a complex spiritual hierarchy.[2] Malevolent entities—such as witches and sorcerers—are viewed as agents of cosmic disruption, intruding into communal life and causing social disharmony.[3] Rituals and divinations led by spiritual leaders seek to restore harmony, expel malevolent forces, and protect communities from harm.[4]

In both frameworks, the cosmic duel is not limited to metaphysical battles but extends into socioeconomic and political struggles.[5] Luke critiques imperial systems that perpetuate exploitation and idolatry, particularly in the portrayal of Rome's greed-driven empire. Figures such as Herod Agrippa (Acts 12:20-23) illustrate how allegiance to oppressive power structures invites divine judgment. ATR similarly condemns colonial domination and the disruption of indigenous spiritual ecosystems, framing the colonial legacy of land dispossession and economic exploitation as a form of spiritual disorder.[6]

Luke's writings and ATR underscore the necessity of spiritual mediation in this cosmic conflict. In Luke-Acts, the Holy Spirit is the transformative agent empowering believers to resist greed and oppression, fostering justice and communal welfare. Disciples such as Peter and Paul act as mediators of divine power, confronting spiritual corruption and imperial oppression through exorcisms, healings, and proclamations of liberation (Acts 8:9-24; 16:16-18). Similarly, ATR emphasizes the role of spiritual leaders—priests, diviners, and elders—who mediate between the spiritual and human realms to counter malevolent forces and uphold communal harmony.[7]

Both traditions also present structured spiritual hierarchies that inform their understanding of power and accountability. In Lukan theology, God is the supreme authority, with Christ as the mediator (son and broker), the Holy Spirit as the source of empowerment, and angels as divine messengers. In ATR, the Supreme Being occupies the highest position, followed by divinities who serve as intermediaries, with ancestors revered as spiritual guardians who ensure communal continuity and moral order.[8]

2. Olupona, "African Traditional Religions," 1.
3. Alolo, "African Traditional Religion," 27.
4. Mbiti, *Introduction to African Religion*, 73-75.
5. Olupona, "African Traditional Religions," 1.
6. Alolo, "African Traditional Religion," 40-43.
7. Lugira, *African Traditional Religion*, 16.
8. Olupona, "African Traditional Religions," 1.

Lukan theology and ATR both emphasize holistic liberation, involving not only the exorcism of malevolent spiritual forces but also the transformation of socioeconomic realities. Paul's exorcism of the enslaved girl in Philippi (Acts 16:16–18) exemplifies this approach, liberating her from both spiritual possession and economic exploitation. Similarly, ATR rituals of deliverance address spiritual afflictions such as illness, infertility, or social discord, highlighting the interconnected nature of spiritual, social, and material restoration.[9]

This cosmic duel extends to the collective memory of divine deliverance. In Luke's writings, the church's remembrance of Jesus's resurrection forms the foundation for resisting spiritual and imperial powers (Acts 4:24–30). Likewise, ATR honors ancestral spirits as custodians of communal memory, providing a moral framework for resilience and communal living.[10] Rituals such as baptism and communal prayers in Luke-Acts symbolize spiritual liberation and solidarity, while ATR ceremonies invoke divine protection and unity.[11]

The African church, drawing from both Lukan theology and the worldview principles of African spirituality, holds significant potential to enhance Christian practice in the cosmic duel against spiritual and sociopolitical oppression. By integrating Luke's critique of greed with ATR's communal ethos, the church can thoughtfully engage indigenous insights without succumbing to uncritical syncretism. Rather than adopting ATR practices wholesale, the church can appreciate its emphasis on collective resilience, sacred responsibility, and spiritual mediation as complementary perspectives that enrich biblical understandings of spiritual warfare.

Reclaiming spiritual warfare within this nuanced framework allows the church to address external systems of exploitation while resisting internal corruption and materialism. Postcolonial and liberation theology further amplify this approach by critiquing neo-colonial structures that perpetuate inequality and framing spiritual deliverance as inseparable from sociopolitical justice. By recognizing how global systems of economic control mirror the exploitative powers condemned in Luke-Acts, the church can foster a prophetic voice that resists both external domination and internal complicity.

This balanced approach fosters a vision of Christian practice that prioritizes justice, communal flourishing, and holistic restoration. It aligns

---

9. Lugira, *African Traditional Religion*, 16.
10. Zimmerman, "General Features of ATRs," 277–79.
11. Ulvestad, "Ubuntu in ATR," 11.

with the marginalized, reimagining spiritual warfare as a call to both personal renewal and systemic liberation, firmly grounded in the distinctives of the Christian faith.

Implications for the Prosperity Gospel

The prosperity gospel, a concept originating from the industrialized United States of America, has rapidly expanded within the African context, representing a form of theological colonialism.[12] By legitimizing wealth and power structures rather than challenging them, the prosperity gospel in Africa reinforces entrenched socioeconomic inequalities under the guise of spiritual favor. Part of the colonial mindset is the equation of divine blessing with material wealth, a theology that perpetuates disparities rather than addressing systemic injustice.

In a prophetic counternarrative, Luke presents wealth not as a blessing but as a moral and spiritual test. Postcolonial thinkers may contrast the prosperity gospel with African indigenous values, reclaiming the communal ethos of *ubuntu* while critiquing the hyper-individualism embedded in prosperity teaching. Often criticized for promoting personal gain over collective justice, the prosperity gospel stands in stark contrast to Luke's vision of Spirit-led community and economic equity.

When evaluated alongside the ethical frameworks of ATRs, the prosperity gospel reveals a significant divergence—it risks perpetuating greed rather than challenging it. ATRs recognize spiritual forces at work in prosperity, power, and misfortune, but Luke-Acts reframes these dynamics, depicting greed as a manifestation of dark spiritual forces. For instance, Judas's betrayal (Luke 22:3) and Ananias's deceit (Acts 5:3) are directly linked to satanic influence. This critique provides African theologians with a robust framework to challenge contemporary teachings that spiritualize wealth accumulation while disregarding socioeconomic justice. Luke portrays false prophets as aligning with greed-driven forces, a trait frequently associated with certain proponents of the prosperity gospel. In Luke-Acts, greed signifies idolatry and allegiance to spiritual powers opposing God's kingdom.

Drawing on Luke's narrative, African theologians can expose how the prosperity gospel often substitutes wealth for God as the ultimate object of worship. Instead, Luke calls for allegiance to God and the empowering

12. Mashau and Kgatle, "Prosperity Gospel and Greed," 1.

Holy Spirit, which disrupts systems of greed and exploitation. This vision insists on a community shaped by justice, generosity, and resistance to oppressive economic ideologies, offering a powerful counternarrative to prosperity teachings that neglect the poor and marginalized.

Appendix B—Further Research Opportunities

THIS STUDY INTERSECTS WITH many broader questions of Lukan theology that cannot be thoroughly addressed within this project; however, the conversations serve as intriguing segues into ongoing research possibilities.

Acts and the Persecuted Community and the Nature of Victory

While this project concludes that Luke presents Paul's arrival in Rome as depicting the Holy Spirit's successful trajectory, history recognizes the struggle for Christians both in Rome and the broader empire. Given that Acts was likely (at the earliest) a late first-century production, the apparent cognitive dissonance of its writer—conveying victory in contrast to ongoing persecution—might be considered in the following ways.

Firstly, how might the divergence of Acts' narrative from historical realities (victory contrasted with persecution) inform its background material, particularly its genre? Luke's possible ignorance of events beyond 62 CE may suggest an earlier dating. However, if he writes to convey ultimate victory to a persecuted community, traditional views of early dating and strict historiographic genre may be challenged. Instead, such a purpose likely reinforces an epic-style narrative intended to encourage the church or support ongoing missional objectives in Rome.

The disconnect between Acts of the Apostles and history may not reflect competing accounts but rather indicate a complex relationship between theology and history in Luke's prophetic historiographic approach. This opens further possibilities for exploration. Rather than seeing theology and history as separate categories, Luke's narrative may reflect an ideological framework in which theological meaning is embedded within historical interpretation. If Luke indeed constructed an eschatological epic, how might readers reconcile his depiction with later historical events? Could Luke have written to a persecuted community not only to clarify the purpose of their suffering but also to bolster their hope in God's ultimate victory in the cosmic conflict? This would integrate historical reality with theological vision.

Perhaps Luke's purpose was to call the church to be faithful witnesses during persecution by revealing the character of the Holy Spirit in confrontation with empire, as reflected within this study. Such a hypothesis presents Luke-Acts with compositional similarities to the Johannine corpus, perhaps even with distinct authors writing in a similar style between Luke and Acts. The Gospel may focus on Jesus's controversies with Jewish opponents, while the second volume addresses a persecuted community afflicted by the empire, depicting God's ultimate triumph.

Such questions also lead into the topic of Lukan eschatology, an ongoing conversation among scholars who assess a potential separation between the Gospel and Acts. Might it be that the Gospel highlights eschatological concerns centered on Jerusalem, while Acts focuses more on the empire (Rome)? In this way, Lukan eschatology is much more contextually framed in the apocalypse of his sociopolitical world.

Moreover, in what ways might Luke-Acts reflect possible theological affirmations of persecution, through which readers may derive hope? Luke's writings record that the kingdom of God is entered through many persecutions (Acts 14:22), while Jesus commissioned his witnesses—literally μάρτυς (Acts 1:8)—a word that later developed into "martyrs." Likewise, suffering is divinely ordained in Paul's life (Acts 9:10–16), and his journey narrative, including his trials and voyage to Rome through Jerusalem, resembles that of Jesus.

Could Luke have intentionally designed Paul's sufferings and presumed death to mirror Jesus's theologically,[13] either to offer a redemptive factor for Jerusalem and Rome or to serve as a prophetic indictment upon their rejection? The sea voyage in Acts 27, with its eucharistic typology and repeated salvation language, followed by Paul's reception in Malta in Acts 28, adds further intrigue. This sequence of events positions Paul's Roman visitation with both optimistic and pessimistic potentials, akin to Jesus's entry into Jerusalem (Luke 19:44).

---

13. Moessner, "'Script' of Scriptures," 251–80.

APPENDIX B

While there has been useful pushback regarding an empire-wide persecution of early Christianity,[14] evidence remains that the great fire of Rome (64 CE) was not too distant from the literary conclusion of Acts. History now attests that Nero was unlikely to have set the fire, and while the church was an unlikely culprit, it still garnered blame from the head of state.[15] The book of Acts, written likely within memory of Nero's persecution, raises at least two intriguing possibilities. The first, discussed in chapter 7, involves Agrippa I's death as a type-scene of judgment upon Nero for various cruel actions. The proposed evidence for this claim was marginal at best, primarily linked to the divine voice. Nevertheless, this potential connection (among other links between Acts and empire) remains a fruitful avenue for ongoing conversation.

Additionally, could Paul, who is clearly and strategically conveyed as a persecutor turned believer in Luke's second volume, represent an indication in Acts of Roman potential to turn to the side of the gospel? Specifically, that while at least certain areas of the empire would persecute the church, could the writer have anticipated that Rome, like Paul, could be persuaded to adopt the faith?

Next, and more daringly, might Luke have intended readers to suspect the fire in Rome as an act of divine or even eschatological rebuke upon the city? This would not be unlike how early Christian traditions attached the fall of Jerusalem to Jesus's prophetic pronouncements. Anthony Barrett notes that, in antiquity, fires were often considered omens of divine displeasure and symbols of greater cataclysmic acts to follow.[16] He leans on Tacitus's perspective, which relates the fire to Nero's displays of dramatic "excess" leading up to the event.[17] Barrett remarks that "although Tacitus does not say so openly, the fire seems a form of divine retribution for the steady decadence of Rome under Nero's stewardship."[18]

While unlikely, might Luke have drawn upon perspectives of Nero's greed and eventual rejection of Paul or the collective Christian mission in connection with the fire in Rome? Luke employs language both comparable to that of the Synoptic writers and uniquely his own when conveying fire imagery. For instance, John the Baptist—described as a politically disruptive

14. Moss, *Myth of Persecution*.
15. Barrett, *Rome Is Burning*.
16. Barrett, *Rome Is Burning*, 127.
17. Tac. *Ann.* 15.37; Barrett, *Rome Is Burning*, 127–28.
18. Barrett, *Rome Is Burning*, 128.

prophetic voice—is associated with fire (Luke 3:9, 16–17). James, the brother of John, who later faced execution under Agrippa I, also appears within this imagery of judgment (Luke 9:54; Acts 12:1–4). Moreover, Jesus himself asserted that he came not as the courier of peace but of fire (Luke 12:49). The Holy Spirit is similarly associated with fire (Luke 3:9; Acts 2:3), while at Ephesus, the church is known for the burning of books (Acts 19:19). Peter declares eschatological signs involving fire (Acts 2:19), and later, in Malta, Paul encounters a viper in association with fire (Acts 28:3, 5).

Chapter 8 considered certain parallels between the rich man and Lazarus (Luke 16:19–31) and Agrippa I. Amanda Miller, who identifies subversive language in Luke's writings, further validates the broader implications of that parable. She describes it as "a text of status reversal that resists the dominant values of Roman imperial society and how it defined wealth, status, and human worth."[19] Remarkably, the wealthy character—who subversively depicts Roman traits—ends up in torturing flames as an eschatological fate.

While some may find this content unconvincing or speculative, the question remains regarding the role of the Jewish Revolt and the Siege of Jerusalem in Luke's writings. Even among those who affirm a later dating, it is reasonable to consider what relationship the writer may have wished to convey regarding the great Roman fire of 64 CE. There remains room for further substantiation of this connection, especially given that the subsequent persecution of Christians by Nero derived a sense of "pity" for the church, which in part aided the movement's growth.[20]

Later Relationship Between the Church and Rome

Another historical variable connected to the theological dimensions of this study is the progression of the relationship between the church and Rome, which initially appears marked by persecution and later by acceptance and even endorsement. Such a transition—from persecution to state approval—is remarkable. One may evaluate this development as either the victory of the church or a critique of its integrity.[21] Moreover, as magic and paganism declined, the church gained social acceptance and became economically

19. Miller, *Rumors of Resistance*, 248.
20. Tac. *Ann.* 15:44.5; Barrett, *Rome Is Burning*, 147.
21. See Stark in both *Cities of God* and *Rise of Christianity* for useful social and historical backgrounds.

viable. The interrelationships of these variables continue to generate ongoing theological reflection.

A theological and historical analysis would trace the trajectory of this transformation. The church moved from persecution and martyrdom under Nero, Decius, and Diocletian to Constantine's Edict of Milan in 313 CE, culminating in Theodosius I's declaration of Christianity as the state religion in 381 CE. This analysis would then examine later implications to assess the nature of this incorporation. Does it represent a theological victory—the fulfillment of Acts' vision, where the gospel triumphs over idolatry and Rome becomes an instrument of God's kingdom? Or does it signal a theological failure, where the church compromises its prophetic identity by adopting imperial structures and power? One must compare Acts' critique of imperial power with the church's eventual embrace of that power, considering whether Acts anticipates this merger or implicitly critiques it through its prophetic stance. Broader perspectives, such as Augustine's *City of God*, which critiques the fusion of church and empire, offer insights into whether this merger aligns with or deviates from the vision of God's kingdom.

As an additional element, MacMullen notes the integration of banditry and threats by the Roman state as a means of creating solidarity for practical purposes.[22] This phenomenon of co-opted banditry offers a helpful analogy for understanding the church's later ambiguous and complex relationship with Roman elites and authorities. This complexity is suggested by the potential patronage of Theophilus in Luke-Acts, possibly reflecting a blurring of lines between opposition and collaboration, or a resistance through integration as the church presents a new order.

The Church in Comparative Analysis with Other Movements

Space limitations prohibit a vital facet of this study's assertions: a comparative analysis with other movements of antiquity. Part of this project's conclusion is that the church, while traditionally argued to be politically compliant, presents itself as congruent with the various threats assessed by MacMullen and others. To establish the genuine uniqueness of the church in Acts, it is crucial to consider other socioreligious and political movements from the Roman period, and possibly from outside this period, to identify similarities and distinctions. Such an approach would help determine the extent to which first-century Rome may have viewed the church

---

22. MacMullen, *Enemies of Roman Order*, 261.

as adopting a threatening posture. In other words, what (if any) movements shared overlap with MacMullen's identified threats yet were not prominently viewed as subversive in character by the empire?

Literary and Narrative Possibilities

One avenue for further exploration is the role of mimesis in Luke-Acts, particularly how Luke appropriates and subverts Greco-Roman literary traditions to construct a counter-imperial narrative. This study has primarily examined the socioeconomic and theological implications of the church's confrontation with greed, idolatry, and imperial structures. Additional research could reinforce the argument that Luke's engagement with Homeric and Vergilian traditions critiques Roman power.

Dennis MacDonald has argued that Luke's writings constitute "a political act," providing the church with "a rival cultural identity by composing a foundational prose epic."[23] If this assessment is correct, it underscores the subversive nature of Luke-Acts. Luke does not just narrate the expansion of the Christian movement but constructs a literary Trojan horse that infiltrates the Greco-Roman worldview with a counternarrative of divine sovereignty centered on Christ. Luke's literary engagement with Homer and Vergil does not simply mirror imperial narratives; rather, it undermines and reconfigures them to assert the superiority of the Christian mission.

Further examination of mimetic elements in the key passages of this study may reinforce how Luke constructs the church's victories over dark forces as a theological and literary challenge to imperial ideology. Acts 12:1–17 and the *Iliad/Aeneid* show how divine intervention to free Peter parallels Hermes and Mercury rescuing mortals. However, unlike these Greco-Roman narratives, God's power is shown to triumph over imperial structures rather than legitimize them.[24] The depiction in Acts 13:4–13 of Elymas's blinding is mirrored in the *Bacchae* by Tiresias's affliction. However, the reversal of Pentheus's fate through Sergius Paulus's conversion highlights Luke's theological inversion—where the Roman official does not perish but embraces the gospel.[25] Acts 16 and Greco-Roman epics present Paul's journey

---

23. MacDonald, *Luke and Homeric Imitation*.

24. MacDonald, *Luke and Homeric Imitation*; see part II, "A Mimetic Commentary on the Acts of the Apostles: Miraculous Escapes; Peter, Priam, and Aeneas (Acts 12:1–17, *Iliad* 24.431–801, and *Aeneid* 4.238–594)."

25. MacDonald, *Luke and Homeric Imitation*; see part II, "Two Rulers and Two Blind Prophets (Acts 13:4–13a and *Bacchae*, passim)."

APPENDIX B

from Troas to Macedonia as echoing Aeneas's divinely directed mission, yet instead of securing Roman imperial dominance, Paul's mission introduces the kingdom of God, subverting expansionist ideologies.[26] Acts 19 and the Asteropaeus episode in the *Iliad* draw a parallel between the defeat of the sons of Sceva by evil spirits and Asteropaeus's failure against Achilles. However, the outcome glorifies Christ rather than reinforcing imperial heroism.[27]

These connections warrant further exploration in understanding Luke's literary strategy as an intentional appropriation and reconfiguration of Roman legitimacy narratives. MacDonald further notes that "if this assessment is correct, it exposes a colossal and catastrophic failure of modern scholarship on Luke-Acts." If scholars have overlooked Luke's deliberate engagement with imperial literary traditions, this suggests an entire layer of narrative resistance and political theology remains underexplored.

This study has argued that Acts portrays the church's victories over greed and dark forces as part of an escalating cosmic duel, culminating in Paul's arrival in Rome as a challenge to imperial power. Additional research could investigate how Luke's mimesis of Homeric and Vergilian literature reinforces this cosmic conflict. This could demonstrate that Luke does not simply narrate the church's triumphs but presents them in a way that mirrors and supersedes Greco-Roman heroism. The overturning of idolatry and economic exploitation in Acts 16 and 19 can be read as a direct challenge to imperial narratives. The Spirit's role in shaping Paul's journey to Rome in Acts 23–28 functions as a theological inversion of Aeneas's mission—where instead of securing Rome's future, Paul confronts it with the ultimate power of God's kingdom.[28]

The study of mimesis in Luke-Acts remains a rich field for further theological and literary analysis. If Luke consciously constructs his narrative to rival Greco-Roman epics, then his engagement with imperial ideology is not only polemical but deeply strategic. The full implications of

---

26. MacDonald, *Luke and Homeric Imitation*; see part II, "Then We Set Sail (Acts 16:9–12, *Odyssey* 9.1–42, and *Aeneid* 3.4–17)"; "Women Worshipping in the Wild: Philippian Women and Maenads (Acts 16:13–15 and *Bacchae* 35–38 and 55–59)"; "Crazed Women (Acts 16:16–18 and *Eumenides* 24–34)," and "More Prison Breaks: Paul and Dionysus (Acts 16:19–40 and *Bacchae* 215–34, 518–801, and 1344–46)."

27. MacDonald, *Luke and Homeric Imitation*; see part II, "Two Lefties: Sceva and Asteropaeus (Acts 19:13–20 and *Iliad* 21.139–214)."

28. MacDonald, *Luke and Homeric Imitation*; see part II, "Divine Directives to Go to Rome: Paul and Aeneas (Acts 23:11 and 27:23–24a and *Aeneid* 2.270–781, 3.116–505, and 4.274–361)."

this mimetic approach—particularly how it reinforces the church's triumph over Rome's power structures, socioeconomic ethics, and theological legitimacy—deserve continued scholarly attention. As MacDonald's assessment suggests, failure to recognize these literary dynamics risks missing a crucial dimension of Luke's theological agenda.

Secondly, further components of Luke's journey motif raise intriguing possibilities observed by this scholar. A textual application of sociocultural, historical, and mythological components offers potential insights. The Acts narrative intersects with Zeus (the supreme deity) and other members of the pantheons of Greece and Rome at multiple locations, either directly or implicitly.[29] Likewise, similar intersections occur implicitly with the imperial cult at multiple destinations. A study of the geographical progression of Acts, focusing on locations of Zeus/Jupiter worship and/or imperial cult presence, could uncover a literary pattern that offers theological opportunities, perhaps in conjunction with mimetic research. For example, Sol, the god of the sun, was also regarded as a patron of the Roman army. This study references the sun multiple times to illustrate the cosmic victory of the Holy Spirit's power (Acts 13:4–11; 27:20).

Thirdly, there may be significant potential to blend Luke's assessed subversive stance with what also appears to be an apologetic posture. This possibility is what this researcher terms the "Trojan Horse" motif. Luke seems to have been influenced and inspired by ancient writings, including those related to the Trojan War. This motif can be explored in at least two ways.

Initially, might Luke have presented the church as a Trojan horse to Rome in narrative form? Such an approach could explain why the church is sometimes read as subversive while simultaneously articulating its innocence to judicial authorities in other moments. The theoretical effectiveness of this posture lies in presenting the church as peacefully compliant, thereby gaining entry into Rome to engage the cosmic conflict.

Alternatively, Acts of the Apostles may have been intended as a Trojan Horse document, presenting Christianity as innocent while subtly conveying its principles. It could thus be intended to compel a Roman elite like Theophilus—if seen as an emerging disciple—to embrace its ethical teachings. This possibility aligns with Luke's evident prioritization of Roman officials.

---

29. As a further example, Paul tell Elymas he would not see the sun (Acts 13:11). The Roman god of the sun, Sol, became a symbol for the imperial army. Moreover, Dionysius (Acts 17:34) and Apollos (Acts 18:24–28) reflect deific names in the Hellenistic context.

Acts as an Apologetic

This project's primary objectives did not include a thorough scholarly critique of theories regarding Lukan writings as an apologetic legitimization of the church toward Rome. Rather, the literature review's engagement with such theories aimed to distinguish this project's unique contribution. Nevertheless, an apologetic reading emerged as a natural conversation partner throughout this study. Clearly, this study's findings—notably as argued in chapter 7—assert the Lukan corpus as a threatening testimony to Rome, possibly not only as an implied perspective but even as an explicit goal.

Space did not allow for a comprehensive engagement with sources that suggest otherwise. Moreover, most apologetic interpretations prioritize texts outside the scope of this study. However, weighing this dissertation's conclusions in dialogue with existing scholarship that affirms a legitimizing view of the church toward Rome in Luke-Acts will likely produce useful critical interaction for both perspectives.

As a subcategory within the apologetic stance, Luke's presentation of the Jews has previously been understood by some scholarship as an apologetic appeal to Rome, leveraging Roman biases against Judaism.[30] However, an alternate perspective arises from the cosmic conflict theme. Following Jerusalem's rejection of Jesus, certain Jewish representatives in Acts appear to function as a collective literary device—as a type of Judas—becoming perpetually stereotyped (though not exclusively) as enemies within the cosmic conflict. While such assertions may not fully address accusations of anti-Semitism, they offer an alternative lens through which to interpret their role as a literary component in Lukan textual development. This could integrate this theme into a more holistic interpretive framework.

Modern Contextual Theology—African Setting

The African context presents several opportunities for scholars to engage the findings of this study. First, among oppressed peoples, liberation theology offers possibilities to rebuke institutions, governments, and ideologies that maintain unjust policies. This project argues that throughout Acts, and particularly in its narrative conclusion, the Spirit's arrival in Rome confronts socioeconomic powers, demonstrating a victory (or expulsion of dark forces) alongside systematic reform.

---

30. Tyson, *Images of Judaism*.

Secondly, this study also segues into postcolonial thought in two ways: (a) it critiques structures of colonial behavior that enable perpetuation of injustices, oppression, and cultural impositions, and (b) it seeks an indigenous reading of the text, instead of relying solely on colonial perspectives. Muñoz-Larrondo's excellent reading provides an example shaped by the experiences of the colonized. Similarly, this study may offer ideal opportunities for readings of Acts where Roman occupation is present in the text, alongside its socioeconomic, political, and historical dimensions.

Portions of this project's textual examination likely reflect limited interpretations found in much Western scholarship. These would greatly benefit from an African (or majority-world) analysis employing a postcolonial methodology. Instances in Acts involving exorcism, magic, prophecy, and idol adherence within the Mediterranean context could engage interestingly with African Traditional Religion(s), known for their sacred view of objects and vibrant relationship with the unseen world. While appropriately respecting cultural traditions, African scholars might consider how comparative analysis or an emphasis on African phenomenology could inform or intersect with the biblical narrative, or vice versa.

United States of America (and Other Industrialized Nations)

Christians in the developed world, particularly in the United States of America, might consider how the principles of this study could enhance a sense of human flourishing in their context by applying sociopolitical criticism. Moreover, the political, economic, and military policies of a nation that exerts itself internationally might be weighed in ways that are, in many respects, congruent with ancient Rome. These findings could apply to macro or corporate issues of colonialism, including debt imposed on nations,[31] military occupation, various forms of political extortion, and other examples of socioeconomic oppression perpetuated by governments or businesses.

Furthermore, the capitalistic environment of the US has produced a unique sense of greed, often described as a "mantra for the American lifestyle."[32] Alongside greed, the rise of individualism associated with the

---

31. Wright, *Surprised by Hope*, 213–19. Wright has targeted the unjust credit extension by Western powers upon unindustrialized nations as a modern equivalent to slavery.

32. Childs, *Greed*, 66–67.

US[33] has likely resulted in both a spiritual fallibility and an ecclesial liability. Likewise, slogans such as "America First" or "Make America Great Again" might be tempered by Luke's theological reversal, which conveys that the first will be last (Luke 13:30).

Additionally, this study repeatedly notes how "great" functions among Luke's portrayal of dark characters, adding further intrigue to his theological perspective on social reversal. Finally, with the rise of Christian nationalism, this study offers avenues for assessing how Luke's depiction of Rome might inform this emerging movement.[34] Themes such as justice, equality, power, inclusivity, allegiance, idolatry, and the imperial cult are particularly relevant for critical reflection.

The Prosperity Gospel and the New Apostolic Reformation

The prosperity gospel, which is growing in prominence and influence among African churches, can be seen as a form of theological colonialism originating from the prosperous US. This study suggests that the Holy Spirit disrupts socioeconomic inequality; however, there is no evidence in Acts that the church's progression enables it to accumulate and harbor wealth. On the contrary, this project serves as a warning to the church regarding the inherent greed associated with wealth, a perspective seemingly incongruent with some contemporary teachings.

Secondly, the New Apostolic Reformation (NAR) affirms the revival of the office of apostle—an office that Luke carefully reserves in his writings. Functionally, the NAR advocates for the takeover of government institutions and businesses for the kingdom of God.[35] In Acts, organizational injustices are indeed confronted by the Holy Spirit. However, the distinction between reform and the hostile takeovers or looting of powers as depicted by the NAR is worthy of further exploration in conversation with the findings of this study.

---

33. See Stewart and Bennett, *American Cultural Patterns*.

34. See Gorski and Perry, *Flag and Cross*; Gagné, *Kingdom, Power, Glory*; Austin, *American Christian Nationalism*; Whitehead, *American Idolatry*.

35. Christerson and Flory, *Rise of Network Christianity*; Pivec and Geivett, *Counterfeit Kingdom*; Geivett and Pivec, *New Apostolic Reformation*.

Demonology, Exorcism, and Spiritual Warfare

Many traditions maintain a view of spiritual warfare, demonology, and exorcisms. This study contributes to these fields by considering how greed operates as a vital component within these categories. Few scholarly sources directly address these variables; however, a commonality among them is the lack of attention to, and general unawareness of, the link between greed and spiritual phenomena.[36] The result is the potential for exploring the intersection of greed and socioeconomic ethics theoretically and practically as either a symptom or a culprit of spiritual phenomena among individuals and organizations.

---

36. See Onyinah, *Spiritual Warfare*; Bellini, *X Manual: Exousia*; Cook and Lawless, *Spiritual Warfare*; Heiser, *Demons*; Rankin and Stetzer, *Spiritual Warfare*; Beilby and Eddy, *Understanding Spiritual Warfare*; Hitchcock, *Answers to Spiritual Warfare*; McDermott, *Demonology*.

Appendix C—Bridging the Gaps: Socioeconomic Ethics, Spiritual Opposition, and Rome in Scholarship

THE CONTENT OF THIS appendix stems from the original dissertation's literature review. Existing scholarly work is loosely organized into three categories relevant to the theme of this book—socioeconomic ethics, spirituality, and Luke's perspective on the Roman Empire. This review identifies the knowledge gap that led to the pursuit of this study but also summarizes each source's relative contribution as a conversation partner to this study.

Socioeconomic Ethics

The initial section of this literature review examines existing sources regarding wealth and socioeconomic ethics in Luke-Acts; however, these publications frequently reflect a targeted focus, either limited to the Gospel material, or just the early sections of Acts rather than the entire book.

1. Primarily limited to the Gospel:

    - Halvor Moxnes's 2004 *The Economy of the Kingdom: Social Conflict and Economic Relations in Luke's Gospel*

    - James A. Metzger's 2007 *Consumption and Wealth in Luke's Travel Narrative*

    - Mija Wi's 2019 *The Path to Salvation in Luke's Gospel: What Must We Do?*

2. Address Acts, yet are limited in their scope:

   - Christy Cobb's 2019 *Slavery, Gender, Truth, and Power in Luke-Acts and Other Ancient Narratives*—examines women and slavery, a specificity that therefore makes only a modest contribution to this literature review

   - Joshua Noble's 2021 *Common Property, the Golden Age, and Empire in Acts 2:42–47 and 4:32–35*—explores Hellenistic idealism, but reduces its focus to two pericopes

   - David D. M. King's 2022 *Reclaiming the Radical Economic Message of Luke*—employs models of Roman economics, but the focus is the extent of Luke's reform rather than specific narrative movements

3. Address Luke and Acts holistically, but with the limitations of generalized content, summarized narratives rather than exhaustive analysis, or surveys of only the earlier sections of Acts, leaving the bulk of narratives in Acts unattended:

   - Luke T. Johnson's 1977 *The Literary Function of Possessions in Luke-Acts*—focuses on early passages in Acts, with the truncated assessment that Acts 9–28 "contain very little about possessions,"[37] a position refuted by Steve Walton (see below)

   - John Gillman's 1991 *Possessions and the Life of Faith: A Reading of Luke-Acts*

   - Thomas E. Phillips's 2001 *Reading Issues of Wealth and Poverty in Luke-Acts*

   - Walter Pilgrim's 2011 *Good News to the Poor: Wealth and Poverty in Luke-Acts*

   - David Peter Seccombe's 2022 *The Poor and Their Possessions: Possessions and the Poor in Luke-Acts*

4. Offer intriguing approaches to the Lukan corpus, with limitations such as a generalized or broad scope, isolating a single aspect of interest, or disproportionate attention to Gospel material:

   - Christopher M. Hays's 2010 *Luke's Wealth Ethics: A Study in Their Coherence and Character*

---

37. Johnson, *Literary Function of Possessions*, 29.

- Joseph M. Lear's 2018 *What Shall We Do? Eschatology and Ethics in Luke-Acts*
- Rachel L. Coleman's 2020 *The Lukan Lens on Wealth and Possessions: A Perspective Shaped by the Themes of Reversal and Right Response*

5. Addresses (in part) the knowledge gap:
   - Steve Walton's 2022 SBL Annual Meeting presentation "Wealth and Poverty According to Acts 11–28"

This project builds upon and further substantiates Walton's position regarding the scholarly neglect of socioeconomic ethics in Acts 11–28.

Spiritual Phenomena

Very little scholarly work specifically addresses either the dark powers and/or the Holy Spirit's intersection with those powers from a strictly Lukan perspective.

1. Prominent literature, but limited in scope:
   - Roger Stronstad's 1984 *The Charismatic Theology of St. Luke*—concentrates on the Holy Spirit without considering its interaction with antithetical forces
   - Todd Klutz's 2004 *The Exorcism Stories in Luke-Acts*—employs a unique socio-stylistic methodology with a very limited textual scope
   - Gonzalo Haya-Prats's 2011 *Empowered Believers: The Holy Spirit in the Book of Acts*—mentions Satan and the devil only once each, and while demonic spirits receive greater attention, the scope is limited to Gospel material
   - Paul Elbert's 2021 *The Lukan Gift of the Holy Spirit: Understanding Luke's Expectations for Theophilus*—does not address spiritual warfare, nor does it explore the historical or literary character of Luke's recipient(s)

2. Advances the conversation of this study:
   - Hans-Josef Klauck's 2003 *Magic and Paganism in Early Christianity: The World of the Acts of the Apostles*—offers value to this study

through its valuable background information regarding sorcery, spells, and idolatry. However, it avoids delving into areas of robust theological significance with a reductionistic view determining an absence of any considerable polemic against magic (evil forces), instead promoting the idea that Luke employs certain narratives to clarify the divergent personality of early Christianity. These conclusions rely on isolating a motif that is read in alienation from other useful factors, failing to take the narrative arc of Acts into account.

- Susan R. Garrett's 1989 *The Demise of the Devil: Magic and the Demonic in Luke's Writings*—demonstrates noticeable distinction in this area of Lukan studies. Garrett engages with three crucial passages from this study: Simon Magus (Acts 8:4–24), Elymas (Acts 13:4–12), and the seven sons of Sceva (Acts 19:8–20). Her thesis is that the narrative progression within Acts indicates that the evil forces grow weaker as the Holy Spirit's power increases. This attestation is paramount as the literary direction toward Rome takes ultimate precedence. While Garrett does not provide further theological implications for her conclusions or any direct application regarding the ending of Acts in Rome, her contribution is notable.

This project expands Garrett's work from three to seven pericopes. It also shows that the progression she identifies throughout the broader narrative arc includes more themes and motifs than magic alone. Moreover, this study's contribution is further solidified by applying the findings (broadly shared by Garrett) to the narrative conclusion, expounding upon the Roman implications.

Luke's View of Rome

The works listed here discuss various aspects of the Roman situation in Luke's writings.

1. Recognize intrinsic economic and political tension in Luke-Acts; offer introductory background material without arguing any conclusive positions:

    - Richard J. Cassidy's 1978 *Jesus, Politics, and Society: A Study in Luke's Gospel*

- Cassidy's 1983 edited volume with Philip J. Scharper titled *Political Issues in Luke-Acts*
- Cassidy's 1988 *Society and Politics in the Acts of the Apostles*

2. Interpret Luke's writings as supporting imperial structures:

   - Philip Francis Esler's 1989 *Community and Gospel in Luke-Acts: The Social and Political Motivations of Lucan Theology*—develops a view from a limited textual analysis
   - Vernon K. Robbins's 1991 "Luke-Acts: A Mixed Population Seeks a Home in the Roman Empire"—bases conclusions on a hermeneutic that likely exceeds Luke's intention

3. Judicial themes; many of these publications tend to adopt a restrictive approach, considering smaller (or micro) textual investigations. Others argue from a limited theological viewpoint (e.g., trial scenes), without embracing the entire narrative arc of Luke-Acts:

   - Paul W. Walaskay's 1983 *"And So We Came to Rome": The Political Perspective of St. Luke*
   - Robert Kenneth Mackenzie's 1984 "Character Description and Socio-Political Apologetic in the Acts of the Apostles"
   - Harry W. Tajra's 1989 *The Trial of St. Paul*
   - Alexandru Neagoe's 2002 *The Trial of the Gospel: An Apologetic Reading of Luke's Trial Narratives*
   - Douglas S. McComiskey's 2007 *Lukan Theology in the Light of the Gospel's Literary Structure*

4. Narrative conclusion of Acts:

   - Conrad Gempf's 2002 essay "Luke's Story of Paul's Reception in Rome"
   - Matthew L. Skinner's 2003 *Locating Paul: Places of Custody as Narrative Settings in Acts 21–28*—while also addressing judicial themes, Skinner argues that the concluding section of Acts has often been overlooked and underappreciated. With a perspective similar to this study, he perceptively highlights how the gospel advances amid political hardships in the latter part of Luke's second volume, ultimately reaching Rome, where Paul (miraculously)

remained unharmed. While this observation aligns in part with this project's interest, Skinner's analysis avoids framing the narrative as inherently victorious. Instead, he emphasizes Paul as a marginalized servant who endures suffering, presenting this as the central focus of the final chapters in Acts.

- Charles B. Puskas's 2009 *The Conclusion of Luke-Acts: The Significance of Acts 28:16–31*

5. Luke's view of empire:

    - Broadly survey Luke's writings (or scholarly assessments of Luke-Acts) to ascertain a view of empire; some result in an inconclusive middle ground:

        a. Steve Walton's 2002 "The State They Were In: Luke's View of the Roman Empire"

        b. Christopher Bryan's 2005 "Followers and the Roman Empire: Luke-Acts, 1 Peter, and Revelation"

        c. Seyoon Kim's 2008 *Christ and Caesar: The Gospel and the Roman Empire in the Writings of Paul and Luke*—interprets Luke's focus as spirituality divorced from political dimensions, undervaluing Luke's strong interest in tangible socioeconomic ethics in favor of a more spiritualized reading of the text

        d. The 2011 volume *Luke-Acts and Empire: Essays in Honor of Robert L. Brawley* edited by David Rhoads et al.—offers a variety of contributions

        e. Pyung Soo Seo's 2015 *Luke's Jesus in the Roman Empire and the Emperor in the Gospel of Luke*

    - Acknowledge the (unsolvable to some) tension associated with Rome located in both Luke-Acts that often generates an essential straddling of the ideological fence:

        a. C. Kavin Rowe's 2010 *World Upside Down: Reading Acts in the Graeco-Roman Age*—critically assesses scholarship's assumed apologetical intention of Luke's writings (for multiple centuries) that have produced contemporary stagnation[38]

---

38. Rowe, *World Upside Down*, 3–4.

b. Dean Pinter's 2013 "The Gospel of Luke and the Roman Empire"

c. Drew J. Strait's 2013 "Proclaiming Another King Named Jesus? The Acts of the Apostles and the Roman Imperial Cult(s)"

d. Bruce W. Winter's 2017 "Paul and Roman Law: 'The Luck of the Draw?'"

- Helpful for advancing the discussion:

  a. Rubén Muñoz-Larrondo's 2011 *A Postcolonial Reading of the Acts of the Apostles*—supplies a vibrant conversation partner and a fresh perspective on existing views of Acts. Muñoz-Larrondo is attentive to subversive themes that emerge through his postcolonial methodology—themes that Western scholars might overlook. Muñoz-Larrondo pivots his critical reading of empire on Agrippa I in Acts 12 and gives attention to most subsequent sections of Acts, applying various postcolonial interpretations. He argues for the subversive tendency of Luke's writing, albeit veiled in necessary cryptic qualities, which can be easily overlooked. His work, however, does not engage the intersection of socioeconomic ethics and spiritual warfare—an area that remains underexplored in postcolonial readings of Luke-Acts.

  b. Matthew Skinner's 2017 "Who Speaks for (or Against) Rome? Acts in Relation to Empire"—identifies the "messy state" of scholarship on Rome in Luke-Acts,[39] observing how divergent methodologies and ideological frameworks have led to a wide range of conclusions. He sees these tensions as opportunities for innovative approaches to the study of empire in Luke's writings.

- Contributions to this study—two essays that, like Skinner's work above, appear in the 2017 edited anthology *Reading Acts in the Discourses of Masculinity and Politics*:

  a. Mikeal C. Parsons's "Empowering, Empire-ing or Engaging? Acts in the Discourse of Politics: A Response"—affirms Skinner's assessment of scholarly fragmentation. He proposes that Luke-Acts may be more critical of Rome than previously considered and calls for further exploration of anti-imperial themes, observing that the literary conclusion of Acts merits more attention.

---

39. Skinner, "Who Speaks for Rome," 107.

b. Barbara R. Rossing's "Turning the Empire (οἰκουμένη) Upside Down"—draws parallels between Acts and Revelation, portraying both as texts that subvert Roman imperial hegemony. She argues that Acts uses judicial and rhetorical strategies to undermine Rome's claims to power, presenting the gospel as a counterforce to imperial control.

Parsons and Rossing both offer material that generates momentum on the topic. Additionally, this project underscores Parsons's encouragement for innovative approaches that also consider the narrative conclusion of Acts.

Knowledge Gap

The resources examined in this literature review reflect a common fallacy in Acts scholarship.[40] Writers often extract themes and motifs from Acts, alienating them from their broader contexts and divorcing their findings from the overarching narrative. Consequently, existing studies tend to isolate socioeconomic ethics and spiritual phenomena, rather than exploring their interplay in shaping the conclusion of Acts and Luke's perspective on Rome.

- Writings engaging in Luke's socioeconomic ethics tends to prioritize the Gospel or restrict attention to the earliest sections of Acts.

- Resources that explore Luke's view of spiritual phenomena tend to concentrate on the Holy Spirit while avoiding significant interaction with the dark forces.

- Many scholarly assessments of Rome in Luke-Acts submit mediating or inconclusive views. The more assertive proposals tend to limit their textual or thematic investigation. Although scholarly stagnation is evident, some works advocate further study using innovative methodologies.

This project contributes to scholarship by examining the intersection of Lukan socioeconomic ethics and spiritual warfare, emphasizing how these intertwined themes inherently position the church in opposition to Roman imperial values. This analysis is substantiated by tracing these themes throughout the narrative arc of Luke's writings, culminating in the literary conclusion set in Rome.

---

40. Gaventa, "Toward Theology," 146–57.

Bibliography

Adams, Samuel L. *Social and Economic Life in Second Temple Judea*. Louisville: Westminster John Knox, 2014.
Ahn, Yong-Sung. *The Reign of God and Rome in Luke's Passion Narrative: An East Asian Global Perspective*. BibInt 80. Leiden: Brill, 2006.
Aldrete, Gregory S. "Cicero: History's Greatest Orator and Roman Secrets of Persuasive Public Speaking." Williams Lecture, Core Curriculum Program, Emory University, Atlanta, Feb. 3, 2016.
Allen, Ronald J. *Acts of the Apostles*. FBPC. Minneapolis: Fortress, 2013.
Alolo, Namawu Alhassan. "African Traditional Religion and Concepts of Development." Religions and Development Working Paper 17, International Development Department, University of Birmingham, 2007.
Arnold, Clinton E., ed. *Acts*. ZIBBC 2B. Grand Rapids: Zondervan, 2007.
Arterbury, Andrew. "Caesarea Maritima." *REHJ* 86–88.
Aune, David. E. "Ephesus." *EDB* 414.
Austin, Michael W. *American Christian Nationalism: Neither Christianity nor Nationalism*. Grand Rapids: Eerdmans, 2023.
Barrett, Anthony A. *Rome Is Burning: Nero and the Fire That Ended a Dynasty*. Princeton: Princeton University Press, 2020.
Barrett, C. K. *A Critical and Exegetical Commentary on the Acts of the Apostles*. ICC. Edinburgh: T&T Clark, 2004.
Bass, Justin W. "Devil." *LBD*.
Bauer, David R. *The Book of Acts as Story: A Narrative-Critical Study*. Grand Rapids: Baker, 2021.
Beale, G. K. *Handbook on the New Testament Use of the Old Testament: Exegesis and Interpretation*. Grand Rapids: Baker, 2012.
Beard, Mary. *Confronting the Classics: Traditions, Adventures and Innovations*. New York: Liveright, 2013.
Beilby, James K., and Paul Rhodes Eddy, eds. *Understanding Spiritual Warfare: Four Views*. Grand Rapids: Baker Academic, 2012.
Bellini, Peter J. *The X Manual: Exousia—A Comprehensive Handbook on Deliverance and Exorcism*. Eugene, OR: Wipf and Stock, 2022.
Bence, Philip A. *Acts: A Bible Commentary in the Wesleyan Tradition*. Indianapolis: Wesleyan, 1998.
Bhabha, Homi. *The Location of Culture*. London: Routledge, 2004.

BIBLIOGRAPHY

Bird, Michael F. *A Bird's-Eye View of Luke and Acts: Context, Story, and Themes*. Downers Grove, IL: IVP Academic, 2023.

Blanton, Thomas R., IV, and Raymond Pickett. *Paul and Economics: A Handbook*. Minneapolis: Fortress, 2017.

Bock, Darrell L. "Acts." In *The Gospels and Acts*, edited by Jeremy Royal Howard, 1044–1251. Holman Apologetics Commentary on the Bible 1. Nashville: Holman Reference, 2013.

———. *A Theology of Luke and Acts: God's Promised Program, Realized for All Nations*. BTNTS. Grand Rapids: Zondervan, 2015.

Bonz, Marianne Palmer. *The Past as Legacy: Luke-Acts and Ancient Epic*. Minneapolis: Fortress, 2000. Kindle.

Borg, Marcus J. *Meeting Jesus Again for the First Time: The Historical Jesus and the Heart of Contemporary Faith*. New York: HarperCollins, 2009.

Borg, Marcus J., and John Dominic Crossan. *The First Christmas: What the Gospels Really Teach About Jesus's Birth*. New York: HarperCollins, 2007.

———. *The Last Week: What the Gospels Really Teach About Jesus's Final Days in Jerusalem*. New York: HarperCollins, 2006.

Bourdieu, Pierre. *Distinction: A Social Critique of the Judgment of Taste*. Cambridge: Harvard University Press, 1984.

Bovon, François. *Luke 2: A Commentary on the Gospel of Luke 9:51—19:27*. Edited by Helmut Koester, translated by Donald S. Deer. Hermeneia: CHCB. Minneapolis: Fortress, 2013.

Brennan, Joseph A. "Artemis and the Ephesian *Haustafeln*: An Examination of the Goddess, Marriage, and the Imago Dei." PhD diss., University of Manchester, UK, 2023.

Bruce, F. F. *The Book of the Acts*. NICNT. Grand Rapids: Eerdmans, 1988.

Brueggemann, Walter. *Money and Possessions*. IRUSC. Louisville: Westminster John Knox, 2016.

———. *Sabbath as Resistance: Saying No to the Culture of Now*. New ed. Louisville: Westminster John Knox, 2017.

Bryan, Christopher. "Followers and the Roman Empire: Luke-Acts, 1 Peter, and Revelation." In *Render to Caesar: Jesus, the Early Church, and the Roman Superpower*, 95–112. Oxford: Oxford University Press, 2005.

Burnett, D. Clint. *Paul and Imperial Divine Honors: Christ, Caesar, and the Gospel*. Grand Rapids: Eerdmans, 2024.

Campbell, William Sanger. *The "We" Passages in the Acts of the Apostles: The Narrator as Narrative Character*. Atlanta: Studies in Biblical Literature, 2007.

Carroll, John T. *Luke: A Commentary*. NTL. Louisville: Westminster John Knox, 2012.

Carter, Warren. *The Roman Empire and the New Testament: An Essential Guide*. Nashville: Abingdon, 2006.

Cassidy, Richard J. *Jesus, Politics, and Society: A Study in Luke's Gospel*. Eugene, OR: Wipf & Stock, 1978.

———. *Society and Politics in the Acts of the Apostles*. New York: Orbis, 1988.

Cassidy, Richard J., and Philip J. Scharper, eds. *Political Issues in Luke-Acts*. Maryknoll, NY: Orbis, 1983.

Charlesworth, James H. *Jesus and Temple: Textual and Archaeological Explorations*. Minneapolis: Fortress, 2014.

Childs, James M. *Greed: Economics and Ethics in Conflict*. Minneapolis: Fortress, 2000.

BIBLIOGRAPHY

Chilton, Bruce. "Annas and Caiaphas." *REHJ* 8–9.

———. *The Herods: Murder, Politics, and the Art of Succession*. Minneapolis: Fortress, 2021.

———. "Historical Criticism." In *Searching for Meaning: An Introduction to Interpreting the New Testament*, edited by Paula Gooder, 5–12. Louisville: Westminster John Knox, 2009.

Cho, Youngmo, and Hyung Dae Park. *Acts, Part One: Introduction and Chapters 1–12*. NCCS. Eugene, OR: Cascade, 2019.

Christerson, Brad, and Richard Flory. *The Rise of Network Christianity: How Apostolic Reformation Is Changing the Religious Landscape*. Oxford: Oxford University Press, 2017.

Cobb, Christy. *Slavery, Gender, Truth, and Power in Luke-Acts and Other Ancient Narratives*. London: Palgrave MacMillan, 2019.

Coffey, Amanda, and Paul Atkinson. *Making Sense of Qualitative Data: Complementary Research Strategies*. Thousand Oaks, CA: Sage, 1996.

Coleman, Rachel L. *The Lukan Lens on Wealth and Possessions: A Perspective Shaped by the Themes of Reversal and Right Response*. Leiden: Brill, 2020.

Conzelmann, Hans. *The Theology of St. Luke*. Translated by Geoffrey Buswell. Philadelphia: Fortress, 1982.

Cook, William F., III, and Chuck Lawless. *Spiritual Warfare in the Storyline of Scripture: A Biblical, Theological, and Practical Approach*. Nashville: B&H Academic, 2019.

Creamer, Jennifer M., et al. "Who Is Theophilus? Discovering the Original Reader of Luke-Acts." *IDS* 48 (2014) 1–7.

Crossan, John Dominic. *The Historical Jesus: The Life of a Mediterranean Jewish Peasant*. New York: HarperOne, 1991.

———. "Roman Imperial Theology." In *In the Shadow of Empire: Reclaiming the Bible as a History of Faithful Resistance*, edited by Richard A. Horsley, 59–74. Louisville: Westminster John Knox, 2008.

Dallaire, Hélène M., and Denise R. Morris. "Joshua and Israel's Exodus from the Dessert Wilderness." In *Reverberations of the Exodus in Scripture*, edited by R. Michael Fox, 18–34. Eugene, OR: Pickwick, 2014.

Daniels, J. W., Jr. "Gossip in the New Testament." *BTB* 42 (2012) 204–13.

Danker, Frederick W. *Jesus and the New Age According to St. Luke: A Commentary on the Third Gospel*. St. Louis: Clayton, 1972.

Davies, Douglas J. "Purity, Spirit, and Reciprocity in the Acts of the Apostles." In *Anthropology and Biblical Studies*, 259–280. Leiden: Brill, 2004. https://doi.org/10.1163/9789004397507_018.

Davies, Eryl W. "A Mathematical Conundrum: The Problem of Large Numbers in Number I and XXVI." *VT* 45 (1995) 449–69.

Davis, John J. "The Rhetorical Use of Numbers in the Old Testament." *Grace* 8 (1967) 40–48.

Derrett, John Duncan M. "Simon Magus (Acts 8:9–24)." *ZNW* 73 (1982) 52–68.

DeSilva, David A. *Honor, Patronage, Kinship & Purity: Unlocking New Testament Culture*. Downers Grove, IL: InterVarsity, 2012.

Douglas, Mary. *Purity and Danger: An Analysis of the Concepts of Pollution and Taboo*. New York: Routledge and Kegan Paul, 1966.

Dunn, James D. G. *The Acts of the Apostles*. Grand Rapids: Eerdmans, 2016.

Edwards, Douglas R. "Tyre (Place)." *ABD* 6:686–92.

Edwards, James R. "Parallels and Patterns Between Luke and Acts." *BBR* 27 (2017) 485–501.

Ehling, Kay. "Zwei Anmerkungen zum ἀργύριον in Apg 19,19" [Two notes on the Argyrion in Acts 19:19]. *ZNW* 94 (2003) 269–75.

Elbert, Paul. *The Lukan Gift of the Holy Spirit: Understanding Luke's Expectations for Theophilus*. Canton, GA: Foundation for Pentecostal Scholarship, 2021.

Elliott, John H. *Greece and Rome*. BtEE 2. Eugene, OR: Cascade, 2016.

———. *What Is Social-Scientific Criticism?* Minneapolis: Fortress, 1993.

Esler, Philip Francis. *Community and Gospel in Luke-Acts: The Social and Political Motivations of Lucan Theology*. SNTSMS 57. Cambridge: Cambridge University Press, 1989.

Ferreiro, Alberto. "The Fall of Simon Magus in Early Christian Commentary." Presentation, 13th International Conference on Patristic Studies, Oxford, Aug. 16–21, 1999.

Ferry, Sara. "Tyre." *LBD*.

Finger, Reta Halteman. *Of Widows and Meals: Communal Meals in the Book of Acts*. Grand Rapids: Eerdmans, 2007. Kindle.

Fitzgerald, John T. *Greco-Roman Perspectives on Friendship*. Atlanta: Scholars, 1997.

Fitzmyer, Joseph A. *The Acts of the Apostles: A New Translation with Introduction and Commentary*. AYBC 31. New Haven: Yale University Press, 2008.

———. *The Gospel According to Luke X–XXIV: Introduction, Translation, and Notes*. AYBC 28B. New Haven: Yale University Press, 2008.

Foerster, Werner. "Εἰρήνη, Εἰρηνεύω, Εἰρηνικός, Εἰρηνοποιός, Εἰρηνοποιέω." TDNT 2:400–420.

Foster, George M. "Peasant Society and the Image of Limited Good." *American Anthropologist* 67 (1965) 293–315.

———. "A Second Look at Limited Good." *Anthropological Quarterly* 45 (1972) 57–64.

Fouts, David M. "A Defense of the Hyperbolic Interpretation of Large Numbers in the Old Testament." *JETS* 40 (1997) 377–87.

———. "The Incredible Numbers of the Hebrew Kings." In *Giving the Sense: Understanding and Using Old Testament Historical Texts*, edited by D. M. Howard Jr. and M. A. Grisanti, 283–89. Grand Rapids: Kregel Academic, 2004.

Fox, Nickolas A. *The Hermeneutics of Social Identity in Luke-Acts*. Eugene, OR: Pickwick, 2021.

France, R. T. *Luke*. TTCS. Ada, MI: Baker, 2013.

Freyne, Seán. "Galilee and Judaea in the First Century." In *The Cambridge History of Christianity: Origins to Constantine*, edited by Margaret M. Mitchell and Frances M. Young, 37–52. New York: Cambridge University Press, 2014.

———. "Galilee: Hellenistic/Roman Galilee." *ABD* 2:897–98.

Friesen, Steven J. *Imperial Cults and the Apocalypse of John: Reading Revelation in the Ruins*. Oxford: Oxford University Press, 2001.

———. "Injustice or God's Will? Early Christian Explanations of Poverty." In *Wealth and Poverty in Early Church and Society*, edited by Susan R. Holman, 17–36. Holy Cross Studies in Patristic Theology and History. Grand Rapids: Baker Academic, 2008.

———. "Poverty in Pauline Studies: Beyond the So-Called New Consensus." *JSNT* 26 (2004) 323–61.

Gagné, André. *The Kingdom, the Power, the Glory: Evangelicals and Extremism*. London: Quercus, 2023.

Gangel, Kenneth O. *Acts*. HNTC 5. Edited by Max Anders. Nashville: Broadman & Holman, 1998.
Gapp, Kenneth Sperber. "The Universal Famine Under Claudius." *HTR* 28 (1935) 258–65.
Garland, David E. *Acts*. TTCS. Grand Rapids: Baker, 2017.
———. *Luke*. ZECNT 3. Grand Rapids: Zondervan Academic, 2011.
Garnsey, Peter, and Richard P. Saller. *The Roman Empire: Economy, Society, and Culture*. Berkeley: University of California Press, 1987.
Garrett, Susan R. *The Demise of the Devil: Magic and the Demonic in Luke's Writings*. Minneapolis: Fortress, 1989.
Gaventa, Beverly Roberts. *Acts*. ANTC. Nashville: Abingdon, 2003.
———. "Toward a Theology of Acts: Reading and Rereading." *Int* 42 (1988) 146–57.
Geivett, R. Douglas, and Holly Pivec. *A New Apostolic Reformation? A Biblical Response to a Worldwide Movement*. Bellingham, WA: Lexham, 2014.
Gempf, Conrad. "Luke's Story of Paul's Reception in Rome." In *Rome in the Bible and the Early Church*, edited by Peter Oakes, 42–66. Grand Rapids: Baker Academic, 2002.
Gillman, John. *Possessions and the Life of Faith: A Reading of Luke-Acts*. Collegeville, MN: Liturgical, 1991.
Glaeser, Edward L. *Triumph of the City: How Our Greatest Invention Makes Us Richer, Smarter, Greener, Healthier, and Happier*. New York: Penguin, 2011.
Glahn, Sandra L. *Nobody's Mother: Artemis of the Ephesians in Antiquity and the New Testament*. Downers Grove, IL: IVP Academic, 2023.
Goldsworthy, Adrian Keith. *Pax Romana: War, Peace and Conquest in the Roman World*. New Haven: Yale University Press, 2017.
Gooder, Paula, ed. *Searching for Meaning: An Introduction to Interpreting the New Testament*. Louisville: Westminster John Knox, 2009.
Goodman, Martin. "The First Jewish Revolt: Social Conflict and the Problem of Debt." *JJS* 33 (1982) 417–27.
———. "The Pilgrimage Economy of Jerusalem in the Second Temple Period." In *Judaism and the Roman World: Collected Essays*, 59–67. Ancient Judaism and Early Christianity 66. Leiden: Brill, 2006.
———. *Rome and Jerusalem: The Clash of Ancient Civilizations*. New York: Knopf Doubleday, 2008.
———. *The Ruling Class of Judaea: The Origins of the Jewish Revolt Against Rome, A.D. 66–70*. New York: Cambridge University Press, 1993.
Gorski, Philip S., and Samuel L. Perry. *The Flag and the Cross: White Christian Nationalism and the Threat to American Democracy*. New York: Oxford University Press, 2022.
Graham, Daryn. "Imperial Responses to the Food Crisis That Began Under Claudius." *Mouseion* 64 (2023) 26–52.
Green, Gene L. "Finding the Will of God: Historical and Modern Perspectives, Acts 16:1–30." In *Mission in Acts: Ancient Narratives in Contemporary Context*, edited by Robert L. Gallagher and Paul Hertig, 209–20. Ossining, NY: Orbis, 2004.
Gupta, Nijay K. *Strange Religion: How the First Christians Were Weird, Dangerous, and Compelling*. Ada, MI: Baker, 2024.
Hadas-Lebel, Mireille. "Caligula, Agrippa Ier et les Juifs." In *Rome, la Judée et les Juifs*, 79–92. Antiquité/Synthèses 12. Paris: Picard, 2009.
Haenchen, Ernst. *The Acts of the Apostles: A Commentary*. Louisville: Westminster John Knox, 1971.

Hamm, Dennis. *The Acts of the Apostles*. NCollBC: NT 5. Collegeville, MN: Liturgical, 2005.

Hammar, Isak. "Making Enemies: The Logic of Immorality in Ciceronian Oratory." PhD diss., Lund University, Sweden, 2013.

Hanson, K. C. "The Galilean Fishing Economy and the Jesus Tradition." *BTB* 27 (1997) 99–111.

———. "Jesus and the Social Bandits." In *The Social Setting of Jesus and the Gospels*, edited by Wolfgang Stegemann et al., 283–300. Minneapolis: Fortress, 2002.

Hanson, Richard P. C. *Cities of God: The Real Story of How Christianity Became an Urban Movement and Conquered Rome*. New York: HarperOne, 2002.

Harvey, David. *Rebel Cities: From the Right to the City to the Urban Revolution*. New York: Verso, 2012.

———. *The Urban Experience*. Baltimore: Johns Hopkins University Press, 1989.

Harvey, Richard. *Judas Iscariot: Betrayal, Blasphemy, and Idolatry in the Gospels and Acts*. Eugene, OR: Wipf & Stock, 2018.

Haya-Prats, Gonzalo. *Empowered Believers: The Holy Spirit in the Book of Acts*. Edited by Paul Elbert, translated by Scott A. Ellington. Eugene, OR: Cascade, 2011.

Hays, Christopher M. *Luke's Wealth Ethics: A Study in Their Coherence and Character*. Tubingen, Ger.: Mohr Siebeck, 2010.

Hays, J. Daniel. *The Temple and the Tabernacle: A Study of God's Dwelling Places from Genesis to Revelation*. Grand Rapids: Baker, 2016.

Heard, W. J., and K. Yamazaki-Ransom. "Revolutionary Movements." *DJG* 789–99.

Heiser, Michael S. *Demons: What the Bible Really Says About the Powers of Darkness*. Bellingham, WA: Lexham, 2020.

Hengel, Martin. *Studien zum Urchristentum: Kleine Schriften VI* [Studies of early Christianity: Selected essays VI]. Edited by Claus-Jürgen Thornton. WUNT I 234. Tubingen, Ger.: Mohr Siebeck, 2011.

Hill, Craig. *Hellenists and Hebrews: Reappraising Division Within the Earliest Church*. Minneapolis: Fortress, 1991.

Hitchcock, Mark. *101 Answers to Questions About Satan, Demons, and Spiritual Warfare*. Eugene, OR: Harvest House, 2012.

Holden, James Herschel. *A History of Horoscopic Astrology: From the Babylonian Period to the Modern Age*. Tempe, AZ: American Federation of Astrology, 2006.

Holladay, Carl R. *Acts: A Commentary*. NTL. Louisville: Westminster John Knox, 2016.

Horsley, Richard A. *Jesus and Empire: The Kingdom of God and the New World Disorder*. Minneapolis: Fortress, 2003. Kindle.

———. *Jesus and the Politics of Roman Palestine*. Columbia: University of South Carolina Press, 2014.

———. *Jesus and the Powers: Conflict, Covenant, and the Hope of the Poor*. Minneapolis: Fortress, 2011.

———. *Jesus and the Spiral of Violence: Popular Jewish Resistance in Roman Palestine*. Minneapolis: Fortress, 1993.

———. *The Liberation of Christmas: The Infancy Narratives in Social Context*. New York: Continuum, 1993.

———. *Paul and Empire: Religion and Power in Roman Imperial Society*. Harrisburg, PA: Trinity, 1997.

———. *Scribes, Visionaries, and the Politics of Second Temple Judea*. Louisville: Westminster John Knox, 2007.

Jennings, Willie James. *Acts*. Belief: TCB. Louisville: Westminster John Knox, 2017.

Johnson, Luke T. *The Literary Function of Possessions in Luke-Acts*. SBLDS 39. Missoula, MT: Scholars, 1977.

Jones, Donald L. "Roman Imperial Cult." *ABD* 5:806–9.

Just, Arthur A., Jr. *Luke 9:51—24:53*. ConcC. St. Louis: Concordia, 1997.

Juvenal. *The Satires*. Translated by A. S. Kline. Poetry in Translation, 2001. https://www.poetryintranslation.com/PITBR/Latin/Juvenalhome.php.

Kauppi, Lynn Allan. *Foreign but Familiar Gods: Greco-Romans Read Religion in Acts*. London: T&T Clark, 2006.

Keener, Craig S. *Acts*. NCBC. Cambridge: Cambridge University Press, 2020.

———. *Acts: An Exegetical Commentary*. 4 vols. Ada, MI: Baker Academic, 2014–2015.

———. *New Testament*. 2nd ed. IVPBBC. Downers Grove, IL: InterVarsity, 2014.

———. "The Plausibility of Luke's Growth Figures in Acts 2.41; 4.4; 21.20." *JGRChJ* 7 (2010) 140–63.

Kellum, L. Scott. *Acts*. EGGNT. Nashville: B&H Academic, 2020.

Kim, Seyoon. *Christ and Caesar: The Gospel and the Roman Empire in the Writings of Paul and Luke*. Grand Rapids: Eerdmans, 2008.

King, David D. M. *Reclaiming the Radical Economic Message of Luke*. Eugene, OR: Pickwick, 2022.

Kistemaker, Simon J., and William Hendriksen. *Exposition of the Acts of the Apostles*. NTC 17. Grand Rapids: Baker, 1990.

Klauck, Hans-Josef. *Magic and Paganism in Early Christianity: The World of the Acts of the Apostles*. Minneapolis: Fortress, 2003. Kindle.

Klein, Neriah. "The Chronicler's Code: The Rise and Fall of Judah's Army in the Book of Chronicles." *JHebS* 17 (2017) 1–19.

Klein, R. W. "How Many in a Thousand?" In *The Chronicler as Historian*, edited by Patrick M. Graham et al., 270–82. JSOTSup 238. Sheffield: Sheffield Academic, 1997.

Klutz, Todd. *The Exorcism Stories in Luke-Acts: A Sociostylistic Reading*. SNTSMS 129. Cambridge: Cambridge University Press, 2004.

Kochenash, Michael. "'Adam, Son of God' (Luke 3.38): Another Jesus-Augustus Parallel in Luke's Gospel." *NTS* 64 (2018) 307–25.

———. *Roman Self-Representation and the Lukan Kingdom of God*. Lanham, MD: Fortress, 2020.

Lear, Joseph M. *What Shall We Do? Eschatology and Ethics in Luke-Acts*. Eugene, OR: Pickwick, 2018.

Levine, L. I. "Jewish War." *ABD* 3:839–45.

Lieu, Judith. *The Gospel of Luke*. Epworth Commentaries. London: Epworth, 1997.

Logan, John R., and Harvey L. Molotch. *Urban Fortunes: The Political Economy of Place*. Berkeley: University of California Press, 1987.

Longenecker, Richard N. "Acts." In *Luke–Acts*, edited by Tremper Longman III and David E. Garland, 663–1102. EBC 10. Grand Rapids: Zondervan, 2007.

Low, Setha M. *On the Plaza: The Politics of Public Space and Culture*. Austin: University of Texas Press, 2000.

Lugira, Aloysius M. *African Traditional Religion*. 3rd ed. World Religions. New York: Chelsea House, 2009.

MacDonald, Dennis R. *Does the New Testament Imitate Homer? Four Cases from the Acts of the Apostles*. New Haven: Yale University Press, 2008.

———. *The Gospels and Homer: Imitations of Greek Epic in Mark and Luke-Acts*. New Testament and Greek Literature. Lanham, MD: Rowman & Littlefield, 2014.

———. *Luke and the Politics of Homeric Imitation: Luke-Acts as Rival to the Aeneid*. Minneapolis: Fortress, 2018.

———. *Luke and Vergil: Imitations of Classical Greek Literature*. New Testament and Greek Literature. Lanham, MD: Rowman & Littlefield, 2014.

———. *Synopses of Epic, Tragedy, and the Gospels*. Claremont, CA: Mimesis, 2022.

Mackenzie, Robert Kenneth. "Character Description and Socio-Political Apologetic in the Acts of the Apostles." PhD diss., University of Edinburgh, 1984.

MacMullen, Ramsay. *Christianizing the Roman Empire: A.D. 100–400*. New Haven: Yale University Press, 1984.

———. *Enemies of the Roman Order: Treason, Unrest, and Alienation in the Empire*. Cambridge: Harvard University Press, 1966.

Malbon, Elizabeth Struthers. "Narrative Criticism." In *Searching for Meaning: An Introduction to Interpreting the New Testament*, edited by Paula Gooder, 80–87. Louisville: Westminster John Knox, 2009.

Malina, Bruce J. "Hands/Feet." *HBSV* 83–85.

———. *The New Testament World: Insights from Cultural Anthropology*. Louisville: Westminster John Knox, 2001.

———. *Windows on the World of Jesus: Time Travel to Ancient Judea*. Louisville: Westminster John Knox, 1993.

Malina, Bruce J., and Richard L. Rohrbaugh. *Social Science Commentary on the Synoptic Gospels*. Minneapolis: Fortress, 1992. Kindle.

Maloney, Linda M., and Ivoni Richter Reimer. *Acts of the Apostles*. WCS 45. Collegeville, MN: Liturgical, 2022.

Marshall, I. Howard. "Political and Eschatological Language in Luke." In *Reading Luke: Interpretation, Reflection, Formation*, edited by Craig G. Bartholomew et al., 157–77. Grand Rapids: Zondervan, 2005.

Martin, Thomas W. "Paulus, Sergius (Person)." *ABD* 5:205–6.

Marx, Werner G. "A New Theophilus." *EvQ* 52 (1980) 17–26.

Mashau, Thinandavha D., and M. S. Kgatle. "Prosperity Gospel and the Culture of Greed in Post-Colonial Africa: Constructing an Alternative African Christian Theology of Ubuntu." *Verbum et Ecclesia* 40 (2019) 1–8.

Mason, Steve. *Josephus and the New Testament*. 2nd ed. Grand Rapids: Baker Academic, 2002.

Massey, Douglas S., and Nancy A. Denton. *American Apartheid: Segregation and the Making of the Underclass*. Cambridge: Harvard University Press, 1993.

Mbiti, John S. *Introduction to African Religion*. London: Heinemann Educational, 1986.

McComiskey, Douglas S. *Lukan Theology in the Light of the Gospel's Literary Structure*. PBM. Eugene, OR: Wipf & Stock, 2007.

McDermott, Gerald. *Demonology for the Global Church: A Biblical Approach in a Multicultural Age*. Bellingham, WA: Lexham, 2023.

McKnight, Scot. *Acts: Participating Together in God's Mission*. New Testament Everyday Bible Study. New York: HarperChristian Resources, 2022.

Meeks, Wayne A. *The First Urban Christians: The Social World of the Apostle Paul*. New Haven: Yale University Press, 2013.

Metzger, James A. *Consumption and Wealth in Luke's Travel Narrative*. Leiden: Brill, 2007.

Miller, Amanda C. *Rumors of Resistance: Status Reversals and Hidden Transcripts in the Gospel of Luke*. ESS. Minneapolis: Fortress, 2014.
Moessner, David P. "The 'Script' of the Scriptures in Acts: Suffering as God's 'Plan' (βουλή) for the World for the 'Release of Sins.'" In *History, Literature, and Society in the Book of Acts*, edited by Ben Witherington III, 251–80. Cambridge: Cambridge University Press, 1996.
Morgan, James M. "Prophetic Historiography as Subgenre and Research Tool: Definition and Relevance for Herodotean and Lukan Research." In *Le corpus lucanien (Luc-Actes) et l'historiographie ancienne: Quels rapports?*, edited by Simon Butticaz et al., 69–96. Théologie biblique 2. Münster: Lit, 2019.
Moss, Candida. *The Myth of Persecution: How Early Christians Invented a Story of Martyrdom*. New York: HarperOne, 2013.
Moxnes, Halvor. *The Economy of the Kingdom: Social Conflict and Economic Relations in Luke's Gospel*. Eugene, OR: Wipf and Stock, 2004.
Muñoz-Larrondo, Rubén. *A Postcolonial Reading of the Acts of the Apostles*. StBibLit 147. New York: Lang, 2011.
Murphy, Frederick J. *Early Judaism: The Exile to the Time of Jesus*. Grand Rapids: Baker Academic, 2010.
Murphy-O'Connor, Jerome. *St. Paul's Ephesus: Texts and Archaeology*. Collegeville, MN: Liturgical, 2008.
Neagoe, Alexandru. *The Trial of the Gospel: An Apologetic Reading of Luke's Trial Narratives*. SNTSMS 116. Cambridge: Cambridge University Press, 2002.
Neyrey, Jerome H. *Honor and Shame in the Gospel of Matthew*. Louisville: Westminster John Knox, 1998.
———. "Limited Good." *HBSV* 103–6.
Noble, Joshua. *Common Property, the Golden Age, and Empire in Acts 2:42–47 and 4:32–35*. London: T&T Clark, 2021.
Nock, Arthur Darby. "Paul and the Magus." In vol. 1 of *Essays on Religion and the Ancient World*, edited by Zeph Stewart, 308–30. Cambridge: Harvard University Press, 1972.
Oakman, Douglas E. "The Countryside in Luke-Acts." In *Social World of Luke-Acts: Models for Interpretation*, edited by Jerome H. Neyrey, 151–80. Ada, MI: Baker Academic, 1991.
———. *Jesus and the Peasants*. MBMC 4. Eugene, OR: Cascade, 2008.
———. *Jesus, Debt, and the Lord's Prayer: First-Century Debt and Jesus' Intentions*. Eugene, OR: Cascade, 2014.
———. *The Political Aims of Jesus*. Minneapolis: Fortress, 2012.
Olupona, Jacob K. "African Traditional Religions." In *Religions and Sects*, edited by Thomas Riggs, 1–22. Vol. 1 of *Worldmark Encyclopedia of Religious Practices*. Detroit: Gale, 2006.
Onyinah, Opoku. *Spiritual Warfare: A Centre for Pentecostal Theology Short Introduction*. Cleveland, TN: CPT, 2012.
Oropeza, B. J. *In the Footsteps of Judas and Other Defectors: The Gospels, Acts, and Johannine Letters*. Apostasy in the New Testament Communities 1. Eugene, OR: Cascade, 2011.
Osborne, Grant R. *Acts Verse by Verse*. ONTC. Bellingham, WA: Lexham, 2019.
———. *Luke Verse by Verse*. ONTC. Bellingham, WA: Lexham, 2018.
Oster, Richard E., Jr. "Ephesus (Place)." *ABD* 2:542–49.
Pagels, Elaine. "The Social History of Satan: From the Hebrew Bible to the Gospels." In *The Origin of Satan*, 35–61. New York: Random House, 1995.

Parsons, Mikeal C. *Acts*. Paideia: CNT. Ada, MI: Baker Academic, 2008.

———. "Empowering, Empire-ing or Engaging? Acts in the Discourse of Politics: A Response." In *Reading Acts in the Discourses of Masculinity and Politics*, edited by Eric Barreto et al., 141–47. London: T&T Clark, 2017.

Perrin, Nicholas. *Jesus the Temple*. Sewanee, TN: SPCK, 2010.

———. *Luke: An Introduction and Commentary*. TNTC 3. Downers Grove, IL: IVP Academic, 2022.

Pervo, Richard I. *Acts: A Commentary*. Edited by Harold W. Attridge. Hermeneia: CHCB. Minneapolis: Fortress, 2009.

———. *Luke's Story of Paul*. Minneapolis: Fortress, 1990.

Peterson, David G. *The Acts of the Apostles*. Pillar New Testament Commentary. Grand Rapids: Eerdmans, 2009.

Petterson, Christina. *Acts of Empire: The Acts of the Apostles and Imperial Ideology*. 2nd ed. CTBS. Eugene, OR: Cascade, 2020.

Phillips, Thomas E. *Reading Issues of Wealth and Poverty in Luke-Acts*. Lewiston, NY: Mellen, 2001.

Pilch, John J. "The Art of Insult." *CHB* 157–62.

———. *The Cultural World of Jesus: Sunday by Sunday, Cycle B*. Collegeville, MN: Liturgical, 1996.

———. "Desert and Wilderness." *CHB* 27–29.

———. "God and Lying Spirits." *CHB* 238–43.

———. *Healing in the New Testament: Insights from Medical and Mediterranean Anthropology*. Minneapolis: Fortress, 2000. Kindle.

———. "Jesus's Healing Activity: Political Acts?" In *Understanding the Social World of the New Testament*, edited by Dietmar Neufeld and Richard E. DeMaris, 147–55. London: Routledge, 2009.

———. "Noble Death." *CHB* 133–38.

———. "Purity." *HBSV* 146–48.

———. "Snakes and Magic." *CHB* 44–45.

Pilgrim, Walter. *Good News to the Poor: Wealth and Poverty in Luke-Acts*. Eugene, OR: Wipf and Stock, 2011.

Pinter, Dean. *Acts*. SGBC 5. Grand Rapids: Zondervan Academic, 2019.

———. "The Gospel of Luke and the Roman Empire." In *Jesus Is Lord, Caesar Is Not: Evaluating Empire in New Testament Studies*, edited by Scot McKnight and Joseph B. Modica, 101–15. Downers Grove, IL: InterVarsity, 2013.

Pivec, Holly, and R. Douglas Geivett. *Counterfeit Kingdom: The Dangers of New Revelation, Prophets, and Practices*. Nashville: B&H, 2022.

Polhill, John B. *Acts*. NAC 26. Nashville: Broadman & Holman, 1992.

Punt, Jeremy. "Countervailing 'Missionary' Forces: Empire and Church in Acts." *Scriptura* 103 (2010) 45–59.

Puskas, Charles B. *The Conclusion of Luke-Acts: The Significance of Acts 28:16–31*. Eugene, OR: Pickwick, 2009.

Putnam, Robert D. *Bowling Alone: The Collapse and Revival of American Community*. New York: Simon & Schuster, 2000.

Rankin, Jerry, and Ed Stetzer. *Spiritual Warfare*. Nashville: B&H, 2010.

Rapske, Brian. *Paul in Roman Custody*. BAFCS 3. Grand Rapids: Eerdmans, 1994.

Reasoner, Mark. *Roman Imperial Texts: A Sourcebook*. Minneapolis: Fortress, 2013.

Reed, Annette Yoshiko. *Demons, Angels, and Writing in Ancient Judaism*. Cambridge: Cambridge University Press, 2020.

Reed, Jonathan L., and Robert A. Wild. "Philippi." *HBD* 794–95.

Reid, Barbara E., and Shelly Matthews. *Luke 1–9*. Edited by Amy-Jill Levine. WCS 43A. Collegeville, MN: Liturgical, 2021.

Reimer, Ivoni Richter. *Women in the Acts of the Apostles: A Feminist Liberation Perspective*. Translated by Linda M. Maloney. Minneapolis: Fortress, 1995.

Reinhardt, Wolfgang. "The Population Size of Jerusalem and the Numerical Growth of the Jerusalem Church." In *Palestinian Setting*, edited by Richard Bauckham, 237–65. Grand Rapids: Eerdmans, 1995.

Rhoads, David, et al., eds. *Luke-Acts and Empire: Essays in Honor of Robert L. Brawley*. PTMS 151. Eugene, OR: Pickwick, 2011.

Richardson, Peter. "Herod (Family)." *EDB* 579–84.

———. *Herod: King of the Jews and Friend of the Romans*. Minneapolis: Fortress, 1999. Kindle.

Ringe, Sharon H. *Luke*. WestBC. Louisville: Westminster John Knox, 1995.

Robbins, Vernon K. "Luke-Acts: A Mixed Population Seeks a Home in the Roman Empire." In *Images of Empire*, edited by Loveday Alexander, 202–21. Sheffield: Sheffield Academic, 1991.

Rodriguez, Darío López. *The Liberating Mission of Jesus: The Message of the Gospel of Luke*. Translated by Stefanie E. Israel and Richard E. Waldrop. PPSJ 6. Eugene, OR: Pickwick, 2012.

Rogerson, John W. *Chronicle of the Old Testament Kings: the Reign-By-Reign Record of the Rulers of Ancient Israel*. London: Thames & Hudson, 1999.

Rohrbaugh, Richard L., ed. *The Social Sciences and New Testament Interpretation*. Peabody, MA: Hendrickson, 1996.

Rossing, Barbara R. "Turning the Empire (οἰκουμένη) Upside Down." In *Reading Acts in the Discourses of Masculinity and Politics*, edited by Eric Barreto et al., 148–55. London: T&T Clark, 2017.

Rowe, C. Kavin. "Luke-Acts and the Imperial Cult: A Way Through the Conundrum?" In *Studies in Luke, Acts, and Paul*, 3–23. Grand Rapids: Eerdmans, 2024.

———. *World Upside Down: Reading Acts in the Graeco-Roman Age*. Oxford: Oxford University Press, 2010.

Sala, Maura. "Sidon." *LBD*.

Saldarini, Anthony J. "Sanhedrin." *ABD* 5:975–80.

Sanders, James A. "The Ethic of Election in Luke's Great Banquet Parable." In *Luke and Scripture: The Function of Sacred Tradition in Luke-Acts*, by Craig A. Evans and James A. Sanders, 106–20. Eugene, OR: Wipf and Stock, 2001.

Sassen, Saskia. *The Global City: New York, London, Tokyo*. Princeton: Princeton University Press, 1991.

Schaper, Joachim. "The Jerusalem Temple as an Instrument of the Achaemenid Fiscal Administration." *VT* 45 (1995) 528–39.

Schnabel, Eckhard J. *Acts*. ZECNT 5. Grand Rapids: Zondervan Academic, 2012.

Schreiner, Patrick. *Acts*. CSC. Nashville: Holman Reference, 2022.

Schweizer, Eduard. *The Good News According to Luke*. Louisville: Westminster John Knox, 1984.

Seal, David. "Ephesus." *LBD*.

Seccombe, David Peter. *The Poor and Their Possessions: Possessions and the Poor in Luke-Acts*. Eugene, OR: Wipf and Stock, 2022.

Seeman, Chris, and Bruce J. Malina. "Envy." *HBSV* 51–53.

Seo, Pyung Soo. *Luke's Jesus in the Roman Empire and the Emperor in the Gospel of Luke*. Eugene, OR: Pickwick, 2015.

Shellberg, Pamela. *Cleansed Lepers, Cleansed Hearts: Purity and Healing in Luke-Acts*. ESS. Minneapolis: Fortress, 2015.

Shepherd, William H., Jr. *The Narrative Function of the Holy Spirit as a Character in Luke-Acts*. SBLDS 147. Atlanta: Scholars, 1994.

Simone, AbdouMaliq. *For the City Yet to Come: Changing African Life in Four Cities*. Durham: Duke University Press, 2004.

Singer, Merrill. "Reinventing Medical Anthropology: Toward a Critical Realignment." *Social Science and Medicine* 30 (1990) 179–87.

Skinner, Matthew L. *Intrusive God, Disruptive Gospel: Encountering the Divine in the Book of Acts*. Grand Rapids: Brazos, 2015.

———. *Locating Paul: Places of Custody as Narrative Settings in Acts 21–28*. AcBib 13. Atlanta: SBL, 2003.

———. "Who Speaks for (or Against) Rome? Acts in Relation to Empire." In *Reading Acts in the Discourses of Masculinity and Politics*, edited by Eric Barreto et al., 107–25. London: T&T Clark, 2017.

Smith, Mitzi J. *The Literary Construction of the Other in the Acts of the Apostles: Charismatics, the Jews, and Women*. PTMS 154. Eugene, OR: Pickwick, 2011. Kindle.

Spencer, F. Scott. *Acts*. Readings—NBC. Sheffield: Sheffield Academic, 1997.

———. *The Gospel of Luke and Acts of the Apostles*. IBT. Nashville: Abingdon, 2008.

———. *Luke*. THNTC. Grand Rapids: Eerdmans, 2019.

Spencer, Richard A. "Philippi." *EDB* 1048.

Stark, Rodney. *Cities of God: The Real Story of How Christianity Became an Urban Movement and Conquered Rome*. New York: HarperOne, 2006.

———. *The Rise of Christianity: How the Obscure, Marginal Jesus Movement Became the Dominant Religious Force in the Western World in a Few Centuries*. San Francisco: HarperSanFrancisco, 1996.

———. *The Triumph of Christianity: How the Jesus Movement Became the World's Largest Religion*. New York: HarperOne, 2012.

Ste. Croix, G. E. M. de. *The Class Struggle in the Ancient Greek World: From the Archaic Age to the Arab Conquests*. Ithaca, NY: Cornell University Press, 1981.

Stein, Robert H. *Luke: An Exegetical and Theological Exposition of Holy Scripture*. NAC 24. Nashville: Broadman & Holman, 1993.

Stewart, Edward C., and Milton J. Bennett. *American Cultural Patterns: A Cross-Cultural Perspective*. London: Quercus, 1991.

Strait, Drew J. "Proclaiming Another King Named Jesus? The Acts of the Apostles and the Roman Imperial Cult(s)." In *Jesus Is Lord, Caesar Is Not: Evaluating Empire in New Testament Studies*, edited by Scot McKnight and Joseph B. Modica, 130–45. Downers Grove, IL: InterVarsity, 2013.

Strauss, Barry. *Ten Caesars: Roman Emperors from Augustus to Constantine*. New York: Simon & Schuster, 2019.

Strauss, M. L. "Sadducees." *DJG* 823–25.

Streeter, Burnett Hillman. *The Four Gospels: A Study of Origins*. London: Macmillan, 1924.

Streett, R. Alan. *Caesar and the Sacrament: Baptism; A Rite of Resistance*. Eugene, OR: Cascade, 2018.
Stronstad, Roger. *The Charismatic Theology of St. Luke*. Peabody, MA: Hendrickson, 1984.
Sullivan, K. P., and P. W. Ferris. "Travel in Biblical Times." *LBD*.
Tajra, Harry W. *The Trial of St. Paul*. Tubingen, Ger.: Mohr Siebeck, 1989.
Talbert, Charles H. *Literary Patterns, Theological Themes and the Genre of Luke-Acts*. Atlanta: SBL, 2006.
———. *Reading Luke: A Literary and Theological Commentary on the Third Gospel*. Macon, GA: Smyth & Helwys, 1982.
Temin, Peter. *The Roman Market Economy*. PEHWW 44. Princeton: Princeton University Press, 2017.
Thiessen, Matthew. *Jesus and the Forces of Death: The Gospels' Portrayal of Ritual Impurity Within First-Century Judaism*. Grand Rapids: Baker, 2020.
Thompson, Richard P. *Acts: A Commentary in the Wesleyan Tradition*. NBBC. Kansas City: Beacon Hill, 2015.
Tomlin, R. S. O. "'The Girl in Question': A New Text from Roman London." *Britannia* 34 (2003) 41–51.
Trainor, Michael. *Acts: About Earth's Children; An Ecological Listening to the Acts of the Apostles*. Earth Bible Commentary. New York: Bloomsbury, 2021.
Tyson, Joseph B. *Images of Judaism in Luke-Acts*. Columbia: University of South Carolina Press, 1992.
Ulvestad, Anja Aga. "Ubuntu in African Traditional Religion." Master's thesis, University of Oslo, 2012, 1–81.
VanderKam, James C. *From Joshua to Caiaphas: High Priests After the Exile*. Philadelphia: Fortress, 2004. Kindle.
Wahlen, Clinton. *Jesus and the Impurity of Spirits in the Synoptic Gospels*. WUNT II 185. Tubingen, Ger.: Mohr Siebeck, 2004.
Walaskay, Paul W. *Acts*. WestBC. Louisville: Westminster John Knox, 1998.
———. *"And So We Came to Rome": The Political Perspective of St. Luke*. Cambridge: Cambridge University Press, 1983.
Wallis, Ian G. *The Galilean Wonderworker: Reassessing Jesus' Reputation for Healing and Exorcism*. Eugene, OR: Cascade, 2020.
Walton, John H., and J. Harvey Walton. *Demons and Spirits in Biblical Theology: Reading the Biblical Text in Its Cultural and Literary Context*. Eugene, OR: Cascade, 2019.
Walton, Steve. *Acts 1—9:42*. WBC 37A. Grand Rapids: Zondervan, 2024.
———. "The State They Were In: Luke's View of the Roman Empire." In *Rome in the Bible and the Early Church*, edited by Peter Oakes, 1–41. Grand Rapids: Baker Academic, 2002.
———. "Trying Paul or Trying Rome? Judges and Accused in the Roman Trials of Paul in Acts." In *Luke-Acts and Empire: Essays in Honor of Robert L. Brawley*, edited by David Rhoads et al., 122–41. PTMS 151. Eugene, OR: Pickwick, 2011.
———. "Wealth and Poverty According to Acts 11–28." Presentation, SBL Annual Meeting, Denver, Nov. 19, 2022.
Walz, Clark A. "The Cursing Paul: Magical Contests in Acts 13 and the New Testament Apocrypha; Acts 13:6–12." In *Mission in Acts: Ancient Narratives in Contemporary Context*, edited by Robert L. Gallagher and Paul Hertig, 167–82. ASMS 34. Maryknoll, NY: Orbis, 2004.
Watson, Duane F. "Devil." *ABD* 2:183–84.

Wenkel, David H. "Sicarii." *LBD*.

———. "The Twelve and the Weaponry of Kingship." In *The Kingship of the Twelve Apostles in Luke-Acts*, 95–108. Basingstoke: Palgrave Pivot, 2018.

Whitehead, Andrew. *American Idolatry: How Christian Nationalism Betrays the Gospel and Threatens the Church*. Grand Rapids: Brazos, 2023.

Wi, Mija. *The Path to Salvation in Luke's Gospel: What Must We Do?* London: T&T Clark, 2019.

Willimon, William H. *Acts*. IBC. Louisville: Westminster John Knox, 2010.

Winter, Bruce W. *Divine Honours for the Caesars: The First Christians' Responses*. Grand Rapids: Eerdmans, 2015.

———. "Paul and Roman Law: 'The Luck of the Draw?'" In *Reading Acts in the Discourses of Masculinity and Politics*, edited by Eric Barreto et al., 126–40. London: T&T Clark, 2017.

Witherington, Ben, III. *The Acts of the Apostles: A Socio-Rhetorical Commentary*. Grand Rapids: Eerdmans, 1998.

Witmer, Amanda. *Jesus, the Galilean Exorcist: His Exorcisms in Social and Political Context*. LHJS 10. LNTS 459. London: Bloomsbury, 2013.

Wright, N. T. *Acts for Everyone, Part 2: Chapters 13–28*. 20th anniv. ed. NTFE. Louisville: Westminster John Knox, 2023.

———. *Jesus and the Victory of God*. COQG 2. Minneapolis: Fortress, 1997.

———. *Paul: A Biography*. San Francisco: HarperOne, 2018.

———. *Surprised by Hope: Rethinking Heaven, the Resurrection, and the Mission of the Church*. New York: HarperOne, 2008.

Zimmerman, Armin. "General Features of African Traditional Religions." *Gema Teologi* 36 (2012) 269–302.

Zukin, Sharon. *Loft Living: Culture and Capital in Urban Change*. Baltimore: Johns Hopkins University Press, 1982.

www.ingramcontent.com/pod-product-compliance
Lightning Source LLC
Chambersburg PA
CBHW070252230426
43664CB00014B/2507